The Enduring Legacy of Ancient China

Chinese Dynasty

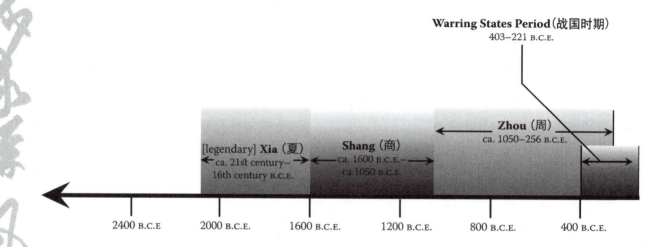

Warring States Period（战国时期）
403–221 B.C.E.

Zhou（周）
ca. 1050–256 B.C.E.

[legendary] **Xia**（夏）
← ca. 21st century–
16th century B.C.E.

Shang（商）
ca. 1600 B.C.E.–
ca. 1050 B.C.E.

2400 B.C.E   2000 B.C.E.   1600 B.C.E.   1200 B.C.E.   800 B.C.E.   400 B.C.E.

B.C.E. (Before Common Era)

Time Line

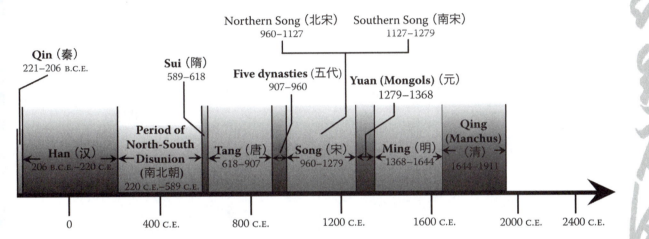

Qin (秦)
221–206 B.C.E.

Han (汉)
206 B.C.E.–220 C.E.

Period of
North-South
Disunion
(南北朝)
220 C.E.–589 C.E.

Sui (隋)
589–618

Tang (唐)
618–907

Five dynasties (五代)
907–960

Northern Song (北宋)
960–1127

Southern Song (南宋)
1127–1279

Song (宋)
960–1279

Yuan (Mongols) (元)
1279–1368

Ming (明)
1368–1644

Qing
(Manchus)
(清)
1644–1911

0   400 C.E.   800 C.E.   1200 C.E.   1600 C.E.   2000 C.E.   2400 C.E.

C.E. (Common Era)

THE ENDURING LEGACY OF
ANCIENT CHINA
Primary Source Lessons for Teachers and Students

Compiled and edited by the curriculum
specialists at Primary Source, Inc.

Foreword by
Michael Puett

Introductory Essay by
Robert E. Murowchick

10 09 08 07 06   1 2 3 4 5 6

Published by
Cheng & Tsui Company, Inc.
25 West Street
Boston, MA 02111-1213 USA
Fax (617) 426-3669
www.cheng-tsui.com
"Bringing Asia to the World"™

Library of Congress Cataloging-in-Publication Data for this work is available.

ISBN 13 978-0-88727-508-1
ISBN 0-88727-508-7

Printed in the U.S.A.

Primary Source dedicates *The Enduring Legacy of Ancient China* to Drs. Anne and John Watt in recognition of the enduring legacy of their work in strengthening teaching about China so that American citizens can better understand Chinese history and culture.

The Enduring Legacy of Ancient China is made possible through the generosity of the Freeman Foundation and the many individuals who contribute to the work of Primary Source.

Contents

IV The Four Accomplishments

V Human Ingenuity

VI Beyond the Borders

Acknowledgments

Primary Source is deeply indebted to Dr. John Watt for his guidance in creating *The Enduring Legacy of Ancient China*. We appreciate the depth and breadth of his knowledge of China, his patience, and his unflagging good humor.

Our sincere thanks to other scholars who have contributed their expertise:

Dr. Robert E. Murowchick, Research Associate Professor of Archaeology and Anthropology and Director of the International Center for East Asian Archaeology and Cultural History at Boston University

Dr. Ronald Knapp, SUNY Distinguished Professor Emeritus, State University of New York at New Paltz

Dr. Huajing Maske, Independent Scholar

Dr. Su Zheng, Associate Professor of Music and East Asian Studies, Wesleyan University

Teacher-Authors:

Cara Abraham, Brookfield High School, Brookfield, CT

Philip Gambone, Head of the Humanities Division, Boston University Academy

Shirley Moore Huettig, Concord Academy, Concord, MA

Peter Lowber, Boston Public Schools

Steven Ratiner, Poet, Independent Scholar

Many thanks to Philip Gambone for reviewing the book and offering advice on student activities.

We also gratefully acknowledge contributions to lessons by:

Michael Abraham, New Milford High School, CT

David J. Buckhoff, Danvers High School, MA

Eugene Dorgan

Jie Gao, Newton Public Schools, MA

Karen Boodro Graham, G. H. Conley School, Boston Public Schools, MA

Joan Hamilton, K–8 librarian, Pierce School, Brookline, MA

Dr. Wei-Tsun Lee, retired teacher/librarian, Oxford Public Schools, MA

Vincent Leung, doctoral candidate, Dept. of East Asian Languages and Civilizations, Harvard University

Paula Winter Lofgren, Pine Hill School, Sherborn, MA

Susan Logsdon, Dover-Sherborn Public Schools, MA

Beatrice Murphy, Boston Public Schools, MA

Anne Mills-Norrie, Silver Lake Regional Public Schools, NH

Kathy Simpson, Cambridge Public Schools, MA
Christine Vaillancourt, Newton Public Schools, MA

Audio:
We thank Kongli Liu for providing the pronunciation of key Chinese words in the lessons.
We are indebted to Shin-Yi Yang, founder of the Boston Guzheng Ensemble, and Jien Bao from Chinese Performing Arts of North America for so generously providing the selections of music.

Primary Source Staff
Several staff members were key to the creation of *The Enduring Legacy of Ancient China*. Wanli Hu, Kongli Liu, and Pamela Tuffley shared their knowledge on all things Chinese, including *pinyin* spelling and Chinese characters. Renee Covalucci contributed artistic expertise by creating various supplementary materials, from maps to time lines.
Liz Nelson, Editor
Ann Black, Administrative Coordinator
Nanette Cormier, Development Director
Renee Covalucci, Program Associate
Dr. Deborah Cunningham, Program Director
Abby Detweiler, Program Manager
Kathleen M. Ennis, Executive Director
Dr. Paul Foos, Web Developer/Bibliographer
Peter Gilmartin, Associate Director, China/World Studies
Al Hope, Program Director, West Africa
Dr. Wanli Hu, Associate Director, China
Jill Jeffrey, Librarian
Eve Lehmann, Permissions Editor
Kongli Liu, Program Associate, China
Mark Lyons, Financial Administrator
Julie Morganstern, Program Associate
Tova Thorpe, Administrative Assistant
Pamela Tuffley, Program Associate
Dr. Anne Watt, Program Director, China/Ancient Civilizations

Interns:
Lucia Carballo, Boston University Graduate School
Bai Kamara, Wellesley College
Deborah Opar, Bates College
Sam Stiegler, Tufts University

十二かへ涌家康風の君の日日

Foreword

Dr. Michael Puett, Department Chair of East Asian Languages and Civilizations,
Harvard University

It is an honor and a pleasure to write a preface to this curriculum guide on the tremendously rich civilization of China. I have been working with Primary Source for many years now, and I have been truly stunned at the extraordinary job that the organization has done in designing curricula for teaching Chinese civilization. This guide represents the culmination of those many years of working with teachers and seeing what works effectively in the classroom. I can say without any hesitation that some of the most inspiring moments for me as a teacher have come in these sessions with Primary Source, and I am tremendously excited that this guide will make that curricula available to a much larger audience.

My excitement concerning the work Primary Source has been doing is only enhanced when I think of my own educational background. When I was a student, China was never part of the educational curriculum. Indeed, I took my first class that dealt with China in my junior year of *college*. I have consequently devoted my life to studying and teaching China, but I often think of my many secondary school classmates who never had this opportunity. And, sadly, I think the implications of these lapses in our earlier education curricula are now clear for all to see. If we train generations of students not to care about learning from other cultures, we create a xenophobic, inward-looking country that fundamentally misunderstands how to deal with other countries.

The vision of Primary Source has been to correct this. Their goal has been to build the study of other cultures into the basic curricula of all K–12 education. The importance of this vision cannot be stressed enough. If we can train the next generations of students to understand the rich civilizations throughout the world, to think of themselves as part of a cosmopolitan world in which it is important to know and care about other cultures, then the implications for the world in which we live will be incalculable.

But why is the study of China in particular so important? Part of the answer to this question is obvious: China is a growing political and economic power that, over the course of the lives of our current students, will only continue to become an increasingly significant force in the world. It is therefore incumbent upon all students to understand the history and culture of such a growing world power.

But there is another reason for studying China as well. Studying the extraordinary history, philosophies, religions, and literatures of China is, quite frankly, life-changing. Indeed, I always start my classes on China with a pledge to this effect. I tell my students that, when studying these traditions, they need to take them seriously—to take the philosophies seriously, take the literature seriously, take the forms of political governance seriously. They don't have to agree with what they will be reading, but they should take them seriously. If they do, they will come to understand different and extremely important ways of thinking, ways of organizing the world, ways of writing a poem. And they will learn to reflect, sometimes critically, on the world they now take for granted. The traditions of China are that rich. So the guarantee I give to my students is simple: if they take these texts seriously, then, by the end of the class, their lives will be fundamentally changed and deeply, deeply enriched. All teachers who use this book should feel free to make the same guarantee.

I want to thank Primary Source for their years of work in designing and implementing curricula for the study of China, and to thank Liz Nelson for bringing that tremendous work together in this guide. I wish that I could have studied this when I was a student, and I am very excited for the next generations of students who will now be able to do so.

Michael Puett
Professor of Chinese History
Chair, Department of East Asian Languages and Civilizations
Harvard University

Introduction

Why China?

The relationship between China and the United States will be one of the greatest challenges and opportunities that our children face in the twenty-first century. With one-fifth of the world's population and the world's most rapidly growing economy, China is poised to become a global superpower. To be contributing, responsible citizens of the world, our students need to learn about China, to appreciate the country's immense contributions, and to understand her people.

For millennia, the Chinese considered themselves the Middle Kingdom—the center of the world. Those beyond their borders they called barbarians, demons and, in more recent times, foreign devils. Surrounded by vast deserts, the world's tallest mountains, and the Pacific Ocean, the Chinese created an enduring civilization, ruled by a succession of dynasties. They saw their imperial regimes as cyclical—when rulers failed to meet the needs of the people, the dynasty failed and was eventually replaced by another. Ancient China had no established religion; instead people fused ancestor worship, local cults, Confucian and Daoist philosophies, and Buddhism, to create a culture that esteemed elders, scholarship, literature, esthetics, and powers that transcended the human order.

The people of the Middle Kingdom invented paper, printing, the compass, gunpowder, the kite, and numerous other technical devices that gradually made their way across the world. They transformed cocoons into silk. They diverted rivers, built vast canals and locks, and constructed the Great Wall. In times of peace, the population flourished and grew. The people also suffered unfathomable horrors as a result of floods, famines, invasions, and civil wars. They celebrated life's gifts and their hopes for prosperity with spectacular lunar festivals. The Chinese have a history like no other people, and they took great pains to record it for posterity.

Our Goal in This Publication

Chinese history is rich and complex. In this book we make no attempt to cover several thousand years of history, though we do provide a chronology of dynasties for reference. The topics have roots in China's ancient civilization. They are ones with which we believe students should be familiar if they are to understand China in the twenty-first century—topics with an enduring legacy. We end the book in the period that saw the ascendancy of European nations. The book is designed so that virtually every lesson can be taught independently of the others. Since they are organized thematically, they can be taught in almost any sequence. Teachers can select the topics that fit best into the time frame they have available.

While this book is designed as a teacher resource, we believe many students, especially with strong reading skills, could use the book directly. As a primary text, *The Enduring Legacy of Ancient China* offers students an engaging and challenging learning approach and direct access to all the primary sources. Before students begin assigned activities, they should be sure to access the full text of the documents on the CD-ROM.

Who Are We?

Primary Source is a non-profit educational resource center offering high quality professional development and curriculum resources to K–12 teachers and school communities. Founded in 1988 by two committed and experienced educators, Anna Roelofs, M.Ed. and Anne Watt, Ed.D., the organization's mission is to promote social studies and humanities education by connecting educators to people and cultures throughout the world.

Primary Source is guided by a commitment to change the way students learn history and understand culture so that their knowledge base is broader, their thinking more flexible and given to inquiry, and their attitudes about peoples of the world more open and inclusive. By equipping teachers with the skills, knowledge, and resources to facilitate this type of learning, Primary Source prepares students for the challenges and complexities of our diverse nation and world. Our main content areas are East Asia, U.S. history with a special focus on African American studies, West Africa, and the Middle East. Although we feel a particular responsibility to social studies teachers, our programs are interdisciplinary, and teachers of all subjects will benefit from a broader understanding of peoples and cultures.

Our professional development opportunities include summer institutes, seminars, workshops, and conferences. All programs are built around participation by scholars and lead teachers. By fostering a climate of intellectual exchange between university scholars and teachers, we acknowledge the pivotal role teachers play in the creation of a more sophisticated and aware American public.

Primary Source also develops publications for use by teachers. In the spring of 2004, Heinemann Publishing, Inc., released *Making Freedom: African Americans in U.S. History*, a series of five curriculum sourcebooks on African American history from the fifteenth century through the Civil Rights Movement. Each book contains primary sources, including diaries, slave narratives, maps, official government documents, autobiographies, cartoons, broadsides, and photographs. We use the same model for *The Enduring Legacy of Ancient China*.

Using Primary Sources

Primary Source, the organization, takes its name from the same term used by historians to distinguish original, uninterpreted material from secondary or third-hand accounts. Thus a photograph, a memoir, or a letter is a primary source, while an essay interpreting the photograph or memoir is usually, though not always, a secondary source. A textbook, still further removed, is a tertiary source.

The Enduring Legacy of Ancient China utilizes a range of primary sources. We include images of artifacts from tombs, ancient texts, illustrations, photographs, scroll paintings, poetry, travelogues, and more. All text has been translated, of course, making it, arguably, no longer a primary source. We have selected translations by eminent scholars to ensure the most accurate reading possible.

While it is imperative to read secondary sources in order to understand context and background, introducing students to "the real stuff" (albeit in translation) raises student interest and curiosity and offers opportunities for students to make discoveries on their own. When textbooks are used as the only source of information, it is much more difficult for students to take ownership, both of their own learning and of a particular body of knowledge. It is difficult to remember other people's generalizations or conclusions. Original source material provides students with rich opportunities for inquiry, the chance to move from concrete to abstract thinking and back again.

How to Use This Book

Each lesson contains:
>
> An Introduction
> The Organizing Idea
> Student Objectives
> Key Questions
> Vocabulary
> Primary Sources
> Student Activities
> Further Student and Teacher Resources
> In the World Today (sidebar)
> Elsewhere in the World (sidebar) (appears in some lessons)

Together, the **context essay** at the beginning of the book and the **introductions** to individual lessons provide background information necessary to understanding the primary sources and engaging in the activities. Teachers can use this introductory material in a variety of ways. For example, they can present the information in a brief lecture, create background information sheets with key points, or, if students have strong reading skills, teachers can have them read the introductions.

Vocabulary lists with topical words are included, and the words are defined in the **glossary**. (The glossary is in the book and on the CD-ROM.) In many instances, given the age of the documents, additional vocabulary lists are provided under supplementary materials to help students better understand what they will read.

Each lesson includes a variety of teaching strategies designed to engage student interest. Each activity is preceded by the related **primary source**(s). Suggested **activities** include study and analysis of primary sources, mapping, research and writing, debating, creation of graphic displays, and various hands-on tasks. When an activity calls for speculation or analysis, it is important to have verifying information available close at hand—in the classroom, the school library, or online. A speculation exercise is not a "stand alone" but, together with research to clarify information and verify a theory, this activity gives students the opportunity to, in effect, become historians.

Because the context essay and lessons were written by a group of scholars and teachers, they offer a variety of writing and instructional approaches. While the format for all of the lessons is the same, we have respected the authors' voices and have not edited them to a uniform length or style. The lessons vary in length and detail and offer a choice of activities.

We do not expect teachers to use every activity in every lesson. Rather, just as they select the lessons, teachers should choose activities that dovetail best into their instructional plan and meet the instructional needs and learning styles of their students. We have set out a buffet—we do not intend for all of it to be consumed by each teacher.

A list of **Further Resources** is provided with most lessons. While every effort has been made to ensure that these Web sites are reputable and current, they change. Any information found on the Internet should be regarded with scrutiny until its accuracy has been verified. Teachers may wish to check URLs before giving students assignments. Students should also be cautioned to carefully evaluate information found in a Web site, checking who is the author and who sponsors the site.

Wherever it is applicable, a lesson includes a sidebar: **Elsewhere in the World**. This informs students what was going on in other parts of the world in the time period(s) addressed in the lesson. **In the World Today**, on the other hand, brings the topic of the lesson into the present.

Some of the **primary source materials** are difficult for students to read. We have selected the most accurate and often quite recent translations, but the students may not be familiar with some of the syntax and vocabulary. **Teacher Resources** on the CD-ROM suggest various ways to help students tackle challenging text. Each teacher will know best how to adapt a lesson to the students' skill level.

The CD-ROM

Most documents have been abbreviated in the book and, in some cases, where many photographs are available, not all appear in the book. All **primary source materials** appear in full on the accompanying CD-ROM and can be printed out for classroom use or projected on a screen. In addition, the CD-ROM includes supplementary materials, a list of recommended historical fiction, an annotated bibliography, teacher resources, and an **audio component**. There are selections of music and, to help teachers and students pronounce key names and terms in the lessons, we include the spoken words on the CD-ROM.

Romanization of Chinese Words

In 1859, Sir Thomas Francis Wade, professor of Chinese at Cambridge University, created a system for the romanization of Chinese characters. His successor Herbert Giles revised it in 1892, establishing the Wade-Giles system, which served as the English language standard until the middle of the twentieth century. In 1953, the People's Republic of China devised its own system called *pinyin*. All older translations use the Wade-Giles spelling, while recent publications have increasingly adopted the *pinyin* spelling. We use *pinyin* throughout *The Enduring Legacy of Ancient China*, with two exceptions. We kept titles of books spelled the way in which they were published, and in the Poetry lesson, poets' names are in Wade-Giles because almost all books of Chinese poetry list them that way. (The *pinyin* spelling appears at the end of the lesson for cross-reference.) In the introductions to the lessons, titles of primary sources, and captions, the first time key words and phrases appear, we include the word written in simplified Chinese characters.

About the Dates Cited

In the academic community, the use of the dating terms "B.C.E." and "C.E." has become increasingly prominent in recent years. This is also the primary dating convention used in *The Enduring Legacy of Ancient China*. However, where original primary sources appear in this text and the CD-ROM, we have left their original dating conventions intact.

"B.C.E." stands for "Before the Common Era" and is equivalent to "B.C.", while "C.E." stands for the "Common Era" and is equivalent to "A.D."

十二億的幾重風の寄る国が法

The Excitement and the Challenge of Understanding China's Past

By Dr. Robert E. Murowchick, Director of the International Center for East Asian
    Archaeology and Cultural History, Boston University

During the past decade, school districts across the United States have increasingly realized the importance of including East Asia—and China in particular—in the K–12 curriculum. In discussions about the focus and content of a China curriculum with teachers, school administrators, and involved and concerned parents, I have heard from many colleagues who strongly feel that these studies should focus mainly—or even exclusively—on "modern" China: the post-1911, post-dynastic period, or even the post-1945 period. It is important, of course, to understand modern China's political, economic, and social developments, and the changing nature and balance of the relationship between China and the West. Some of this emphasis is driven by concerns about China's economic juggernaut and the seemingly endless loss of American jobs to lower-wage Chinese producers, or by the fear of what is seen as China's growing military strength in the Asia-Pacific region, or by the familiarity that many Americans have with certain events and people from China's recent past and present: Chairman Mao, the Great Proletarian Cultural Revolution, "Ping-Pong diplomacy," Deng Xiaoping, "One Child Per Family," the military crackdown in Tiananmen Square, Hong Kong 1997, and the 2008 Beijing Olympics. Modern China represents, however, only one part of a much larger panorama. If a focus on "modern" China comes at the cost of not studying China's past, then the deep and fascinating foundations upon which contemporary China is based will not be understood, and the truly amazing story of how China evolved will be missed.

It is not useful to consider "modern" China as a stand-alone period, somehow divorced from its own history. As *The Enduring Legacy of Ancient China* will show, there are intricate networks of continuity and development, and of cultural interaction and exchange, that bind past and present. There are many aspects of traditional Chinese society today—religious beliefs, literature, the arts, education, architecture, cuisine, bureaucracy and governmental structure, to name just a few—that began to take shape in the deep antiquity of the Neolithic and Bronze Age periods many thousands of years ago, and evolved through the often tumultuous twists and turns of China's dynastic rule and its relationships with the "outside" world. For example, the roots of the Chinese language can be found in the divination texts of the Shang culture of 3,200 years ago. The origins of traditional construction techniques and architectural layouts, both of individual residences and of towns and cities, can be seen in the late Neolithic and Bronze Age periods. Some of the "hallmark" handicrafts that many people associate with "Chinese civilization" are clearly seen in the archaeological record covering the period from about 2000 B.C.E. to the unification of China during the third century B.C.E. under the Qin dynasty. These include the production of magnificent bronze ritual vessels during the Shang (ca. 1600–ca. 1050 B.C.E.) and Zhou (ca. 1050–256 B.C.E.) dynasties, and the production of exquisite silks and lacquerware, especially during the Eastern Zhou period (ca. 450–256 B.C.E.). Several key periods in China's past—such as the Han and Tang dynasties—saw the growth of international diplomacy and exploration, and of technological and economic achievements, that connected it with its contemporary cultures elsewhere in the Old World. Many of these developments helped to mold the China that we see today, and many others had significant effects on the development of the countries of Central, Northeast, and Southeast Asia, and of Europe.

Ongoing scholarship in archaeology, history, and related fields have provided an incredibly exciting and ever-growing source of primary data about ancient China that needs to be considered and evaluated, and our interpretations revised as appropriate. Studying ancient China, and understanding it well enough to clearly convey the important points to one's students, can seem overwhelming when faced with an ever-increasing amount of information, dates, places, and names. As teachers, we must weigh the importance of the details against the potential problems introduced through oversimplification. Textbooks and "introductory" articles are often filled with sweeping statements that are exaggerated in their presentation as "fact" of issues that are still highly debated. For example, "China is one of the world's two oldest continuous civilizations" is a broad generalization that is misleading in its simplicity. Other statements, such as "China's civilization developed over a long period in considerable isolation," are riddled with inaccuracies because they are outdated, their authors unaware of new discoveries and rapidly—and sometimes radically—changing interpretations. Other errors occur because writers unwittingly perpetuate ideas that have their basis not in factual data, but in the biased interpretations and presentations of scholarship guided by political and nationalistic motivations during certain periods of the past three thousand years. It is important that we all keep in mind a number of key points as we study the development of China, and as we figure out how to present this material to our students.

(1) What is "Chinese civilization"? We must be aware of the pitfalls of discussing "Chinese civilization" as if it were a clearly defined, monolithic entity. What does one mean by "China" and "Chinese," and at what point in prehistory or history can one define a "China"? We often see presentations of China's past that focus on the emergence of "civilization" in the North China Plain with the sequential rise and fall of the Sandai, or "Three Dynasties" of Xia, Shang, and Zhou, as if this were a simple linear, sequential series of states that then lead to the well-known sequence of dynasties from Qin (221–206 B.C.E.) through Qing (1644–1911 C.E.). This linear presentation of China's past is reinforced by countless "time lines" in books and classrooms across the country that show the appealingly simple (but highly misleading) sequence from Neolithic to Xia to Shang to Zhou to Qin, and eventually to the last two dynasties, Ming and Qing. Using such time lines is a useful starting point to give students a sense of the time spans involved in these cultural and political developments, and to increase their familiarity with dynastic names and approximate dates. Teachers must take care, however, to explain that the "linearity" suggested by the timeline is an oversimplification of the actual situation.

The area that today is modern China was filled in the past with a fascinating mosaic of cultures, some of which are well known, and others that are only now beginning to be recognized. The boundaries of "China" have changed considerably during different time periods. A rather traditional view of "China" sees the North China Plain of the middle and lower Yellow River as the crucible of "Chinese civilization," and this view is understandable in many ways: numerous ancient texts, written by historians based in this area, provide detailed histories of these early states and their rulers, establishing early on a sense of "center" versus "periphery" in the approach taken in the study of ancient China. This North China Plain–centric view was further reinforced by the discovery and study of oracle bones (divinatory texts) and subsequent field archaeology in the 1920s and 1930s that corroborated the existence of the early Bronze Age Shang state in present-day Henan Province. This developed into what I see as a self-feeding cycle of misinterpretation (or at least biased interpretation): the early texts talk about the North China Plain as being the home of China's foundational ancient states, which leads to field archaeology that indeed finds glorious evidence of at least some of these states, which are interpreted based largely on what the ancient texts say. This development leads us to the increasingly uncomfortable situation of trying to understand "ancient China" while wearing scholarly blinders, and to the fact that:

(2) **Maps can lie.** Maps show us what their creators want to show us, and they don't show us anything else. A belief in the simple, linear sequence of early "dynasties" can lead to the creation of highly misleading maps that visually reinforce a false understanding of China's past. To pick but one example, consider the following: a map showing the supposed boundaries of the "Shang Dynasty" in a glaring, bold color with distinct borders against a blank, white background of China. The dangers of such a presentation are numerous. First of all, efforts to create boundaries of the Shang state (ca. 1600–ca. 1050 B.C.E.)—or any ancient culture or polity—are often based on the archaeologically-derived distribution of artifacts (such as certain types of bronze ritual vessels) that we somehow define as markers of "Shang" because similar pieces were found at the site of the last Shang capital city near Anyang, in northern Henan Province. Does the discovery of such artifacts along the Yangtze River, hundreds of miles south of Anyang, indicate that this was part of the Shang state, as the maps suggest? Or are these items traded long distances between contemporaneous cultures? Shouldn't we really be talking about a much smaller Shang "state," a larger area of possible "Shang influence" or "Shang interaction sphere," and a still larger area where we find what we think are "Shang-related" objects, while acknowledging that there are many interpretations about how or why they got there?

The huge blank areas of these maps outside of the "Shang borders" also visually suggest that these parts of what is now China were either uninhabited in the past, or were culturally insignificant. The "traditional" picture of ancient China suggests a "center" ("us," interesting, important, sophisticated, influential) vs. "periphery" ("them," unimportant, of no consequence to China's development, "barbarian," unsophisticated). During the past fifty years, the rapidly developing field of archaeology has shown us that the true picture of ancient China was much more complex—and much more interesting! The cultural landscape of ancient China was an unbelievably rich array of cultures stretching across the entirety of what today is modern China. Some of these cultures are mentioned in early histories and other ancient texts, but most are known only through archaeological discoveries and study. Where ancient texts generically describe the "Southern Barbarians" or the "Southwestern Barbarians," archaeological exploration now shows dozens of Neolithic and Bronze Age cultures that are unique in many ways, and that share many features with their neighbors. The ancient landscape was alive with social, economic, ritual, and military life, with alliances between neighbors, and with warfare among others; with farming, cities, transport and trade; and with short- and long-distance interactions that we have not yet even come close to understanding. In our efforts to understand China's past, we must be patient and we must be flexible, because:

(3) The past is a moving target. We "know" details of many of the cultures that made up ancient China because we have archaeological and other types of evidence about them. As new finds are made, however, we are often forced to reevaluate what we know, or what we think we know. In many cases, this is a long-term process of using new finds to fine-tune our understanding. In other cases, surprising new discoveries require us—sometimes literally overnight—to simply throw out earlier ideas and start fresh. This is a frustrating fact of life for archaeologists, but it is this sense of discovery that makes the field so fascinating. While new discoveries are responsible for changing our understanding of China's past, other revisions are necessary because we recognize that:

(4) It is really hard to avoid errors in reasoning. Some of these biases result from the very nature of archaeological data. It is sometimes said that doing archaeology is like trying to put together an enormous jigsaw puzzle, only you don't know how many pieces there are in the puzzle, nor do you know which pieces are missing, nor do you know what the finished puzzle is supposed to look like. Archaeological research can tell us much about ancient cultures, but we must remember that only a tiny portion of an ancient culture survives to be discovered. At most ancient sites (including settlement sites, tombs, and manufacturing sites), certain artifact categories (e.g., ceramics, stone, and bronze) are well preserved because they are naturally resistant to decay. Organic materials (including bodies, bones, textiles, wood, and bamboo) are only preserved under certain environmental conditions that inhibit decay, including highly arid sites (e.g., Egyptian mummies or the mummies of the desert sites of Xinjiang in northwest China), waterlogged sites (including the famously well-preserved corpses from the site of Mawangdui and other Han-period burials along the central Yangtze River valley), and frozen sites (e.g., mastadons frozen in Siberian tundra, or Otzi, the Neolithic "Iceman" from the Alps). The presence of well-preserved organic remains presents a much more complete picture of the site under study, and can profoundly impact our interpretation of an ancient culture. But its absence doesn't necessarily mean that we cannot draw certain interpretations and conclusions, as long as we recognize that our picture is never a complete one.

Archaeological research in China and elsewhere can also be skewed by the types of sites that are studied. Traditionally, archaeology has focused on ancient tombs—especially richly furnished tombs of ancient rulers and their court. While this provides beautiful jades, bronzes, and other objects for museum exhibitions, it obviously presents a picture of the ancient elite at the expense of our understanding of the majority of the population of an ancient culture. Also, many sites are excavated after being discovered accidentally during modern construction work. This can present a false picture of the actual distribution of the sites of an ancient culture, with many ancient sites apparently located near modern cities (where construction projects are most likely to be).

Archaeological research and interpretations can also be biased because of political or nationalistic pressures that guide the work. This has an impact not only on the way that the archaeologists undertake their work, but also on the media that reports it, and on consumers of this information. Archaeological work in every country in the world has seen such biases, and China's archaeology is a fascinating case study of such pressures. Just to mention one such aspect, archaeology in China from the 1950s through 1970s was seen as a very useful tool with which to inform the Chinese public about its past, in that it could provide material evidence in support of the prevailing doctrines of Marx, Engels, and Mao concerning the evolution of societies through stages of "Primitive Society," "Slave Society," "Feudal Society," and so forth. Archaeological discoveries were fitted into this evolutionary scheme, and history museums across China organized their archaeological exhibits according to these same templates. Assumptions were presented as "facts" to both Chinese and non-Chinese museum visitors, and many of these ideas continue to weigh heavily on our understanding of China's past.

Historians and other scholars have shown an interest in China's past for more than two thousand years. Historical texts on bamboo slips and in later paper editions describe China's ancient legendary heroes and sage kings. Tomb art from the Han dynasty and beyond visually presents many of these same stories. At least as early as the Song dynasty in the eleventh century, scholarly studies of antiquities resulted in printed catalogues showing woodblock-printed pictures of the artifact, a textual description of the object, and in many cases some comment about how these objects corroborate our understanding about certain ancient rituals, or about the moral authority of rulers, or about other matters. Since the early twentieth century, the science of archaeology has witnessed explosive growth in China, especially during the past two decades. However, we must keep in mind that:

(5) A diamond might be forever, but the past isn't. China's modernization has produced many benefits for its people, and continues to raise China's position as one of the major world leaders for the next century. This modernization, however, brings with it profoundly destructive forces that threaten to forever obliterate the very information that can help us to better understand where China has come from. Economic development wipes out sites, many of them as yet undiscovered and virtually all of them as yet unstudied. In some situations, the accidental discovery of ancient sites results in the suspension of construction while archaeologists undertake their study, collection, and preservation of the remains. In many projects, however, the pressures of time and money take precedence over scholarly endeavors. In some cases, this results in the loss of individual sites; in other cases—such as the Three Gorges Dam hydropower project along the central Yangtze River—this involves untold thousands of archaeological and historical sites, some known, most not yet discovered.

China's past is also being rapidly destroyed in a much more targeted, intentional way: the rape of the ancient landscape by thieves looting tombs and other sites in the search for valuable objects to sell and resell into the international antiquities market. In spite of national and international efforts to enforce antiquities laws meant to protect such sites, the situation in China—and indeed, in much of the world—is veering out of control. Unscrupulous dealers, collectors, and some museums care not that the objects that grace their cases and mantels arrive there only as the final stage of a highly destructive process that obliterates the past that they claim to cherish so dearly. Tombs and other sites are destroyed in the search to find a few pieces of marketable jade, gold, bronze, or lacquer. Those pieces are torn from the context of their original setting, the all-important associations that might have allowed us to understand why, how, when, and where they were made. The end result is an object about which not much information can ever be gleaned, and sites that had survived for thousands of years are destroyed forever in the course of a few hours of stealthy nighttime digging. Given the dramatic changes in our understanding of ancient China that have resulted from archaeological studies over the past seventy years—since the advent of the field in China in the 1920s—it is truly depressing to think of all of the irreplaceable information that has been permanently lost, and that continues to be destroyed at a rapidly escalating rate.

The study of ancient China in all of its many forms—its ancient archaeological remains, literary and artistic masterpieces, philosophical traditions, religious and ritual activities, educational and governmental frameworks—provides a strong foundation to more fully understand China today, and where it might be going in the future. Complementary information about China's past cultures is being provided by fields as diverse as archaeology, geography, history, literature, art history, and anthropology. Together they provide more pieces of the puzzle that is ancient China. Just as our understanding of China's past today is quite different from that presented in textbooks from forty years ago, there are still many, many aspects of ancient China that are not yet well known. Countless surprises still remain buried deep beneath the earth, awaiting discovery and interpretation by our students—and by their students.

Dr. Robert E. Murowchick
Director of the International Center for East Asian Archaeology and Cultural History
Boston University

The image of a carp is, in Chinese tradition, a symbol of perseverance. In the third moon of each year, the fish swim up the *Huang He* (the Yellow River), struggling against the current. The ones who succeed in getting beyond the rapids of Lungmen are transformed into dragons. As a result of their fortitude and resilience, carp represent scholarly achievement.

Lesson 1 CD-ROM Contents

Primary Sources

THE CHINESE QUESTION.—[See Page 147.]

COLUMBIA.—"Hands off, Gentlemen! America means Fair Play for all Men."

Lesson 1
Stereotypes

Across human history people have been suspicious of and often hostile to strangers. Those of other cultures are "others," people different from us. For a variety of reasons, we stereotype and label "others," usually with derogatory terms, though not always. For example, many people "know" that Asian students excel in academics, especially the sciences. Do they?

Our Stereotypes

The assumption of this lesson is that most non-Asian students have some stereotypes about Asians embedded in their consciousness. These stereotypes are usually oversimplified ideas about people who are different from us. We absorb these misconceptions from the media, the street, our families, and from books. Before they leave elementary school, most children of Asian heritage have heard at least one of the following slanders and phrases: "slant eyes," "yellow," "math genius," "sneaky," "chink," "coolie," "they all look alike." Non-Asian peers may pass individuals of Asian heritage on the street or in the mall and pull up the outer corners of their eyes. They may imitate the cadence of an Asian language.

Conversely, the Chinese have held strong stereotypes of non-Asian people for centuries. They referred to them as barbarians, even in official documents. Chinese immigrants to the West Coast of the United States called Americans "demons." Many Chinese think of Westerners (Americans and Europeans) as blunt to the point of rudeness, lacking in respect, and devoid of culture. In short, still barbarians.

The Teacher's Role

Our job as teachers and students is to uncover the ethnic and racial prejudices that exist in our institutions, our culture, and in ourselves and to explore history in a careful, inclusive, and truthful manner. Depending on the composition of the class, there may be students who feel particularly vulnerable or targeted by the material discussed on a given day. Students who are of mixed ethnicity may feel conflicted. All students should be encouraged to express their thoughts and feelings; students learn a great deal from each other.

Giving students ample time to reflect in writing on what they have learned is a good outlet for feelings, and also a way to discover a student who may be having an especially difficult time. A piece of private, reflective writing may reveal conflicts appropriate for the whole class to discuss, or individual conflicts that need to be responsibly addressed by the teacher.

Students seldom have the opportunity to engage in critical, analytical discussions about ethnicity and race. Our role as educators is to provide them with information and tools to do so constructively. Students can be engaged in setting class guidelines for discussion of controversial subjects. Some examples follow.

• All opinions and expressions of feelings and emotions are accepted and respected in class, whether other students share them or not.

• Opinions and feelings expressed on sensitive topics should be kept within the confines of the classroom.

• Students should speak from their own experience, using "I-statements" as much as possible. This simply means that students should start with the phrase, "I think, I heard, I believe, I feel…" rather than "You're wrong because…". The latter can feel like a direct attack on another speaker.

• Students should know also that it would be fine to choose not to speak.

Organizing Idea

Stereotyping "others," usually in derogatory fashion, is a common human characteristic. To counter racial stereotyping we need to explore its roots and raise our awareness.

Student Objectives

Students will:

- become aware that we all have prejudices
- begin to understand the reasons behind why people stereotype others
- identify hurtful stereotypes of Chinese and other Asian peoples
- develop approaches to counter racial and ethnic stereotyping

Key Questions

- Why do people stereotype "others"?
- How is stereotyping destructive?
- How are racial and ethnic stereotypes created?
- How can we learn to respect and appreciate differences?

Vocabulary

barbarian
ethnic
prejudice
stereotype

Student Activities

›› Activity 1: Getting Labels Out in the Open

Distribute scraps of paper to students and ask them to write on each piece of paper one ethnic label or slur that they've heard used against any ethnic or racial group. (You may need to define what a slur is, give an example, and explain that slurs can be both ethnic and racial.) Collect all the scraps and list the words on the board.

- Ask students what types of words these are. What, if anything, do the words have in common?
- Have them categorize the terms.
- Which words on the list have they heard used to describe people of Hispanic origin, African Americans, people of European descent, people from Asia, from the Middle East, from Africa?
- Where have they heard these terms used?
- Why are ethnic and racial labels created?
- In what other ways, besides verbal assaults, are people stereotyped? (For example, ethnic jokes, cartoons, movies, etc.)
- At the end of the discussion, throw all of the scraps of paper in the trash.

PRIMARY SOURCES related to Activity 2

Document 1.1: Illustration, "The Chinese Question," *Harper's Weekly*, 1871

» Activity 2: Examining 19th-Century Illustrations

Divide the students into small groups and distribute the two illustrations from *Harper's Weekly* (1.1 and 1.2). Students should discuss their responses to the images and take notes.

Document 1.1:

- What is happening in this illustration? (Note also how the Irishman is depicted.)
- How are the men on the right dressed? How is the individual on the left dressed?
- List the words from the sign that describe men from China.
- Why might there have been such an outpouring of negative sentiment toward Chinese immigrants in the early 1870s? (See http://memory.loc.gov/learn/features/immig/chinese6.html for information about the Chinese Exclusion Act of 1882.)

Document 1.2: Illustration, "Ching Cartoon," *Harper's Weekly*, 1894

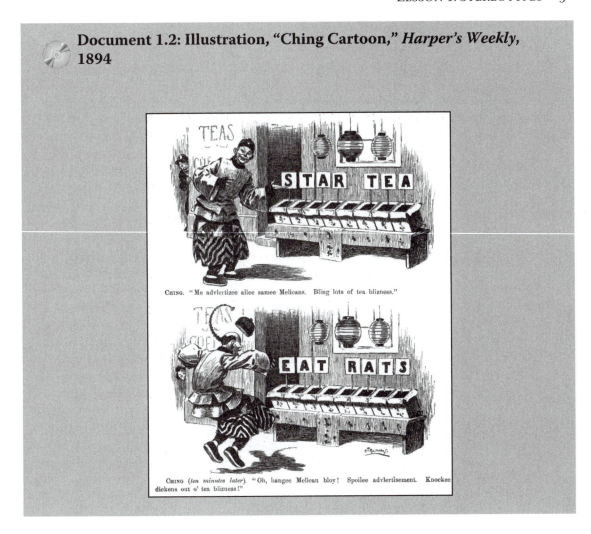

CHING. "Me advlertizee allee samee Melicans. Bling lots of tea blizness."

CHING (*ten minutes later*). "Oh, hangee Melican bloy! Spoilee advlertisement. Knockee dickens out o' tea blizness!"

Document 1.2:

- Explain what you see in the cartoon.
- Why is the spelling of the captions odd?
- How is the man dressed? Why?
- What is each person in the two images doing?
- What messages about the Chinese does this cartoon convey?

After students have shared their observations and conclusions with each other, ask them what the artists' intent was in each illustration. Read the "In the World Today" sidebar at the end of Lesson 16 to learn more about Chinese men and the building of the Transcontinental Railway. What can students conclude about the attitude of people of European descent toward individuals from China in the 19th century? Based on their examination of these illustrations and the list of ethnic slurs they generated, discuss how much has and has not changed in over a century.

PRIMARY SOURCES related to Activity 3
Document 1.3: Excerpts from *Dragonwings* by Laurence Yep

Eight-year-old Moon Shadow leaves China to join his father in San Francisco. After living in Chinatown for a few months, he and his father move into an area populated by Americans of European descent. Moon Shadow is about to meet their landlady for the first time.

Father took my hand as if he knew I needed the support, and we started toward the demon house. . . . [W]e went up the back steps and knocked on the door. Under my shirt, I wore the charm to keep demons away.

I think that the demoness had been waiting for us, because Father had no sooner knocked once than she opened the door. She was the first demoness that I had ever seen this close up, and I stared. I had expected her to be ten feet tall with blue skin and to have a face covered with warts and ear lobes that hung all the way down to her knees so that her ear lobes would bounce off the knees when she walked. And she might have a potbelly shiny as a mirror, and big sacs of flesh for breasts, and maybe she would only be wearing a loin cloth.

Instead I saw a petite lady, not much bigger than Hand Clap [*a relative*]. She had a large nose—but not absurdly so—and a red face and silver hair; and she wore a long dress of what looked like white cotton, over which she had put a red apron. The dress was freshly starched, and crinkled when she moved and smelled good. . . .

"Well," she said. "Well." I looked at her eyes and saw a friendly twinkle in them that made her seem even less threatening. There were demons, after all, who could be kindly disposed. I suddenly felt calm and unafraid as I stood before her.

❯❯ Activity 3: Views of Westerners from Historical Fiction

Students should read the excerpts from Laurence Yep's and Peter Hessler's books (1.3 and 1.4).

- How do Chinese children and young adults view Westerners?
- Is their view accurate?
- Why might they have this view of people other than the Chinese among whom they live?
- How do stereotypes come to exist and how are they perpetuated?

In small groups have students generate ideas for countering ethnic and racial stereotyping. What can each student do? What can students do as a class? What can the community do?

Document 1.4: A journal entry by a Chinese student in 1996 from *River Town: Two Years on the Yangtze* by Peter Hessler

Peter Hessler spent two years (1996–98) as a Peace Corps volunteer in Fuling, Sichuan Province. He taught English Literature at a Chinese Teachers' College. He observed many aspects of life in China. This journal entry was written by one of his students.

People in the west like the girl who is elegant or the girl who is sexuality? But I always heard a view that girl in the east is famous for her elegance and the girl in the west is famous for her sexuality.

The girls in China, most of them are elegant, refined, and kind. They always do something following rules. It's the Chinese tradition.

But the girls in the west are very open to outside. They can marry anyone and get divorced whenever. Don't mind the appraise of others. They can do everything that she wants to do, not concern about whether it's wrong or right. They lead a loose life.

I think I like the statue and virtue of the girl in the east. They are elegant, refined.

» Activity 4: Searching for Stereotypes in the Media

Ask students to find at least two examples of ethnic or racial stereotyping in magazines, television commercials or programs, or movies. They should bring in printed materials and create a collage of these examples or write brief descriptions of other examples from the media. Discuss as a class what stereotypes are being reinforced.

» Activity 5: A Connection to Literature

Have students read *The Kite Rider* by Geraldine McCaughrean, an award-winning British novelist. As McCaughrean explains, man-carrying (or boy-carrying) kites probably did not exist in the 13th century, but other details in the book are historically accurate. One of the threads the author weaves through the book is the attitude of the Chinese toward the invading Mongols. Students can witness the main character's, Haoyou's, changing perspective and reflect on why his attitude changes. The story also lends itself to careful examination of the value of traditions, the roles of children and adults, and the definition of character traits such as loyalty, greed, and courage.

Further Student and Teacher Resources

Choy, Philip P., Lorraine Dong, and Marlon K. Hom, eds. *Coming Man: 19th Century American Perceptions of the Chinese.* Seattle: University of Washington Press, 1994.

Wong, Vivian Wu and Yoshihisa Tak Matsusaka. *Early Chinese Immigration and the Process of Exclusion.* A Unit of Study for Grades 8–12. The National Center for History in the Schools, University of California, Los Angeles, 1998.

Web Sites

http://www.askasia.org/teachers/Instructional_Resources/Lesson_Plans/index.htm (lesson plans designed to broaden students' view of Asian countries and cultures, includes lessons on stereotyping)

http://www.pbs.org/inthemix/whatsnormal_index.html (site for *In the Mix*, a PBS program for teenagers on overcoming obstacles and stereotypes. It includes teens talking, video clips, and various episodes.)

www.caaav.org (site for the Committee Against Anti-Asian Violence, which is especially active in New York City)

http://en.wikipedia.org/wiki/Chinese_Exclusion_Act_of_1882 and http://www.mtholyok.edu/acad/intrel/chinex.htm (for information on the Chinese Exclusion Act of 1882)

In the World Today

Media Portrayals of Asian Americans

Media Action Network for Asian Americans has among their goals "to advocate and provide reinforcement for fair, accurate, sensitive, and balanced depictions of persons of Asian Pacific descent in all facets of the media." The following is from the group's Web site, www.manaa.org.

"For decades, American entertainment media have defined the Asian image to all the world. And usually, that image has been shaped by people with little understanding of Asian people themselves—and with little foresight into how such images would impact the Asian American community. Despite the good intentions of individual producers and filmmakers, limited and unbalanced portrayals of Asians have traditionally been the norm in the entertainment industry.

"Too often, an Asian face or accent is presented as a shorthand symbol for anything antithetical to American or Western culture. Too often, no distinctions are made between Asian Americans—acculturated U.S. citizens with deep roots in this nation— and Asian nationals who may or may not have any loyalty to the United States. Too often, the media insinuate that Asian Americans don't belong in their own country.

"Not all Hollywood projects with Asians are objectionable, however. In fact, some Hollywood movies—such as *Dragon: The Bruce Lee Story* and *The Joy Luck Club*—have been widely welcomed by Asian American audiences. But Hollywood typically restricts its portrayals of Asians to a limited range of cliched stock characters. And this has affected how Asian Americans are perceived and treated in the broader society."

For a list of common stereotypes, students can click on the site's "Stereotype Busters" link. Discuss as a class how ethnic stereotypes in the media can best be addressed.

Lesson 2 CD-ROM Contents

Primary Sources

- Document 2.1a–k: Photographs of landscape in Gansu, Shaanxi, Yunnan, Guizhou, and Anhui provinces
- Document 2.2: "The Land," chapter describing land cultivation from *River Town: Two Years on the Yangtze* by Peter Hessler
- Document 2.3: Excerpt describing government response to flooding during reign of Emperor Shun, approximately 2255 B.C.E., in *Records of the Historian* (《史记》) by Sima Qian (司马迁), written between 105 and 90 B.C.E.
- Document 2.4: Excerpt describing a flood from *Ju Lin Wai Shih* (*Informal History of the Forest of Scholars*, 《儒林外史》) by Wu Ching-tzu (吴敬梓), written in mid-1700s
- Document 2.5: Excerpt from *Forty-five Years in China. Reminiscences by Timothy Richard*, describing a famine
- Document 2.6: Image of water pump, 12th century
- Document 2.7: Painting of men maintaining dikes along the Yellow River, 1700s

Suplementary Materials

- Item 2.A: Outline map of the world
- Item 2.B: Outline map of China
- Item 2.C: Average yearly precipitation in China
- Item 2.D: Excerpts describing a flood from *The Good Earth* by Pearl Buck

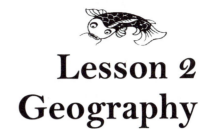

Lesson 2
Geography

Lesson Contents
- Landform
- Rivers
- Climate

Geography is one of the factors that affects the history, culture, and daily lives of a people. The natural environment provides both opportunities and challenges to overcome. China's location, coastline, landforms, rivers, and climate play a crucial role in its history and culture. In the interaction of people and nature, each contributes to the shaping of the other.

Landform

The people of ancient China (中国), in their quest to open new lands to agriculture and to ward off devastating floods and droughts, changed their environment through great cooperative human effort. They built terraces on hills, drained marshes, created new waterways by building canals, and contained rivers by building dikes. Even level areas, such as the plains and banks of rivers, have been modified by human action.

China contains some of the highest mountains of the world, although most of China's uplands are hills and plateaus. Over 60 percent of the land is more than a mile above sea level. The Himalayas, the world's highest mountains, are on China's southwest border. Physical barriers, such as high mountains and deserts, at times isolated China from other civilizations. On the other hand, China's large size, geographical diversity, and natural resources have enabled the country to create and maintain rich and varied cultures.

Today more than 1.3 billion people live in China—more than one out of five of the people on our earth. While China is essentially the same size as the United States, only about 13 percent of its land is suitable for growing crops (compared with approximately 40 percent of U.S. land). In addition, China is a country where natural disasters—floods, droughts, and earthquakes—have occurred frequently, exacting a huge human toll.

Rivers

Two major rivers, both of which flow for thousands of miles from west to east, are China's most prominent geographic features. The northernmost of these is the *Huang He* (黄河), or Yellow River. The 3,395-mile-long (5460 km) river gets its name from the amount of yellow earth—*loess* (黄土)—in the water. *Loess* is the fine, yellow, wind-blown soil of North China, which blows in from the Gobi Desert and provides a fertile base for agriculture. Vast quantities of loess are eroded by rainfall, carried into streams, and then into the *Huang He* as dense sediment that gives the river its color and name. In the lower reaches of the *Huang He,* the deposits of the eroded sediment constantly raise its level. In some areas, because natural and manmade banks keep compensating or being built higher, the river itself actually flows above the level of the fields. When the river breaks through its banks, floods devastate the surrounding countryside and ruin the crops and livelihood of many farmers who live along it. As a result, *Huang He* has earned the name "China's sorrow." However, the water and loess it carries have also made agriculture possible for millennia. In recent decades, the flow of the river has decreased substantially in the lower reaches of the *Huang He,* so instead of flooding there is now only a trickle of a stream. Indeed, it is in the rich soil of the river's bottom that farmers now till their fields.

Another major river system is called the *Chang Jiang* (长江), the Yangtze River. It is the longest river in China and one of the five longest rivers in the world. It rises in Tibet and flows 3,494 miles (6300 km) down through Central China to the coast at Shanghai. Fed by snowmelt and heavy rain, this river and its tributaries (more than 3,000) provide the major transportation system for this region of China. Approximately 40 percent of China's grain and 70 percent of its rice production occur in the river's huge basin. For these reasons, many of China's important cities have developed here and made it one of the most densely populated areas in the world.

Climate

China has great climatic differences resulting from the large size of the country, the variety of its natural features, and the monsoon-like wind system that controls precipitation. Although China does not experience the prominent monsoons of South Asia, there is a monsoon-like seasonal reversal of winds in East Asia. This is especially true in winter, when winds blow out from Central Asia, carrying cold, dry air toward the sea in North China, extending into some areas of southern China. To some degree, this is like the arrival of the bitterly cold and dry Arctic air masses that *sometimes* affect the winter weather of the northern United States. In China, this occurs throughout every winter. From late spring to early fall, on the other hand, moist and hot air blows inland from the sea, leading to substantial rainfall when the air rises over the hills and mountains. Because of these monsoon-like seasonal reversals of winds, more rain falls in summer than in winter throughout China. Most parts of the country receive more than 80 percent of their rainfall from May to October. Moreover, far more rain falls south of the Yangtze River than on North China. In North China rainfall occurs mostly in the summer, but it is unpredictable and varies from year to year, often creating drought or flooding. Life is much harder for farmers in North China than in South China.

Temperatures in China vary greatly from region to region. Northern and western China have cold and long winters like those in north-central United States. In South China winters are usually mild. Summer temperatures average about 80–90 degrees Fahrenheit (26–32 degrees Celsius) throughout much of China, but in southeastern China summers are also extremely humid.

Land formation and climate in China determine which crops are grown in different regions. This has, in turn, dictated people's diet. The staple foods in the north are noodles and dumplings made of wheat and other hardy grains, such as millet and sorghum; even steamed bread is commonly eaten. In southeastern and eastern China, on the other hand, people generally eat rice rather than wheat. Rice, too, can be made into noodles and dumplings in addition to being steamed. Poultry and pork are preferred meats because raising these animals requires little land, unlike the grazing of cattle. China's environment has influenced every aspect of its history and culture, from the location of major cities to innovative farming practices to the food people eat.

Organizing Idea

China's diverse landscape and dramatic climatic events have influenced the course of her history. For centuries the Chinese people have found ingenious solutions to the challenges their environment presents.

Student Objectives

Students will:

- learn basic facts about the location and topography of China
- create a Big Map and their own desk maps
- place major rivers, deserts, and mountains on the Big Map and their own desk maps
- identify major factors that affect climate
- identify main climate regions in China
- understand how topography and climate determine people's diet

Key Questions

- Where is China?
- What are China's topographic characteristics?
- How does China's topography affect people's ability to grow food?
- Where in China do most people live? Why?
- What are some differences between the climates of North and South China?
- What are monsoons and how do they affect the climate of China?
- What solutions have Chinese people found for environmental challenges?
- How has China's environment affected what crops people in different regions grow and eat?

Vocabulary

arable
climate
dike
drought
irrigation
loess
monsoon
plateau
river basin
steppe
temperate
terrace
topography

Supplementary Materials

Item 2.A: Outline map of the world
Item 2.B: Outline map of China
Item 2.C: Average yearly precipitation in China
Item 2.D: Excerpts describing a flood from *The Good Earth* by Pearl Buck

Student Activities

» Activity 1: What Do You Know?

Ask students the following questions and record their various answers (right and wrong) on the board.

- Where is China?
- Compared to the United States how big is China?
- What type of topography does it have?
- What crops do the Chinese grow and what animals do they raise?
- What have been the students' sources of information?

PRIMARY SOURCES related to Activity 3

Document 2.1a–k: Photographs of landscape in Gansu, Shaanxi, Yunnan, Guizhou, and Anhui provinces

Photo by Renee Covalucci

2.1e Loess plateau, Yaodong, Shaanxi (陕西) Province

Photo by Michael Abraham

2.1j Qing Man village in Guizhou (贵州) Province, with rice paddies in the valley

Photo by Kongli Liu

2.1b Huang He, in downtown Lanzhou, Gansu (甘肃) Province

Photo by Ronald G. Knapp

2.1k Mountain village in Anhui (安徽) Province

• *The remaining photos are available on the CD-ROM* •

» Activity 2: China on a World Map

Using an overhead projector, project an outline map of the world onto a large piece of paper. Create a Big Map, following the instructions in Teacher Resources on the CD-ROM. Ask students to take turns and to label continents and oceans on the map. Then identify the United States, Mexico, Canada, Russia, India, China, Vietnam, Korea, Taiwan, and Mongolia. Hang the map in a prominent place in the classroom. Discuss some obvious physical features of China, such as its neighbors and the ocean.

» Activity 3: A Photographic Exhibit—An Introduction to the Topography of China

Display the photographs of Chinese landscape (2.1a–k) around the classroom. Explain that these photographs were taken in China in the past ten years but that what they see is largely unchanged from the way it's been for centuries. Have students examine the images and jot down notes about exactly what they see in each photograph. Reconvene as a class and discuss:

- What types of temperate zones do the photographs show?
- What crops are being grown?
- What is the climate likely to be in Gansu Province (2.1a)? In the loess plateau of Shaanxi Province (2.1d)? In Guizhou Province (2.1i)?
- What surprised them about the photographs? What else would they like to know and where can they find answers?

›› Activity 4: Creating a Topographic Map of China

Students should read the introduction to the lesson, or the teacher can present a short lecture.

- Identify a river near where the students live. How long is it from its source to the mouth? How does that compare to either the Yellow River or the Yangtze River?
- Are there mountains in the vicinity? What's the tallest mountain in the United States? How does the height of these compare to that of Mount Everest?
- Then project an outline map of China (Item 2.B) onto a large piece of paper. Follow the instructions for making a Big Map in Teacher Resources on the CD-ROM. At the same time, students will work on individual outline maps at their desks. Students should establish map keys and a color code. Using their atlases or Internet resources, they then add basic land formations—rivers, river basins, mountain ranges, lowlands, plateaus, deserts—to their maps. One option is to sponge paint each temperate zone in a different light color. Ask students to note on their maps (and on the Big Map) the places where the photographs were taken (2.1a–k).

Note: Students may be interested to learn that Chinese has two words for river: *he* (as in *Huang He*, the Yellow River) and *jiang* (*Chang Jiang*, the Yangtze River). *He* is a relatively quietly flowing river, such as the Mississippi River in the United States. *Jiang*, on the other hand, is more tumultuous like the Colorado River.

›› Activity 5: What Can a Topographic Map Teach Us?

Based on their maps, ask the students to speculate:

- Where is the best farming land in China? Why?
- What are the advantages and disadvantages of the major rivers?
- How might the mountain ranges and the deserts affect farming? How might it have affected contact with people in other lands?
- How did people travel in the past?
- Where were towns and cities built? Why?
- Ask students to find out what conditions are needed to cultivate rice and wheat. Then identify where these probably grow in China.
- Why does two-thirds of the population live in the eastern and southeastern third of the country?

In an atlas or online, look at maps that show agriculture of China. Have students verify their hypotheses and then add information to the Big Map and their own maps indicating where various crops grow.

» Activity 6: Mapping the Climate

Define climate and list the characteristics of the students' regional climate. Find out what the average rainfall is in your area and when most of it comes. Define and discuss monsoon. Create a new Big Map using the chart of China's rainfall (Item 2.C) and information from an atlas. Students can use light water-based paints and sponges to sponge-paint different areas of precipitation. They can also add symbols to show hot and cold regions. Which climate of China does their own climate most closely match?

PRIMARY SOURCE related to Activity 7

Document 2.2: "The Land," chapter describing land cultivation from *River Town: Two Years on the Yangtze* by Peter Hessler

May 5

Along the southern shoulder of the mountain a long thin field is being harvested; workers are piling the wheat stalks into bundles and tying them with reeds. The bundles weigh more than fifty pounds each, and they must be carried to shelters where they will be kept dry. A young man takes a long sturdy stick and stabs it into the heart of a bundle, lifting it onto his shoulder. He uses its weight to help him stick the other end deep into another bundle, and then he lifts both bales, adjusts the load, and carries them balanced across his back. He walks quickly, moving with a loose-kneed bouncing gait, heading toward home.

May 11

After six days the harvested wheat field is unrecognizable. It has been flooded and half filled with rice shoots, their green tips poking above the water like drowning blades of grass. In less than a week, the wheat field has been turned into a rice paddy.

• Full text available on CD-ROM •

≫ Activity 7: Reading about Land Cultivation

Have students read "The Land," a chapter in Peter Hessler's book (2.2). Divide the class into groups and ask each group to address one of the questions below. Then reconfigure the groups so that the new groups have at least one member each of the original groups. Ask students to share the answer to their question with members of the new group.

- Compare the old and new methods of transplanting rice seedlings.
- What crops do farmers grow in the area near Fuling, where Hessler lived?
- Describe how farmers harvest wheat and what they do with it afterwards.
- What conditions are necessary to grow wheat? What conditions are necessary for rice cultivation? How can the same field be used for both?
- What happened in August of the year about which Hessler writes? Why?

As a follow-up assignment, students can choose to:

- write a description of one aspect of land cultivation they learned about in this chapter
- illustrate one of the scenes Hessler describes in the chapter
- write a poem in response to the chapter

≫ Activity 8: The Effects of Climate on Human Life

The climate of a region and long rivers such as the Yangtze and Yellow Rivers can have constructive and destructive effects on human life. The history of China is filled with accounts of floods and droughts and the resulting famines. As recently as 1998, flooding in the *Chang Jiang* (Yangtze River) valley killed some 3,656 people and left 14 million homeless. Divide the class into small groups and have each group read one of the descriptions of flood and/or famine (Documents 2.3–2.5 and secondary sources, Items 2.D and 2.E). Ask students to take notes in response to the questions that apply to their selection and to prepare a brief summary.

- What does the author/character describe seeing and hearing?
- What are some of the ways people responded to famines?
- How did government officials respond to the crisis?

Have the students share their summaries with their classmates. Then discuss what appears to have caused the famines. Why did government response vary? Ask students to suggest additional possible approaches to prevent the crises and/or solutions once they occur.

PRIMARY SOURCE related to Activity 8

Document 2.3: Excerpt describing government response to flooding during reign of Emperor Shun, approximately 2255 B.C.E., in *Records of the Historian* (《史记》) by Sima Qian (司马迁), written between 105 and 90 B.C.E.

Sima Qian (145–ca. 90 B.C.E.) worked as court historian during the Han (汉) dynasty (206 B.C.E.–220 C.E.), and compiled Records of the Historian, *the first official history of China. The work of 130 chapters was based on all the documents recording Chinese traditions and legends that were available to him at the time. Sima Qian began the history of China with the legend of the Yellow Emperor, Huangdi (黄帝).*

In this excerpt the historian described how the legendary Great Yu (大禹) had been chosen by Emperor Shun (舜) (believed to have come to power around 2255 B.C.E.) to "open up the nine provinces" of China, to make "the roads communicable," bank "up the marshes," and to survey the hills. "Yu in this way worked for the mutual convenience of the respective districts as regards the distribution of the wealth and resources of the country." According to legend, Yu is credited with extensive water-control projects. Seventeen years before he died, Emperor Shun chose Yu as his successor. Emperor Yu is said to have founded the Xia (夏) dynasty (ca. 21st century–16th century B.C.E.).

Yu said, "When the flood assailed the heavens, and in its vast expanse encompassed the mountains and overtopped the hills, so that the common people were overcome by the water, I traveled on dry land in a carriage, went about on the water in a boat, in miry places I used a sledge, while in going over the hills I used spikes. All along the hills I hewed paths through the woods, and together with Yi supplied the people with paddy [rice] and fresh meat. In order to drain the nine streams into the four seas, I deepened the channels and canals, and connected them with the rivers, and together with Millet [prince of one of the provinces] and the people in general when it was difficult to obtain food, and when food was scarce I bartered the surplus stock to make up for deficiencies, and removed the stores. Thus the people were quieted, and the various states properly governed."

Document 2.4: Excerpt describing a flood from *Ju Lin Wai Shih* (*Informal History of the Forest of Scholars*, 《儒林外史》) by Wu Ching-tzu (吴敬梓), written in mid-1700s

One day in the clear early dawn [Wang Mian] was sitting in his room when he was amazed to see a great crowd of men and women shrieking and wailing as they moved down the street. In the baskets that hung from their shoulder poles, some had pots and household things and some had children. All were gaunt and ragged. They streamed past, rank and rank, filling up the street. Some sat on the ground and begged. Asked why they were here, they said they had come from the shires and counties along the Yellow River. Their fields and homes had been swept away, they said, when the river broke through the dikes and flooded the countryside. They were ordinary folk fleeing a disaster for which the government had no concern. So they could only take to the road to survive.

Document 2.5: Excerpt from *Forty-five Years in China. Reminiscences by Timothy Richard*, describing a famine

February 2. At the next city was the most awful sight I ever saw. It was early in the morning when I approached the city gate. On one side of it was a pile of naked dead men, heaped on top of each other as though they were pigs in a slaughterhouse. On the other side of the gate was a similar heap of dead women, their clothing having been taken away to pawn for food. Carts were there to take the corpses away to two great pits, into one of which they threw the men and into the other the women…For many miles in this district the trees were all white, stripped clean for ten or twenty feet high of their bark, which was being used for food…

• Full text available on CD-ROM •

Item 2.D: Excerpts describing a flood from *The Good Earth* by Pearl Buck

There were no harvests of any kind that year and everywhere people starved and were hungry and were angry at what had befallen them yet again. Some went south, and some who were bold and angry and cared nothing for what they did joined the robber bands that flourished everywhere in the countryside. These even tried to beleaguer the town so that the townspeople locked the gates of the wall continually except for one small gate called the western water gate, and this was watched by soldiers and locked at night also. And besides those who robbed and those who went south to work and to beg, even as Wang Lung had once gone with his old father and his wife and children, there were others who were old and tired and timid, and who had no sons, like Ching, and these stayed and starved and ate grass and what leaves they could find on high places and many died upon the land and water.

• *Full text available on CD-ROM* •

» Activity 9: Looking at Solutions to Challenges Created by Climate and Landforms

Explain to students that besides the extensive irrigation projects constructed on the plains bordering the Yangtze River as far back as the 5th century B.C.E., the Chinese have tried many ways to temper the devastating effects of their climate. In 321 C.E. men created two giant reservoirs near what is now Jinjiang in Jiangsu Province to counter periodic droughts. Many canals have been dug, in part to facilitate transportation of grain to areas struck by famine. Distribute copies of the image of men working a water pump and men maintaining dikes along the Yellow River (Documents 2.6 and 2.7). Discuss:

- How does the water pump work?
- Why might it be useful?
- What is the purpose of the dikes?
- Based on this painting, how were dikes constructed? What work has already been done that is not shown in the painting?
- What are men carrying in the containers?
- How labor-intensive does this work appear to be?

Keeping in mind all that you've learned about the climate and about how both rivers have broken through dikes and flooded the countryside hundreds of times, how could dike building be improved?

What major floods have occured in other countries in recent times? What caused the flooding?

Item 2.E: Excerpts describing effects of a flood from *The Examination* by Malcolm Bosse

This young adult historical novel tells the story of two brothers, Chen and Hong, traveling hundreds of miles across China so the elder brother can take advanced levels of the civil service exams. This event takes place on the final leg of their journey.

The little man smiled grimly. "You'll be going through flooded country. Remember that. Water's been in everything. Every storage bin, every grain cellar, every pot and jar has either been buried in mud or washed away or ruined by water. That means nothing to eat. That means when two young fellows like you come along, looking well fed and healthy, people will just naturally want what's in the bundles you're carrying."…

When the brothers reach the flooded area, they are horrified by what they see floating in the river: household goods, farm tools, sections of homes, and bloated corpses. Then they hear voices behind them and see two women leaning against the wall of a hut. They offer them some rice.

[T]he young woman refused to eat, refused even to acknowledge the offer, the older woman lifted her rice-filled hand and munched slowly. To swallow seemed painful. After she had chewed awhile, eating a small portion of the rice, she poured the rest carefully into the pocket of her blouse. "May the gods bless you," she muttered at Chen. "We got here I don't know how." She seemed confused by what she was saying. "Our whole village went down. My granddaughter drowned, I think. My daughter"—she glanced at the younger woman—"this one—was swept away. No, not this one. I have three daughters, good girls, and two sons, and four grandchildren, one girl, three boys. It filled up everything until everything washed away. Two horses, goat, some dogs, I think. They were taken straight across the field, swept away like twigs, swept away by so much water I wonder where it came from. We lived on tree bark. Ah yes, that's when granddaughter died. She didn't drown. She was one that starved. Another one did, probably all the others did. And Two Daughter [her second born daughter] here has stopped eating. Look at her. She won't eat again." The woman shook her head sadly. "No, my Number Two girl won't ever eat again."

PRIMARY SOURCES related to Activity 9
Document 2.6: Image of water pump, 12th century

Courtesy of Smithsonian Freer Gallery of Art

Officials during the Song (宋) dynasty (960–1279 C.E.) wanted to promote the best in agricultural technology and had artists draw twelve illustrations to show the steps peasants should follow. Foot-powered water pumps, such as this one, came in various designs. Many needed only one person to operate the pump.

Document 2.7: Painting of men maintaining dikes along the Yellow River, 1700s

Photo: Thierry Ollivier. Réunion des Musées Nationaux/Art Resource, NY.

Keeping the dikes along the Yellow River (黄河) in good repair meant that periodically the government enlisted large numbers of farmers for the work.

›› Activity 10: Growing Beans on Terraces

This activity lends itself to collaboration with a science teacher.

Materials

- Two plastic tubs that will not leak
- Soil
- Beans or other quick-growing seeds
- Rulers or materials of hard plastic, which can be used to form walls
- Rocks
- Water

Have students follow the instructions for creating two planting environments:

In the first tub, pile soil up against one side of the tub, sloping it from top to bottom and leaving one-third of the tub's bottom without soil.

In the second tub, use the rulers and rocks to build several levels of terraces. Build the terraces from the bottom up. Lay a ruler on its side lengthwise and bury it halfway with soil. If necessary, use the rocks to stabilize and extend the wall. Fill in the uphill side with soil to the top of the ruler. Bury another ruler halfway in the soil several inches back from the first. Fill in the uphill side with soil to the top of the ruler and stabilize with rocks. Continue this process until the tub is terraced. Make sure the land in each terrace is fairly level. The walls should be strong enough that they will not collapse when seeds and seedlings are watered.

Plant the beans or other seeds in each tub. Water regularly. Erosion and slippage should begin to appear in the tub without terracing. Students should also notice water running off the slope and pooling in the bottom of the tub. Once the seeds have been planted students should not rearrange the dirt. Just let things take their natural course.

After the plants have begun to grow, ask students to write about what they have observed. What are the advantages of terracing on steep slopes?

›› Activity 11: Essay Writing—A Wrap Up

Have students write an essay in which they address one of these topics:

- a description and comparison of two major temperate zones in China, where they are located, and how people live in each zone
- the most important features of the country and how they affect the people in positive and negative ways
- the advantages and disadvantages of China's physical borders

Further Student and Teacher Resources

Budnick, Dan et al. (photography), Kevin Sinclair (text). *Over China*. Los Angeles: Knapp Press, 1998. (includes hundreds of aerial photographs of China's topography taken from a hot air balloon)

Dai, Qing. *The River Dragon Has Come! The Three Gorges Dam and the Fate of China's Yangtze River and Its People*. New York: M. E. Sharpe, 1998. (compilation of essays and field reports)

Hayman, Richard Perry. *Three Gorges on the Yangzi, Grand Canyons of China*. New York: Odyssey Publication, Ltd, 2000. (includes many photographs and information on the dam)

Hong, Qiu Yao, trans. *Origins of Chinese Food Culture*. Singapore: Asiapac Books, 2003.

Lynn, Madeleine, ed. *Yangtze River: The Wildest, Wickedest River on Earth*. New York: Oxford University Press, 1997. (collection of writing, spanning thirteen centuries, about the Yangtze River)

The Three Gorges on the Yangtze River. Haifeng Publishing House, 1994. (text in Chinese and English with many photographs)

Van Slyke, Lyman P. *Yangtze: Nature, History, and the River*. Reading, Mass.: Addison-Wesley Publishing Co., 1988. (tells the story of China from prehistory to the present through the life of the river)

Winchester, Simon. *The River at the Center of the World: A Journey Up the Yangtze and Back in Chinese Time*. New York: Henry Holt & Co., 1996.

Web Sites

For maps

http://academic.brooklyn.cuny.edu/core9/phalsall/images.html

http://www.lib.utexas.edu/maps/china.html

http://depts.washington.edu/chinaciv/geo/land.htm

http://www.worldatlas.com (gives major geographical landforms)

http://afe.easia.columbia.edu/china/geog/maps.htm (an excellent site for maps, information, and assessment tools)

http://depts.washington.edu/chinaciv/geo/yangtze.htm (for information on and images of the Yangtze River)

http://depts.washington.edu/chinaciv/geo/yelriver.htm (for information on and images of the Yellow River)

Video

Yellow Earth (1984), directed by Chen Kaige, is set in the 1930s with evocative cinematography of northern China and the Yellow River.

Three Gorges: The Biggest Dam in the World (1999), Discovery Channel, 52 min. (With great footage of the Gorges and the dam, this film presents mainly a positive view of the controversial project.)

In the World Today

The Three Gorges Dam Project

When completed, the Three Gorges Dam Project will be the world's largest hydro-electric dam. Its stated goal is to prevent the Yangtze River from flooding and to provide energy in a quantity that would rival the production of about eighteen nuclear power plants. At 610 feet high, 1.3 miles wide (185 m high, 2 km wide), and with a reservoir that stretches for 400 miles (640 km) up the river, the completed dam will be an impressive display of engineering comparable to the Great Wall (*Changcheng,* 长城). While many are impressed by the magnitude of this project, it is highly controversial.

Critics of the dam point to a number of issues that have resulted from the construction thus far, and those they believe will result from the completion of the dam. Some are concerned with the cost of the project, predicting that the money, time, and energy put into the project will all be in vain as cheaper sources of energy arise in the future. The dam project is displacing hundreds of thousands of people from their homes and towns. Environmentalists argue that the dam will cause water pollution, deforestation, and coastline erosion. Archaeologists and historians are horrified by the fact that the new reservoirs will permanently destroy historical sites. To counter such criticisms, the Chinese government emphasizes the need to prevent future floods, the value of hydroelectric power, and the prestige that such a large technological success would bring to China. Officials expect the Three Gorges Dam to be finished in 2009.

Ask students to explore online the controversy surrounding this massive project and to debate the pros and cons. Information can be found on the following sites:

http://www.chinaonline.com/refer/ministry_profiles/threegorgesdam.asp
http://www.pbs.org/itvs/greatwall/dam.html
http://news.bbc.co.uk/go/pr/fr/-/2/hi/asia-pacific/2953420.stm

Lesson 3 CD-ROM Contents

Primary Sources

- Document 3.1: Excerpt from *Records of the Historian* (*Shiji*, 《史记》), chapter 1, describing the Five Emperors, by Sima Qian (司马迁), written between 105 and 90 B.C.E.

- Document 3.2: Excerpt from *Records of the Historian* (*Shiji*, 《史记》), chapter 2, "The Xia (夏) Dynasty," by Sima Qian (司马迁), written between 105 and 90 B.C.E.

- Document 3.3: The legend of "The Nine Sacred Cauldrons of Yu" (*Jiu ding chuanshuo*, 九鼎传说) from *The Zuozhuan* (《左传》), written in approximately 300 B.C.E.

- Document 3.4: Photograph of a bronze *jue* (爵), 15th–14th century B.C.E.

- Document 3.5: Photograph of a bronze *lei* (罍), 15th–14th century B.C.E.

- Document 3.6: Photograph of a bronze four-ram *fang zun* (方尊), 13th–11th century B.C.E.

Supplementary Materials

- Item 3.A: Additional vocabulary for primary sources
- Item 3.B: Diagrams showing casting process

Lesson 3
Emergence of a
State-level Society

Lesson Contents

- Defining "civilization" or "state-level society"
- China's Bronze Age
- Uses for bronzes in ancient China

"China has the world's longest continuing civilization" is a statement frequently found in books. But what exactly is "civilization," and how do scholars determine that the civilizations of China began about 3,500 years ago? While we recognize a complex society as a civilization, there is no universal agreement on what exact elements are necessary for a particular people and place to be described in that way. Because the word "civilization" is considered value-laden, some scholars prefer the phrase "state-level society" or "complex society" to describe the shifts toward social complexity that have occurred in many cultures. In China, these shifts signaled the beginning of what is popularly known as the dynastic phase of Chinese history.

State-level Societies

Archaeological work has added a great deal to our understanding of the changes that took place thousands of years ago. Some cultures that had been based on village agriculture, hunting, and gathering gradually moved toward state-level societies. Many important social changes took place during this transition. A ruling elite emerged, who controlled many resources, including human labor. Craft specialists began producing the fine ceramics, metallurgy, jades, and architecture needed by the king and his court. Urban centers arose to serve as political and ritual centers, and also to house a population growing dramatically because of improvements in agricultural practices that produced a food surplus. Writing was developed for the purpose of record keeping and as a way for the elite or ruling class to communicate with guardian powers (ancestors and ruling gods). In addition, the elite could influence the recording of history by making sure that what was written was beneficial to their purpose. In short, writing and record keeping in early state-level societies often served as a tool to legitimize the power of the ruling class. It was not used to educate the ordinary individual.

For centuries, knowledge of China's ancient civilizations was limited to what we now refer to as that of the Han (汉) Chinese living around the North China Plain. This knowledge was based on early written records, of which the most famous is Sima Qian's *Shiji (Records of the Historian,* 《史记》) compiled between 105 and 90 B.C.E. Beginning in the twentieth century, however, spectacular archaeological finds not only confirmed many written records but revealed secrets of ancient China previously unknown. Ancient bronzes and oracle bones (see Lesson 5) unearthed in Henan Province (河南) on the floodplains of the Yellow River (黄河), coupled with the remains of tombs and city sites (see Lesson 11), offer proof of a complicated mosaic of settled and organized societies, dating back 3,500 years and more.

Bronze

One of the most interesting and informative products of state-level society in ancient China is bronze metallurgy, which played a key role in the ritual activities of many of the ancient cultures there. Bronze is an alloy (or mixture) of copper and tin, and the production of bronze vessels involved a very complicated series of steps. First, men had to find and mine the ores that contain these metals. The ores had to be crushed and smelted in a special furnace to separate the copper and tin from the non-metal parts of the rock. Large quantities of the resulting metals were then transported often hundreds of miles to workshops where workers once again melted the metals and mixed them in the right proportions to create bronze. Finally, large numbers of highly skilled craftsmen created bronze vessels of extraordinary beauty using complicated pottery molds for the casting process. This sophisticated bronze industry, supported by the ruling elite, produced military equipment such as helmets, chariot parts, spears, arrowheads, and knives, as well as a variety of vessels used in important state rituals. The importance of bronze both in ritual and in warfare further reinforced the power of the ruling elite that produced them.

In 1980–81 "The Great Bronze Age of China: An Exhibition from the People's Republic of China" toured the United States. In her essay by the same name, Dr. Emily Sano wrote, "Besides revealing the superb skills of ancient artists," the items in the exhibition "enabled us to reconstruct the religious, political, economic, and cultural aspects of civilization which developed at about the same time that Stonehenge was being built in England and the principles of Judaism were being framed."

Organizing Idea

State-level society in China dates back approximately 3,500 years. Legends, ancient histories, and excavated artifacts such as bronze vessels inform us of many aspects of those ancient civilizations.

Student Objectives

Students will:

- become familiar with elements scholars use to recognize a shift to a state-level society
- learn about the complex process of creating a bronze vessel
- understand how archaeological evidence from the Bronze Age of China provides a better understanding of its ancient civilizations
- learn how bronze was related to power and divinity in ancient China

Key Questions

- What are key elements scholars use to recognize a shift to a state-level society?
- What types of cultural changes must have occurred in a society in order for people to be able to create bronze artifacts?
- Who was the Great Yu and for what achievements is he remembered?
- What purposes did bronze vessels serve in ancient China?

Vocabulary

alloy
archaeology
bronze
cauldron
civilization
copper
elite
hierarchy
inscription
ritual
smelt
specialization
subsistence
surplus
tin
vessel

Supplementary Materials

Item 3.A: Additional vocabulary for primary sources
Item 3.B: Diagrams showing casting process

PRIMARY SOURCES related to Activity 1 and 2

Document 3.1: Excerpt from *Records of the Historian* (*Shiji*, 《史记》), chapter 1, describing the Five Emperors, by Sima Qian (司马迁), written between 105 and 90 B.C.E.

Sima Qian (145–ca. 90 B.C.E.) worked as court historian during the Han dynasty (206 B.C.E.–220 C.E.), and compiled Records of the Historian, *the first official history of China. The work of 130 chapters was based on all the documents recording Chinese traditions and legends that were available to him at the time. Sima Qian began the history of China with the legend of the Yellow Emperor, Huangdi (黄帝). Huangdi was the first of the legendary Five Emperors (五帝), said to have ruled from 2697–2597 B.C.E.*

He appointed a chief and deputy superintendent over international affairs, and the various states being at peace, he worshipped the demons and spirits of the hills and streams with the feng and shan ceremonies in numbers. He obtained a valuable tripod, and made calculations of future events, appointing 'Chief of the winds,' 'Strength-governor,' 'Everfirst,' and 'Great Swan,' to direct the people to act in accordance with the celestial and terrestrial arrangements, the dark and bright prognostications, the disputations on life and death, the planting of the crops, plants, and trees in their seasons, and the transformations of birds, beasts, insects, and moths. He also prepared a record of the movements of the sun, moon, and stars; the flow of the tides; and the properties of clay, stones, metals, and gems. He devoted much careful attention to these things, and his observation was applied to ascertaining how fire, water, wood, and other elements could be used economically. There was an auspicious omen of the earth's energy, and he was therefore called 'Yellow god.'

• *Full text available on CD-ROM* •

Student Activities

›› Activity 1: Creating a Time Line

For many students, the concept of 4,500 years can be incomprehensible. One approach is to suggest that we can think of two days (forty-eight hours) as representing the years Before the Common Era (B.C.E.) and the Common Era (C.E.). Yesterday represents Before the Common Era, midnight was Year 1, and today is the Common Era. See Teaching Resources for a time line, which can be used as a guide. Also on the CD-ROM is a template of a dragon that students can use to create their own time lines or a large one that can be displayed in the room. Once students have created the time line and read the introductions to Documents 3.1 and 3.2, ask them to indicate approximately when Huangdi and Yu are said to have ruled. Later they will also add information about the Shang dynasty and the Bronze Age. Many of the lessons include information about events that were happening elsewhere in the world. Students can add these to the class time line as well.

Document 3.2: Excerpt from *Records of the Historian* (*Shiji*, 《史记》), chapter 2, "The Xia (夏) Dynasty," by Sima Qian (司马迁), written between 105 and 90 B.C.E.

In this excerpt the historian described how Yu (禹) had been chosen by Emperor Shun (舜) (ca. 2255 B.C.E.) to work for the "mutual convenience" of the nine districts "as regards the distribution of the wealth and resources of the country." Seventeen years before he died, Emperor Shun chose Yu as his successor. Emperor Yu is said to have founded the Xia dynasty (ca. 21st century–16th century B.C.E.).

Yu, then in company with Yi and Prince Millet, having received the Emperor's orders, bade the princes and people raise a gang of men "to make a division of the land, and following the line of the hills hew down the trees and determine the characteristics of the high hills and great rivers."…When travelling along the dry land he [Yu] used a carriage, on the water he used a boat, in miry places a sledge, while in going over the hills he used spikes. On the one hand he used the marking-line, and on the other the compass and square. Working as the seasons permitted, and with a view to "open up the nine provinces," he made the roads communicable, banked up the marshes, surveyed the hills, told Yi and his band that paddy [rice] should be planted in low damp places, and directed Lord Millet and his band when it was difficult to obtain food, or when food was scarce, to barter their surplus stock in exchange for what they had not, so as to put all the princes on an equal footing…

• *Full text available on CD-ROM* •

›› Activity 2: Recognizing the Achievements of Legendary Kings

Have students read the introduction to the lesson or present the information as a lecture. Students need to have a firm understanding of the elements that indicate a shift to a state-level society before they begin work with the primary source documents. The reading material is challenging, and teachers may wish to divide Documents 3.1 and 3.2 among pairs of students, where each pair is responsible for two or three sentences. Ask students to read the sentences and to determine what is being said about the achievements of either Huangdi (Yellow God or Emperor) or the Great Yu (who is said to have founded the Xia dynasty).

The students then report their findings to the class and compare the achievements to the list of elements that help define a state-level society. Discuss:

- Could China as described in these legends be called a state-level society?
- Is it valid to use a history that is based on legends, oral traditions, and other ancient written records as factual?
- What overall impression do you get of human accomplishment in China during the third millennium B.C.E.?

Add relevant information to the class time line. Finally, students should write a short essay describing six achievements of this period that suggest a shift to a state-level society.

PRIMARY SOURCE related to Activity 3

Document 3.3: The legend of "The Nine Sacred Cauldrons of Yu" (*Jiu ding chuanshuo,* 九鼎传说) from *The Zuozhuan* (《左传》), written in approximately 300 B.C.E.

Large-scale production of bronze began during the Shang dynasty (ca. 1600–ca. 1050 B.C.E.). However, the presence of bronze in China predates the Shang (商) dynasty. The legend of the Nine Cauldrons (ding, 鼎) was first officially recorded in The Zuozhuan. *This is China's oldest narrative history. The legend suggests that bronze already existed when Yu is said to have founded the Xia (夏) dynasty 600 years earlier. Archaeologists have found bronze vessels that date back to 1800 B.C.E. and a bronze knife from Gansu Province (甘肃) from about 3000 B.C.E., making it more than 5,000 years old.*

Long ago...people from distant areas made illustrations of objects and creatures and made tributary offerings of metal to the nine regional stewards [lords]. So [Yu collected metals from the stewards and] forged cauldrons in the image of these creatures. He took precautionary measures against all living things on behalf of the people, to make sure that they knew where were the malign spirits. Therefore, when the people went on rivers or entered marshes, or went on mountains or into forests, they never came across adverse beings; neither goblins or trolls could ever run into them. They also enjoyed the grace of harmony between Heaven above and earth below, and received blessings from Heaven. Jie [of the Xia] was wicked, so the cauldrons and their sovereign power passed over to the Shang for six centuries. [The last ruler of the Shang] was a harsh despot, so the cauldrons passed over to the Zhou. If the virtue of the ruling house is pure and true, even thought the cauldrons might be small, they weigh heavily. If the ruling house is perverted and prone to instability, even though the cauldrons may be large, they are lightweight. Heaven protects pure virtue and keeps it safe.

In 1976, a bronze vessel was discovered with an extraordinary inscription. It reads that the object was commissioned eight days after the defeat of the Shang dynasty (1027 B.C.E.) and the capture of the Nine Cauldrons, also known as the Auspicious Bronzes of the State. To date, the nine cauldrons have not been found.

>> Activity 3: Analyzing the Legend of the Nine Cauldrons

The ancient Chinese believed that if a king possessed the sacred nine cauldrons (*ding*) it was proof that Heaven had bestowed upon him the right to rule. Have students read the introductory material and the legend (3.3), then gather in groups of three and write down all that they have learned from this document. Consider:

- How did the Great Yu create the nine cauldrons?
- How did the cauldrons protect the people?
- What was the relationship between the cauldrons and a king's authority to rule?
- What symbolic role did the cauldrons play?

Discuss the information as a class. Ask the students: If bronze existed at the time of the Great Yu, and based on archaeological digs as far back as 3000 B.C.E., what might this indicate about how society was developing in China at that time? The Great Yu was the founder of the legendary Xia dynasty. Where can the legend be placed on the time line?

PRIMARY SOURCES *related to Activity 4*

Document 3.4: Photograph of a bronze *jue* (爵), 15th–14th century B.C.E.

Courtesy of the Cultural Relics Bureau, Beijing and The Metropolitan Museum of Art

Unlike in other cultures, where bronze was first used primarily for tools and weapons, in China it was not only used for military equipment and weapons, but also for creating enormous quantities of vessels for food and wine used in rituals. Chinese kings believed their right to rule was dependent on good relationships with the spirits of their ancestors, who controlled what would happen to the kingdom. Based on inscriptions on vessels from a later era and on ancient texts, we know that kings and nobles had bronze vessels cast so they could offer food and wine to their ancestors at ceremonial banquets. The *jue* was used for offering wine.

Document 3.5: Photograph of a bronze *lei* (罍), 15th–14th century B.C.E.

Courtesy of the Cultural Relics Bureau, Beijing and The Metropolitan Museum of Art

Chinese kings believed their right to rule was dependent on good relationships with the spirits of their ancestors, who controlled what would happen to the kingdom. Men in power used enormous resources and manpower to have ceremonial bronze vessels made. Each vessel was made for a specific purpose and was meant for a special food or drink. Wine was offered to ancestors in a *lei* at ritual banquets.

Document 3.6: Photograph of a bronze four-ram *fang zun* (方尊), 13th–11th century B.C.E.

Courtesy of the Cultural Relics Bureau, Beijing and The Metropolitan Museum of Art

Like the *jue* the *zun* was used to offer wine to one's ancestors during ritual ceremonies. This bronze vessel was found by peasants digging in hilly countryside, and so scholars believe it must have been cast in a foundry in the southern provinces rather than in the capital city near Anyang. Increasingly, bronze vessels reflected highly sophisticated technical and artistic achievement.

» Activity 4: Examining Photographs of Ancient Bronzes

Indicate the period of the Shang dynasty on the time line (ca. 1600–ca. 1050 B.C.E.). Based on archaeological finds, this is the first period of large-scale production of bronze in China. Share with the class information in the introduction describing the process of creating something out of bronze. Then have students work in small groups, with each group responsible for one photograph of a bronze vessel (3.4–3.6). Each student should have his or her own copy of a photograph. Within each group, further divide the photograph into thirds or quarters, and ask each student to examine that section of the bronze. (Use magnifying glasses if possible.)

- Have the students describe to each other exactly what they see.
- How do they think this vessel was made?
- Ask them to consider all that goes into making something out of bronze. What does the creation of this item suggest about the shift to state-level societies in ancient China?

As a class, collate all the information the students have on bronzes during the Shang dynasty. Now ask students to look at Item 3.B, which describes the unique casting system the Chinese used in making bronze containers. Have students go back to the vessels they examined and reassess how each was probably created.

» Activity 5: Extended Research

Have the students work in small groups and use books and online references to research one of the following topics:

1. The Bronze Age in China lasted some 2,000 years. Explore how the creation of bronze items and their use changed over time.
2. Create a chart showing the step-by-step process of creating a bronze vessel, beginning with the mining of the metals.
3. The discovery of ancient mines has added to our knowledge about mining. What have archaeologists found?
4. Read about the Xia or Shang dynasties and identify the highlights.

Students can share their findings with classmates in a short presentation that includes visual aids.

Further Resources for Students and Teachers

"Ancient China Teaching Kit," created by The International Center for East Asian Archaeology and Cultural History at Boston University includes overheads, lesson plans, and precise replicas of ancient artifacts. It can be rented from the Boston Children's Museum, 800-370-5487, Ext. 231.

Bussagli, Mario. *Chinese Bronzes*. New York: Paul Hamlyn Publishing Group Limited, 1966.

Fong, Wen, ed. *The Great Bronze Age of China*. New York: The Metropolitan Museum of Art, Alfred A. Knopf, Inc., 1980.

Sarin, Amita V. "The Nine Sacred Caldrons of Yu," *Calliope*, Cobblestone Publishing, Inc., October 1997.

Web Sites

For additional information about the Bronze Age in China and ancient Chinese bronze vessels, visit:

http://afe.easia.columbia.edu/china/art/tch_brnz.htm

http://home-2.worldonline.nl/~staalman/China/bronze.html

http://www.nga.gov/education/chinatp_bze.htm

http://www.chinavoc.com/arts/handicraft/bronze.htm

http://www.humanities-interactive.org/ancient/bronze/brochure_bronze_age.htm

http://depts.washington.edu/chinaciv/archae/2tommain.htm (includes lots of information about ancient tombs and excavated artifacts)

Elsewhere in the World

During the Shang dynasty of China, when large scale production of bronze began:

- **the Mycenean civilization developed in Greece (1600 B.C.E.)**
- **Minoan palaces were destroyed in Crete (1450 B.C.E.)**
- **in Phoenicia a phonetic alphabet was developed (ca. 1400 B.C.E.)**
- **the Egyptian empire was at its height (ca. 1300 B.C.E.)**
- **the Hitite empire in Middle East was at its peak (1300 B.C.E.)**
- **the Olmec civilization in Mexico existed (ca. 1200 B.C.E.)**
- **the Exodus of Jews from Egypt occurred (ca. 1240 B.C.E.)**
- **the Trojan War took place, Greece vs. Troy (ca. 1200)**

In the World Today

Tomb of Fu Hao

The tomb of Fu Hao was uncovered in 1976 not far from Anyang (安阳), the location of the last Shang (商) dynasty capital. While many other Shang tombs had already been discovered at Anyang, Fu Hao's was the only royal tomb so far discovered that had not been looted. Oracle bones discovered around Anyang describe Fu Hao not only as the wife of a Shang king, but also as a military leader and powerful figure. Her tomb contained almost 2,000 objects, including hundreds of jade artifacts, more than 200 bronze vessels (the most complete group from the Shang dynasty), and nearly 7,000 cowry shells (the Shang currency). The discovery of Fu Hao's and others' tombs was evidence that the Shang dynasty had in fact existed. Fu Hao's tomb, intact and full of so many valuable artifacts, gives historians extraordinary insight into the kind of wealth that was likely buried in all royal tombs.

Archaeological digs have enjoyed significant support from the People's Republic of China. In his article "Rediscovering China," Professor Albert E. Dien writes, "Archaeology fosters pride in the past and a sense of self-identification, while demonstrating the indigenous nature of Chinese culture. It provides grounds for celebrating what is said to be the genius of the common people, the anonymous creators of the artifacts archaeologists uncover" (*Archaeology*, March/April 1999). For additional information, students should visit these Web sites:

http://www.nga.gov/education/chinatp_fu.htm
(National Gallery of Art. "Teaching Chinese Archaeology" describes what was found in the tomb of Fu Hao.)
http://depts.washington.edu/chinaciv/archae/2fuhmain.htm
(includes pictures of the excavation of the tomb along with a short article describing what was found there, the significance of the discovery, as well as a little history)

Lesson 4 CD-ROM Contents

Primary Sources

- Document 4.1: Photograph of terracotta warriors standing in rank, excavated from pit 1 at the First Emperor's burial site, Shaanxi (陕西) Province
- Document 4.2: Photograph of terracotta charioteer, Qin (秦) dynasty (221–206 B.C.E.)
- Document 4.3: Photograph of terracotta archer, Qin (秦) dynasty (221–206 B.C.E.)
- Document 4.4: Photograph of terracotta general, Qin (秦) dynasty (221–206 B.C.E.)
- Document 4.5: Photograph of bronze chariot, charioteer, and four horses, Qin (秦) dynasty (221–206 B.C.E.)
- Document 4.6: Excerpt describing Qin Shi Huangdi's tomb from *Records of the Historian* (*Shiji*, 《史记》) by Sima Qian (司马迁), written between 105 and 90 B.C.E.

Supplementary Materials

- Item 4.A: Additional vocabulary for primary sources
- Item 4.B: Images of terracotta warriors, without captions

Lesson 4
Archaeology Unlocks the Past

Lesson Contents
- Archaeologists at work
- Qin Shi Huangdi's burial site and Terracotta Warriors

Archaeological discoveries of the twentieth century have transformed our understanding of ancient China. In the past, historians relied on written texts, but were unsure of how to distinguish fact from legend. For example, archaeologists still have not found documentary proof that the Xia (夏) dynasty (21st century to 16th century B.C.E.), to which ancient histories refer, really existed. However, the unearthing of ancient burial sites proves unequivocally that there was a Shang (商) culture that flourished from about 1600 to about 1050 B.C.E., just as historians of ancient China had written. The archaeological digs of the past century have, in some cases, confirmed information in ancient texts. They have also brought to light previously unknown aspects of life in ancient China, and, inevitably, raised questions for scholars to explore further.

Archaeologists at Work

Over time, objects we use and places where we live get buried by layers of dirt and debris. Many have had the experience of finding a long lost toy buried under layers of decomposed leaves in the back yard. Locally, there may be places where foundations of houses remain, partially visible and partially buried by soil. Archaeologists call this accumulation of layers stratification. Sometimes this is a very gradual process: After hundreds of years, many layers can cover places where people lived. In other cases, a single event, such as a major flood or a volcanic eruption, can bury evidence of the past under thick blankets of silt, ash, or other materials.

When archaeologists suspect or know they have found a site where people once lived or were buried, they begin to excavate. They dig very carefully. Generally, the deeper they go, the older the discoveries are likely to be. Archaeologists are like detectives, scientists, and historians blended into one. They may uncover pieces of pottery, which, like a puzzle, they fit back together into a vase. They may excavate foundations of city walls and bronze foundries. Or they may discover stunning burial sites, containing lost documents, tapestries, and other fascinating materials. In China, as elsewhere in the world, some of the most dramatic discoveries have been in tombs.

The Discovery of Qin Shi Huangdi's Burial Complex

In 1974, during one of China's many droughts, farmers were digging a new well about twenty miles east of the city of Xi'an (西安) in Shaanxi (陕西) Province. One shovelful of dirt included a head of clay. The men reacted with horror, believing they had found "a ghost who drank all the water meant for the crops," said Yang Jungeng, one of the farmers. They had actually found what many refer to as "the greatest archaeological find of our time," or even "the Eighth Wonder of the World": the burial complex planned by China's First Emperor, Qin Shi Huangdi (秦始皇帝), to protect his tomb.

Royal Tombs

Usually, the more powerful and wealthy the individual, the more elaborate the plans for the burial site. Concerned about their spirit and safe passage in the afterlife, the powerful spent much of their lives planning and building a tomb. Royalty of the Shang dynasty were buried with exquisite bronzes (see Lesson 3), ceramics, weapons, amulets, and ornaments. Human beings and animals were sacrificed and buried with them to accompany and serve them in their afterlife. In the Zhou (周) dynasty (ca. 1050–256 B.C.E.) complicated burials continued, but gradually wood and clay figurines replaced human sacrifices.

The Terracotta Warriors

To the best of our knowledge, no one planned a more elaborate burial site than the victorious king of Qin (秦), who ruled as "first emperor" (Shi Huangdi) between 221 and 210 B.C.E. (For information on Qin Shi Huangdi's accomplishments, see Lesson 16.) Historians refer to it as a necropolis, a city of the dead. Seven hundred thousand men are said to have worked for about forty years to create this necropolis that covers twenty-two square miles (35 km square). The emperor's grave itself has not yet been excavated, but parts of the huge area surrounding it have. The site includes almost one hundred underground pits and tunnel galleries, containing everything from terracotta grooms and skeletons of horses, to clay models of birds and plants. Three pits stand out. Pit 1 contains thousands of terracotta soldiers standing in ranks, terracotta horses, and the outlines of some 40 wooden chariots. Pit 2 has about 1,400 figures of cavalrymen, infantry, and horses, along with 90 war chariots. Pit 3 holds 68 additional figures. The face of every one of the emperor's terracotta soldiers was individually crafted. From tiny paint chips, archaeologists have concluded that the warriors were originally painted in thirteen different colors. It appears that the pits were once looted and burned, probably when the Qin dynasty collapsed in 206 B.C.E. Looters smashed figures and stole some weapons. Nevertheless, archaeologists unearthed more than 30,000 weapons, including dagger-axes, double-edged swords, crossbows, sho-lances, and curved swords, giving historians an excellent idea of the type of weapons used by the Qin army.

The discovery of the First Emperor's terracotta army provides us with additional information about how the ancient Chinese viewed life and death, the clothing and weaponry of Qin soldiers, and the emperor and his resources, among many other details. The discovery reconfirmed the extraordinary ability of archaeologists to unlock the past.

Organizing Idea

Archaeological excavations in China have both confirmed information in ancient texts and brought to light previously unknown aspects of life in ancient China. Among the most spectacular finds is that of the First Emperor's buried terracotta warriors.

Student Objectives

Students will:

- understand the work of archaeologists
- compare and contrast burial practices in ancient cultures
- understand the scope and significance of the discovery of the First Emperor's burial site

Key Questions

- How do archaeologists work?
- How does the work of archaeologists add to our understanding of the lives of people who came before us?
- Why do people refer to the discovery of the First Emperor's burial site as "the greatest archaeological find of our time," and "the Eighth Wonder of the World"?
- What is the relationship between burial practices and people's beliefs?

Vocabulary

archaeology
excavation
provenance
site
stratification
terracotta

Supplementary Materials

Item 4.A: Additional vocabulary for primary sources
Item 4.B: Images of terracotta warriors, without captions

Student Activities

›› Activity 1: Planning for an Archaeological Dig of the Future

Students should be familiar with the information in the introduction to this lesson, either from a class lecture or by reading the material. Next, as a homework assignment, ask students to select one item that they would like to bury for archaeologists to discover 1,000 years in the future. Students should come to class prepared to explain how this item will inform people in the year 3010 about our lives, customs, and beliefs. Like the Qin emperor, students should not feel restricted by size or expense; however, they do need to limit themselves to one item. In class, gather in small groups and decide on how these items together will be useful to future historians. Students may wish to change their selections so that as a group they leave representative objects that complement each other.

Each group should present their selection of items to the class without any explanation.

Invite classmates to choose the objects of any group (other than their own) and to become archaeologists. Ask students to imagine it is the year 3010. Have them write a short essay describing the objects unearthed and explaining what this discovery says about the people of ca. 2007.

Ask students to read a few essays aloud in class and ask the group that chose the objects to respond. Did the archaeologist discover what the group members intended for him or her to discover? Did he or she conclude something unexpected? How valid are the conclusions based on archaeological discoveries? Are there ways to confirm scholars' conclusions?

›› Activity 2: Simulating One Task Done by Archaeologists

Materials

- Eight to ten old pottery items of no value (flower pots, vases, bowls, mugs, etc.). It is best if the items are decorated with a pattern. Break them with a hammer, so that each is in about sixteen pieces. (The more pieces, the bigger the challenge. You can also use chipped pottery and/or intentionally throw out a couple of pieces.) Store each broken item mixed with sand in a separate box.
- Any substance that will allow students to temporarily glue pieces of pottery together (play dough, plasticine)
- Trays to use as work surfaces

Have students work in pairs or groups of three. Distribute one box of broken pottery to each group and ask students to reassemble the pieces using the gluey substance to keep them in place. After they have reconstructed the item, have students write a paragraph describing the process. How did they go about it? What was most difficult or frustrating? At what point did they recognize what they were reassembling? Remind them that archaeologists often work on sites where the fragments of a number of items are all mixed in together.

The task can be made more challenging still by mixing pieces of three items in one box so that students first have to decide which fragments go together before they begin to reassemble the item.

» Activity 3: Exploring Local Archaeological Discoveries

Counties and states across the country employ archaeologists, as does the National Park Service. Ask students to research who the local archaeologists are and on what projects they are working. If possible, invite an archaeologist to come in to speak to the students, visit a site, or view an exhibit of recently unearthed items.

» Activity 4: Comparing and Contrasting Funeral and Burial Practices

Ask students what they know about burial traditions in other cultures. What are some similarities and differences? (Refer to the introduction to Lesson 1, regarding respect for alternate ethnic traditions. It is also of paramount importance to be sensitive to any loss students in the class may have experienced.) Using Venn diagrams, students can compare and contrast present-day Chinese burial customs with those of other cultures. Discuss the relationship between burial practices and cultural and religious beliefs.

Next have students research burial traditions of the Shang dynasty (ca. 1600–ca. 1050 B.C.E.) and those of another ancient culture, such as Egypt. They should compare information such as how bodies were prepared for burial, what objects were found in the tombs, and how the tombs were constructed. Again, ask students to consider the relationship between the traditions and beliefs of the people at that time.

PRIMARY SOURCE related to Activity 5

Document 4.1: Photograph of terracotta warriors standing in rank, excavated from pit 1 at the First Emperor's burial site, Shaanxi (陕西) Province

Photo by Liz Nelson

The first pit is larger than two football fields. It holds more than 6,000 soldiers and horses, of which about one-sixth have been excavated. The soldiers appear to have been placed to counter an attack from any direcion. Most face east. Those on the far right and left face outward, to block the enemy from either side. The rear guards stand with their backs to the rest, to prevent an attack from behind.

» Activity 5: Exploring the Creation of the First Emperor's Burial Site

Distribute copies of the photograph showing the ranks of terracotta warriors that were buried in pits close to Qin Shi Huangdi's tomb (4.1). Explain to students that in his ancient history of China, *Shiji (Records of the Historian)*, Sima Qian wrote that of the artisans and workers who labored on the First Emperor's tomb "not one was allowed to emerge alive." Whether this included those who worked on the terracotta army we don't know. Neither Sima Qian nor any other historian of the past make mention of the buried army. Its discovery was a complete surprise to present day historians. Ask students to work with a partner and to examine the image. Have them divide it visually into quarters and look at one section at a time.

- What exactly do they see?
- How are the figures positioned? Why?
- Note the ridges on the earth dividing the warriors. What might have caused this? *(Answer: The terracotta army was originally buried in underground chambers, the roof of which was supported by wooden beams. When the burial chambers were looted and then burned, the roof collapsed and crushed the terracotta soldiers. The ridges show where the original support beams were located.)*
- What might have been the purpose of this buried terracotta army?

Discuss the students' findings as a class. Also discuss why this army might have been kept so secret.

PRIMARY SOURCES related to Activity 6

Document 4.2: Photograph of terracotta charioteer, Qin (秦) dynasty (221–206 B.C.E.)

Terracotta Warrior Museum

The actual chariots, once made of wood, have rotted away, but the impressions of the vehicles remain in the dirt. The chariots were pulled by four horses, of which there are many terracotta statues in the pits.

Document 4.3: Photograph of terracotta archer, Qin (秦) dynasty (221–206 B.C.E.)

Terracotta Warrior Museum

Some 160 kneeling archers were found in pit 2. It appears that they knelt to reload their crossbows before standing up to fire. The Chinese were using crossbows as early as 400 B.C.E.

Document 4.4: Photograph of terracotta general, Qin (秦) dynasty (221–206 B.C.E.)

Terracotta Warrior Museum

The terracotta general was created to stand taller than other soldiers in the army. This figure was one of several of high-ranking officers found in pit 1.

» Activity 6: Comparing the Terracotta Warriors

Without describing who they are, teachers may wish to first show images of the terracotta warriors on a screen. (Documents 4.2–4.4 without titles and captions are available as Item 4.B on the CD-ROM.) Ask students to speculate who is represented by each statue. How can they tell? Then divide the class into small groups and distribute copies of the photographs to each group. Remind students that every one of the terracotta soldiers unearthed is different. Ask students to compare and contrast the warriors' posture, headgear, hand positions, facial expression, and clothing.

- Describe and explain the posture.
- Why are their hands positioned in that way?
- What purpose does the clothing serve? Does each figure have the same amount of clothing? Whose clothing is the most elaborate? Why?
- What surprises students about the statues?
- What would they like to know more about and where can they find answers?

» Activity 7: Planning a Burial Site

Have students study the bronze chariot buried near Qin Shi Huangdi's tomb (4.5) and read Sima Qian's description of how Qin Shi Huangdi planned his tomb (4.6).

- What is remarkable about the chariot and what is the significance of it being created and then buried near the tomb?
- What is remarkable about the description of the tomb project?
- What surprises students about the two primary sources?
- What questions do they have, and where can they find answers?

Next, ask students to choose someone they admire. They are to imagine they have just been employed to plan and design a tomb for this person, just as the First Emperor planned his. There are no limits on cost, what is included in the tomb, or the number of people required to complete the project. Students will need to

- learn about the person and write a brief biography
- decide what objects of value should be placed in the tomb
- choose the location for the tomb
- design its appearance
- choose the materials from which it will be constructed

Students should present their finished work on a poster.

PRIMARY SOURCES *related to Activity 7*

Document 4.5: Photograph of bronze chariot, charioteer, and four horses, Qin (秦) dynasty (221–206 B.C.E.)

Terracotta Warrior Museum

In 1980, archaeologists unearthed two bronze chariots twenty meters west of the First Emperor's tomb. They are the oldest bronze chariots found to date in China. Chariots, charioteers, and horses are all half life-size. The chariots were created out of more than 100 sections and like the horses are decorated with hundreds of gold and silver ornaments. An imperial chariot, such as this one, would have been responsible for clearing the road for the emperor's entourage. Archaeologists suspect that because Chinese design is often symmetrical, they will find more ancient treasures in this area of the burial site.

Document 4.6: Excerpt describing Qin Shi Huangdi's tomb from *Records of the Historian (Shiji,《史记》)* by Sima Qian (司马迁), written between 105 and 90 B.C.E.

Sima Qian (145–ca. 90 B.C.E.) worked as court historian during the Han (汉) dynasty (206 B.C.E.–220 C.E.), and compiled Records of the Historian, *the first official history of China. The work of 130 chapters was based on all the documents recording Chinese traditions and legends that were available to him at the time.*

As soon as the First Emperor became the king of Qin, excavations and buildings had been started at Mount Li, while after he won the empire more than seven hundred thousand conscripts from all parts of the country worked there. They dug through three subterranean streams and poured molten copper for the outer coffin, and the tomb was filled with models of palaces, pavilions and offices, as well as fine vessels, precious stones and rarities. Artisans were ordered to fix up crossbows so that any thief breaking in would be shot. All the country's streams, the Yellow River and the Yangtze River were reproduced in quicksilver and by some mechanical means made to flow into a miniature ocean. The heavenly constellations were shown above the regions of the earth below. The candles were made of whale oil to ensure their burning for the longest possible time...

After the interment someone pointed out that the artisans who had made the mechanical contrivances might disclose all the treasure that was in the tomb; therefore after the burial and sealing up of the treasures, the middle gate was shut and the outer gate was closed to imprison all the artisans and labourers, so that not one came out. Trees and grass were planted over the mausoleum to make it seem like a hill.

» Activity 8: Extended Research

Using books and Internet resources, students can work in small groups to conduct research on

- The First Emperor, Qin Shi Huangdi, who unified China
- Archaeological sites in China, such as the tombs of Fu Hao, Prince Liu Sheng, Marquis Yi of Zeng, and the Marquess of Dai, and excavations at Sanxingdui in Sichuan Province

» Activity 9: The Science of Archaeology or How Do We Know It's That Old?

Teachers can work with colleagues in the science department to have students explore the specifics of how archaeologists work. Among the topics to research: radiocarbon dating, thermoluminescent dating, potassium argon dating, isotopic analysis, dendrochronology, infrared photography, magnetometers, and satellite imagery in archaeology.

Further Teacher and Student Resources

"Ancient China Teaching Kit," created by The International Center for East Asian Archaeology and Cultural History at Boston University includes overheads, lesson plans, and precise replicas of ancient artifacts. It can be rented from the Boston Children's Museum, 800-370-5487, Ext. 231

Debaine-Francfort, Corinne. *The Search for Ancient China.* New York: Harry N. Abrams, Inc., 1999.

"China's First Emperor: Shi-Huangdi," *Calliope*, Cobblestone Publishing, Inc., October 1997.

Dig. Cobblestone Publishing Co., Peterborough, N.H. (archaeology magazine for upper elementary and middle school students)

Guisso, R.W. L. and Catherine Pagani with David Miller. *The First Emperor of China.* Toronto, Canada: Birch Lane Press, 1989.

Lindesay, William. *The Terracotta Army of the First Emperor of China.* Hong Kong: Odyssey Publications Ltd., 1998.

Murowchick, Robert E., ed. *Cradles of Civilization: China.* Norman: University of Oklahoma Press, 1994.

O'Connor, Jane. *The Emperor's Silent Army: Terracotta Warriors of Ancient China.* New York: Viking, 2002.

Wen, Qin and Zhao Runze, eds. *The Subterranean Army of Emperor Qin Shi Huang.* Beijing, China: Morning Glory Publishers, 2002.

Web Sites

http://archnet.asu.edu (directory of archaeology)

http://www.digonsite.com and www.dig.archaeology.org (information on archaeology geared to upper elementary and middle school students)

http://www.nga.gov/education/chinatp_pt4.htm and http://www.nga.gov/education/chinatp_emp.htm (for additional information on archaeology in China)

http://www.nga.gov/education/chinatp_act.htm (includes lots of teaching activities)

http://www.carleton.ca/~bgordon/Rice/ (site about the Ancient Chinese Rice Archaeological Project, which has been exploring the roots of Chinese human civilization through examination of rice at excavation sites)

http://www.chineseprehistory.org/ (site for the Center for the Study of Chinese Prehistory, looks into fossil evidence throughout Chinese human evolution) http://archaeology.about.com/library/atlas/blchina.htm (site with links to many different archaeological sites in China, along with information about the current researchers and other history and general information)

For more information on Terracotta Warriors:

http://www.utexas.edu/courses/wilson/ant304/biography/arybios98/smithbio.html (information about the tomb, where the warriors were found, and about the warriors themselves)

http://hubcap.clemson.edu/~eemoise/ch02tca.html (includes a lot of pictures)

http://depts.washington.edu/chinaciv/archae/2tommain.htm (includes images and information about several ancient tombs)

Video

The First Emperor of China, National Film Board of Canada/China Xi'an Film Studio, 40 min. (good overview of Qin Shi Huangdi, including information about the terracotta warriors)

Elsewhere in the World

While Qin Shi Huangdi was in power (221–210 B.C.E.):

- **Hannibal was also alive (247–182 B.C.E.)**

- **Rome fought Carthage in the Second Punic War (218–202 B.C.E.)**

- **The Paracas culture existed in Peru (700–200 B.C.E.)**

- **Latin drama emerged with Plautus (225–184 B.C.E.)**

- **In Greece, scientist and mathematician Eratosthenes was alive (276–194 B.C.E.)**

In the World Today

Smuggling of Antiquities

In the spring of 2002, twenty minutes before bidding was to begin, Sotheby's, a prestigious auction house in New York City, removed six Chinese figurines from the list of available items. Why? They had been stolen from the tomb of Empress Dou. In 1998, the Chinese displayed more than 3,000 recovered stolen artifacts in the National Museum of Chinese History. Scotland Yard had confiscated all of them from warehouses in London. These examples of theft from temples and tombs are far from isolated. Officials at China's National Cultural Relics Bureau estimate that between 1998 and 2003 at least 220,000 ancient Chinese tombs had been broken into (*Time*, "Spirited Away," October 20, 2003). Despite a United Nations resolution whereby museums agree not to acquire archaeological objects for which the provenance (history of ownership) is unknown, global antiquities smuggling now rivals that of drugs and weapons. Pillaged items include heads cut off of precious clay sculptures in a temple, and wall panels and ancient bronzes from tombs. The final destination of stolen artifacts is often a private collector, who purchases it from an unethical dealer, who has purchased it from other middlemen, who in turn have bought the item from someone often living in abject poverty. Ironically, though a collector may value the stolen artifact for its artistic beauty, as soon as such an object is stolen from its site, it loses much of its scientific value. No one can vouch for its origin or its history. The object has been separated from its historical and scientific context. The world at large loses the story that goes with the object.

Students can find out more about ongoing efforts to stem international trade in stolen antiquities on http://www.archaeology.org. Have students research looting in places such as Sicily, Turkey, Cyprus, Peru, Cambodia, and Central America. Discuss in class what the repercussions are of this illegal market. Have students suggest ways to prevent it.

Lesson 5 CD-ROM Contents

Primary Sources

- Document 5.1: Photograph of an oracle bone, recorded as having been excavated in Anyang, 13th century B.C.E.
- Document 5.2: A chart showing different styles of script
- Document 5.3: Photograph of bamboo slips from between 202 B.C.E. and 9 C.E., excavated in Shandong Province
- Document 5.4: "The Tiger Behind the Fox" (*Hu jia hu wei*, 狐假虎威), a folk tale, including Chinese characters
- Document 5.5: Photograph of a name chop, Han (汉) dynasty (202 B.C.E.–220 C.E.)
- Document 5.6: "The Missing Seal" (*Shi yin ji*, 失印记), a folk tale retold by Chinghua Tang (唐庆华)

Supplementary Materials

- Item 5.A: Chinese characters from "The Tiger Behind the Fox" (*Hu jia hu wei*, 狐假虎威), translated into English
- Item 5.B: Chinese male and female names

Lesson 5
Language

Lesson Contents
- Chinese written language
- Oracle bones
- Ancestor worship
- Bamboo scrolls
- *Pinyin*

A shift in mindset is necessary to understand the Chinese language, spoken or written. Chinese is a tonal language. The tone affects the meaning. For example, *ma* means mother (妈), hemp (麻), horse (马), or to scold (骂), depending on whether a speaker uses high tone, a rising tone, a low-rising tone, or a falling tone. These variations give spoken Chinese its musical sound. For speakers of European languages, this can seem confusing. The Chinese, on the other hand, find verb tenses, plural endings, and gender words (such as he, she, it) perplexing since those don't exist in their language.

In so large a country, divided by rivers and mountain ranges, different dialects inevitably developed, as different from each other as Spanish, Italian, and Portuguese. In the nineteenth and early twentieth centuries, most Chinese immigrants who came to the west coast of the United States were from the area around Guangzhou (广州) (also known as Canton), and so the dialects most often heard in the U.S. at that time were forms of Cantonese. Mandarin, a North China dialect, was spoken by government officials in past centuries. Since early in the twentieth century, government leaders have promoted it as the official language of China. Approximately three-quarters of China's citizens speak Mandarin, also known as *putonghua* (普通话, common speech).

Written Language
Though variations among dialects continue to exist in spoken Chinese, the First Emperor of Qin, Shi Huangdi (秦始黄帝)

(reigned 221–210 B.C.E.) ordered the unification of writing into two standard forms. Modern Chinese styles of writing developed from this unified writing system. Unlike European languages, Chinese does not use an alphabet. Chinese is written using characters, which represent ideas or images. The writing began with pictographs, drawings that look like the objects they represent. For example, the character for a bird looked like a drawing of a bird. The character for sun looked like the sun. As Chinese writing developed, the characters became more abstract and symbolic and less like the object they represented.

Many ideas, thoughts, and feelings are expressed by combining two or more characters to form a new character with a new meaning. The character for tree (木), for instance, written twice means forest (林). The character for sun (日) and the one for moon (月) written together means bright (明). These types of characters are called ideograms. In addition, two or more characters can be written consecutively to form another meaning, but they still remain separate characters. The character for fire (火) followed by the character for mountain (山) form a two-character term meaning volcano (火山). Written language is a defining characteristic of civilization or state-level society. That of China dates back more than 3,500 years. It is one of the earliest known writing systems.

Ancestor Worship

During the Shang (商) dynasty (ca. 1600–ca. 1050 B.C.E.), in a practice known as ancestor worship, the kings looked to their ancestors and their ancestral god for support and guidance when facing difficult decisions. This belief of honoring one's predecessors and asking for their support and guidance continued among the Chinese for millennia. Many practice a form of it today. Three thousand years ago, the Shang kings communicated with their ancestral god by using oracle bones.

Oracle Bones (甲骨)

On flat bones, such as the shoulder blades of oxen or the lower shell (plastron) of turtles, questions and sometimes answers to those questions were written. For example, the inscriptions might ask about whether the king should go into battle or not, future weather patterns, or when to go hunting. The bones were heated, which caused cracks to appear. Someone, likely the king himself or a diviner, interpreted the cracks. At the present time, historians are not sure in what order this took place. Why do some oracle bones have no writing? Why do some only have the question but no answer? Future archaeological evidence may answer these questions.

About 150,000 fragments of oracle bones have been found, but only those from the last Shang capital city at Anyang carry any written inscriptions. The writing includes more than 4,000 different characters, about half of which historians have identified. The highly developed vocabulary shown by the sheer number of characters leads historians to conclude that written language existed in China for a long time before it was recorded on the oracle bones.

Bamboo Scrolls (竹简)

In the twenty-first century, many cannot imagine communicating without computers and certainly not without paper. Paper didn't exist, however, until the Chinese created it around 100 B.C.E. (see Lesson 17). In the centuries before that, people in China wrote on bamboo and wood strips. The strips were held together with string and rolled up like scrolls. Using a hard brush or stick, men wrote the characters in vertical columns, to fit on the strip, and from right to left, which accounts for the traditional method of writing. Because bamboo is light, cheap, and portable, writing began to be used for purposes other than ceremonial and historical ones. People also wrote on wooden tablets, jade, bronze vessels and, later, on silk cloth.

Archaeologists have found examples of writing on bamboo strips in tombs, dating back 2,500 years. Historians know older ones existed, however, because images of bamboo strips appear in some oracle bone inscriptions from about 3,000 years ago. In most burial conditions, bamboo or wood strips and silk are more destructible than bones, bronze, and pottery. So far archaeologists have not found any actual specimens of these older examples of writing.

A Chinese dictionary of the twenty-first century contains more than 50,000 words. To be functionally literate—to read signs, buy groceries, and so on—a person must be able to read about 3,000 characters, but to read a book or newspaper he or she must recognize closer to 5,000 characters. To learn the same number of words in the English vocabulary, a person would have to memorize one-eighth of the American Heritage Dictionary. Clearly, learning to read and write Chinese requires years of study and practice for Chinese and non-Chinese students.

Note: This lesson is best taught in conjunction with Lesson 12 on calligraphy.

Organizing Idea

Chinese is a family of several distinct spoken languages. Oral Chinese and the written language, based on characters, have evolved over 4,000 years.

Student Objectives

Students will:

- learn about the earliest writing in China and how it changed over time
- learn to write several Chinese characters using the traditional tools of Chinese writing
- become familiar with Chinese naming practices
- create a name chop with their chosen Chinese name
- practice reading a folk tale that includes Chinese characters

Key Questions

- How were oracle bones used? How might the reading of oracle bones have affected the power of a leader?
- Over time what materials have been used for writing?
- How do Chinese people choose and write their names?
- What is a name chop? What is its cultural significance, and when is it used?

Vocabulary

bamboo
calligraphy
character (in Chinese writing)
dialect
diviner
ideogram
Mandarin
name chop
oracle bone
pictograph
shaman

Supplementary Materials

Item 5.A: Chinese characters from "The Tiger Behind the Fox" (*Hu jia hu wei*,
  狐假虎威), **translated into English**
Item 5.B: Chinese male and female names

Student Activities

›› Activity 1: Examining Oracle Bones

Ask students to look at the photograph of an oracle bone (5.1) and to speculate on what this might be. Does the caption give any clues? Have students copy two or three of the symbols. Explain these are pictographs, and ask students to work with a partner to try to figure out what the markings might represent. Have students share their hypotheses.

Now share the introduction to the lesson or have students read it independently. Explain that the inscriptions on this oracle bone concern an invasion of northern tribes, the king's order to lords under his control, as well as hunting and astronomical phenomena. Discuss as a class:

- In light of what students know about Chinese beliefs, why would it have been important for kings to predict the future?
- Why did they turn to their ancestors and ancestor gods for guidance?
- Do leaders and citizens in the world today try to predict the future in any way? Consider economists, stockbrokers, and meteorologists. What tools do they use?

PRIMARY SOURCE *related to Activity 1*

Document 5.1: Photograph of an oracle bone, recorded as having been excavated in Anyang, 13th century B.C.E.

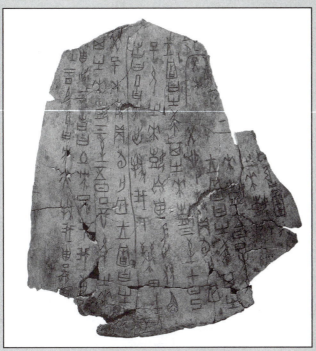

Courtesy of National Museum of China, Beijing

Oxen bones, such as this one, were occasionally found by peasants tilling their land in the region of Anyang (the last capital of the Shang dynasty, ca. 1600–ca. 1050 B.C.E.). Recognizing them as something unusual, they considered them dragon bones and sold them to traditional medicine shops, where they were ground up for therapeutic purposes.

- How would a king's ability to predict the future affect his standing among the common people?
- What else would you like to know about oracle bones and where can you find the answers?

≫ Activity 2: Examining Changing Scripts

After 200 C.E. the Regular Script (*kaishu*) became the standard script for all formal use, but several other styles existed and were in use. Have the students look at the chart (Document 5.2) and compare and contrast the script styles, beginning with the one found on oracle bones.

- Which most closely resembles the ideas or images that the characters represent? Which is the most complicated?
- If they had to pick one for street signs, banknotes, and official documents, which would they choose and why? (The Chinese use the clerical or official script.)
- Why do students think different styles evolved? Do we have different styles of writing? What are they?

PRIMARY SOURCE related to Activity 2

Document 5.2: A chart showing different styles of script

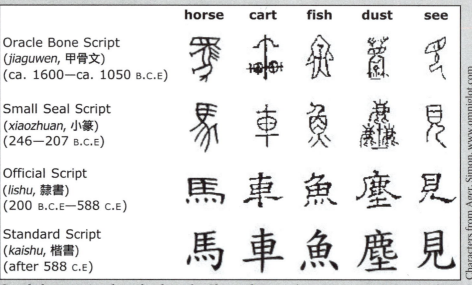

	horse	cart	fish	dust	see
Oracle Bone Script (*jiaguwen*, 甲骨文) (ca. 1600—ca. 1050 B.C.E)					
Small Seal Script (*xiaozhuan*, 小篆) (246—207 B.C.E.)					
Official Script (*lishu*, 隸書) (200 B.C.E—588 C.E)					
Standard Script (*kaishu*, 楷書) (after 588 C.E)					

Characters from Ager, Simon, www.omniglot.com

Oracle bone script dates back to the Shang dynasty (ca. 1600–ca. 1050 B.C.E.). Seal script was first developed during the Zhou dynasty and standardized again under Qin Shi Huangdi (秦始皇帝) into what is known as small seal script (*xiaozhuan,* 小篆). Clerical or official script (*lishu,* 隸书) became standardized in the 1st century B.C.E. Regular style (*kaishu,* 楷书) became the accepted formal script after 200 C.E., and was taught in all schools.

›› Activity 3: Examining Bamboo Scroll

Ask students to examine the photograph of the bamboo scroll (5.3). Discuss:

- How are the characters similar to and different from the characters on the oracle bones?
- Which style do they most closely resemble, oracle bone characters or one of the later styles (see Document 5.2)?
- Why was bamboo used? What would have been the advantages and disadvantages of writing a book on bamboo strips?

PRIMARY SOURCE *related to Activity 3*

Document 5.3: Photograph of bamboo slips from between 202 B.C.E. and 9 C.E., excavated in Shandong Province

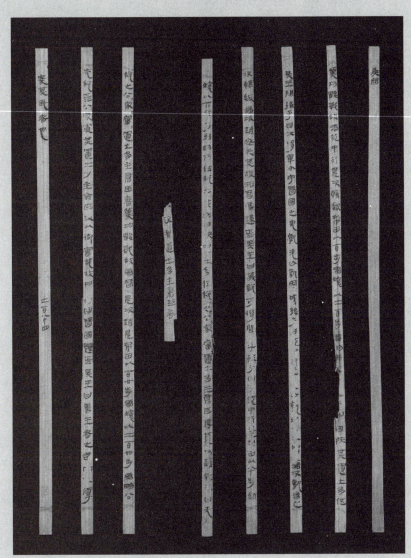

Courtesy of National Museum of China, Beijing

These bamboo strips are part of 4,942 complete and incomplete strips unearthed in 1972. The book *The Art of War* (《孙子兵法》) had been copied onto 300 of the strips and included all 13 chapters of that work.

PRIMARY SOURCE related to Activity 4

Document 5.4: "The Tiger Behind the Fox" (*Hu jia hu wei*, 狐假虎威), a folk tale, including Chinese characters

A 老虎 caught a 狐狸. The 狐狸 said, "You wouldn't dare eat me! The gods in Heaven made me the 大王 of all animals. It would be a violation of the gods' mandate for you to make a 餐 of me. If you doubt it, let me walk in front, and you follow to see if any animal dares stand his ground." The 老虎 consented and followed the 狐狸, 鼻子 to heels. Every animal that saw them fled. Amazed, and agreeing that the 狐狸 was 大王 of all animals, the 老虎 went on his way.

» Activity 4: Reading a Folk Tale with Chinese Written Characters

Hand out copies of "The Tiger Behind the Fox" (Document 5.4) and the list of translated characters (Item 5.A). Have students work with a partner, together reading the tale using the translation guide. Ask them to practice reading several times until they no longer need the guide. Then ask them to write an original sentence using as many of the characters as possible, filling in English words where necessary. (This is done using a regular pen, not in calligraphy.) Ask students to write their sentences on the board so they can share their creative use of Chinese characters.

Ask the students whether the folk tale seems familiar. Do they know of ones from other traditions where animals are used to make a point (for example, Aesop's Fables and Uncle Remus stories)?

» Activity 5: Creating a Name Chop

Begin by explaining to students that a typical Chinese name consists of two parts: a surname (family name) and a given name. In China, the family name comes first. This expresses the belief that the family is more important than the individual. The given name has one or two characters. When parents choose a name for a baby, it represents what they hope his or her character will be or the baby's destiny. In addition, as Laurence Yep writes in *Dragonwings*:

A [Chinese] man can have several names. He has a family name and a personal name given to him at birth. He can have another name given to him when he comes of age, a nickname from his friends, and if he is a poet, he can have a pen name. We are not like the demons [Caucasians], who lock a child into one name from birth—with maybe a nickname if he is lucky. We feel that a man should be able to change his name as he changes, the way a hermit crab can throw away his shell when it's too small and find another one. (*pp. 31–2*)

PRIMARY SOURCE *related to Activity 5*

Document 5.5: Photograph of a name chop, Han dynasty (202 B.C.E.–220 C.E.)

Courtesy of Shanghai Museum

The use of name seals or name chops originated during the Zhou dynasty (ca. 1050–256 B.C.E.). Name seals made of jade, stone, wood, metal, glass, porcelain, or ivory continue to be used to prove ownership and are considered more reliable than a signature. Old paintings are often covered with seals made by name chops, showing who owned them over the centuries. Name chops themselves are often considered works of art.

Have students look at the photograph of a seal print (5.5) and note how the characters are centered and fill the seal. Be sure to mention that unlike real seals, such as this one, the name chops students make will only have their first name on them, not their family name. Ask the students to look at the list of male and female names (Item 5.B) and to choose two characters for themselves that reflect their personal characteristics and interests. Students should practice writing the characters of their Chinese names with paper and pencil until they are comfortable with the strokes and recognize their names by sight.

Materials

- Pencils with dull points
- Tracing paper, cut into 2-inch (5 cm) squares
- Flat sheet of ¼-inch (½ cm) thick foam board cut into 2-inch (5 cm) squares
- Cardboard cut into 2-inch (5 cm) squares
- ½-inch x 3-inch (1½ cm x 8 cm) strip of corrugated cardboard for each chop
- red tempera or acrylic paint
- small brushes and trays for paint

Distribute foam board and cardboard squares, and have students glue them together back to back as one piece. On the cardboard side, have students write their initials and the Chinese name they have chosen along the outside edges. Next students write their Chinese names on the small squares of tracing paper. Remind them to look at the name seal as a guide. Normally, a given name such as Moon Flower is written as one word by joining the characters for moon and flower side by side. Students should turn the tracing paper upside down on top of the foam board and trace the characters again, bearing down into the foam. This creates a mirror image impression that will produce the characters on the seal. Finally, students make a handle for the name chop by folding a thin strip of corrugated cardboard in half and turning each end about ½ inch (1½ cm) outward in opposite directions. Using a fast-drying glue, have them attach the two flaps to the center on the cardboard side of the chop.

Ask students to place a small amount of red paint on a tray and brush it onto the foam side of the name chop, not too thickly. Test the name chop on scrap paper. If necessary, retrace the characters to make deeper impressions.

Finally ask students to write a one- to two-paragraph story, using as many characters from the lesson as they can. (Students may consult Chinese-English dictionaries to build their vocabularies.) When they have finished, have them "sign" their work with their new name chop. Students should keep their name chops and use them to sign all subsequent work they do as part of their study of China.

≫ Activity 7: Discussing a Chinese Folk Tale

Have students read "The Missing Seal" (5.6). Discuss:

- What do you learn about the use of seals from this story?
- Which character traits are admired and which are not by the storyteller? How can you tell?

PRIMARY SOURCE *related to Activity 7*

Document 5.6: "The Missing Seal" (*Shi yin ji*, 失印记), a folk tale retold by Chinghua Tang (唐庆华)

"The imperial inspector has arrived at this country," the mayor continued. "I have a hunch that he is going to make trouble for me. I want you to go to his yamen and get his official seal for me. Without the seal, he cannot carry out his official mission and he will lose his job at that. I'll give you 100 ounces of gold for your work."

"No problem, Your Honor. I'll get it to you in no time."

Later that night he returned with the seal and the mayor was elated.

"You've done a wonderful job," the mayor said, giving the thief the gold as he had promised. "Now there is no point for you to hang around here. You'd better leave as soon as possible."

"Your Honor, you are generous with me. I'd like to offer you a word of advice before I leave?"

"What is it?" asked the mayor.

"When I was hidden on top of the beam, in his office, " said the thief, "I could not help noticing the way His Lordship worked, going through the documents quickly and writing down his instructions without a break. It seems to me that you are up against an extremely capable and sharp-witted man. A man of that caliber is not to be fooled. I think it would be the best for you if you hand back the seal tomorrow. Just tell him that it was found by your night patrols but the thief had run off. Even if the inspector smelled a rat, he would think twice before picking on you."

"It doesn't make sense to return the seal," said the mayor. "The seal means authority. With his seal in hand, he'd be able to do whatever he likes with me. You'd better go home and leave me alone."

He locked the seal box and put it back, and bade his subordinates not to breathe a word about the theft. Then he said he was ill. For the next few days, he did not go to work.

When the mayor called upon him, the inspector seemed in good mood. They talked over a cup of tea about administrative matters, local customs, taxes and budget and what not. The mayor started to feel a bit embarrassed seeing the inspector totally unsuspecting and hospitable. Just as they were chatting, a servant rushed in.

"Fire, fire! Your Honor, the kitchen is on fire."

The inspector's face changed color. He jumped up from the couch. Grabbing the seal box, he handed it to the mayor. "We have to get out. Take care of this for me. Please get more help to put out the fire."…

• Full text available on CD-ROM •

❯❯ Extended Activities: Research Topics

Working in small groups, students can conduct research on several ancient literary works.

The Classic of Poetry (*Shijing,* 《诗经》)

The Classic of Changes (*Yijing,* 《易经》)

The Classic of Documents (*Shujing,* 《书经》)

The Spring and Autumn Annals (*Chunqiu,* 《春秋》)

The Record of Rites (*Liji,* 《礼记》)

The Art of War (*Sunzi bingfa,* 《孙子兵法》)

The Historical Records (*Shiji,* 《史记》)

Admonitions for Women (*Nüjie,* 《女诫》)

The Three Kingdoms (*Sanguo yanyi,* 《三国演义》)

The Marsh Heroes (*Shuihu zhuan,* 《水浒传》) (also titled *The Water Margin,* based on traditional stories)

The students' finished projects can be presented orally, as exhibits, or as papers. Each should include an excerpt of writing from the book, a description of the book and its author, and the significance of the work in China's history and schools of thought.

Further Resources for Students and Teachers

A Dream of Red Mansions: An Abridged Version. Boston: Cheng & Tsui Co., 1998. (Original Chinese text by Hsueh-chin Tsao and Ngo Kao; translated by Yang Hsien-yi and Gladys Yang)

Aria, Barbara. *The Nature of the Chinese Character.* New York: Simon and Schuster, 1991.

Bordahl, Vibeke and Jette Ross. *Chinese Storytellers: Life and Art in the Yangzhou Tradition.* Boston: Cheng & Tsui Co., 2002.

Chang, Raymond and Margaret Scrogin Chang. *Speaking of Chinese.* New York: W. W. Norton & Co., 1978.

Chiang, Gregory. *Language of the Dragon 1: A Classical Chinese Reader.* Boston: Cheng & Tsui Co., 1998.

———. *Language of the Dragon 2: A Classical Chinese Reader.* Boston: Cheng & Tsui Co., 1999.

Eberhard, Wolfram. *A Dictionary of Chinese Symbols.* New York: Routledge and Kegan Paul, 1986.

Fazzioli, Edoardo. *Chinese Calligraphy—The Pictograph to Ideogram: The History of 214 Essential Chinese/Japanese Characters.* New York: Abbeville Press, 1986.

Hansen, Valerie. "The Chinese Writing System," *Calliope*, Cobblestone Publishing, Inc., May 2004.

Lo, Chiung-yu. *Chinese Characters for Beginners.* Taiwan: Panda Media Co., 2002.

Ma, Y. W. and Joseph S. M. Lau. *Traditional Chinese Stories: Themes and Variations.* Boston: Cheng & Tsui Co., 1991. (Language)

Moore, Oliver. *Chinese.* Berkeley: University of California Press, 2000. Published by arrangement with the British Museum Press. (Highly illustrated. Excellent coverage of oracle bones and writing through the Bronze Age.)

Ramsey, S. Robert. *The Languages of China.* Princeton: Princeton University Press, 1987.

Shi, Bo. *Between Heaven and Earth: A History of Chinese Writing.* Boston and London: Shambhala, 2003. (short book that covers many topics, highly illustrated)

Young, Ed. *Voices of the Heart.* New York: Scholastic Press, 1997.

Web Sites

http://www.chinaknowledge.de/ (excellent site for information on Chinese language, literature, calligraphy, oracle bones, and more)

http://www.askasia.org/teachers/Instructional_Resources/Lesson_Plans/ (long list of lesson plans includes one on Chinese dialect)

http://afe.easia.columbia.edu/china/language/teach.htm (excellent introduction to the Chinese language; includes practice in saying a few words and an exercise in finding the meanings of the names of provinces and cities in China)

http://www.chinapage.com/classic1.html

In the World Today

Pinyin

At about the same time as the government of the People's Republic of China established Mandarin as the common language of China, taught in all schools and used in national news broadcasts, they also created a standardized system for transcribing the Chinese language using the roman alphabet. *Pinyin* is taught to younger children and illiterate adults—and to foreigners trying to learn Chinese—as a bridge to learning Chinese characters. When a child completes elementary school, he or she should be able to read Chinese both in *pinyin* and in approximately 3,000 simplified Chinese characters. Most Western media, publications, libraries, and governments have adopted the *pinyin* system as the standard spelling of Chinese using the Roman alphabet. Ask students to discuss what the advantages and disadvantages might be of the *pinyin* system within China.

Lesson 6 CD-ROM Contents

Primary Sources

- Document 6.1: Excerpts from myths describing Nüwa (女娲), written between the 2nd century B.C.E. and 3rd century C.E.
- Document 6.2: Excerpts of a creation myth describing Yin (阴) and Yang (阳), written around 139 B.C.E.
- Document 6.3: Symbol that represents concept of Yin (阴) and Yang (阳)
- Document 6.4: Excerpts from myths describing Fuxi (伏羲), written between the 1st century B.C.E. and 3rd century C.E.
- Document 6.5: Rubbing of stone carving from Han (汉) dynasty (202 B.C.E.–220 C.E.) of Nüwa (女娲) and Fuxi (伏羲)
- Document 6.6: Excerpts from myths describing Huangdi (黄帝), the Yellow Emperor, written between the 2nd century B.C.E. and 4th century C.E.
- Document 6.7: Excerpts from myths describing The Great Yu (大禹), 4th century B.C.E. to 4th century C.E.

Supplementary Materials

- Item 6.A: Additional vocabulary from primary sources

Lesson 6
Early Chinese Mythology

Lesson Contents
• Creation myths
• Mythical heroes

Myths are "sacred narratives," writes Anne Birrell in *Chinese Myths*, that "embody the most deeply felt spiritual values of a nation" (p. 7). Myths have played a large part in shaping Chinese culture. Mythic heroes who overcame demons, "discovered" writing, promoted agriculture, controlled floods, and established virtuous government, highlight accomplishments central to traditional Chinese history.

Early Chinese myths were first recorded in classical texts written between the sixth and third centuries B.C.E., but the stories they tell date much earlier. The tales were most likely based on ancient oral tradition, Birrell explains. Unlike in some other cultures, one rarely finds a complete Chinese myth written down. Rather, various Chinese writers told bits and pieces of the myths as part of their philosophical or historical writings. They include them to make a point or to illustrate an idea.

Early myths became more solidified during the Han (汉) dynasty (202 B.C.E.–220 C.E.). The myths of this era sum up important lessons learned from the past and are recorded as part of the history of the land. Early historians and other writers did not clearly differentiate between what was myth and what was actual history. Indeed, in their minds, it is quite possible that the "myths" actually were part of history. There are stories of heroic exploits—some supernaturally so and clearly not factual—of legendary kings, and of the mystical births of clan founders who would later become the rulers of the Xia (夏),

Shang (商), and Zhou (周) dynasties (ca. 21st century B.C.E.–ca. 256 B.C.E.). While these stories are mythological, in the literature they merge with historical descriptions of the reigns of real kings for whom we have strong corroborating archaeological evidence. While this reminds us that myth and history have much in common, one of the results is that many generations have learned a mix of fact and legend about "ancient China," and the perpetuation of many of these stories has often served political purposes.

Myths from all corners of the world reflect the particular concerns of each culture. As the concerns and values change, so do the myths. For example, among China's early creation myths is one of a goddess named Woman Gua (*Nüwa*, 女娲). She is both a creator and savior of mankind. During the Han dynasty, though, when Confucianism (see Lesson 7) became the state ideology, the creation myth of Pangu (盘古)—a male—supplanted that of Nüwa. This both reflected and inspired the increasingly patriarchal society. Nüwa's extraordinary feats in damming flood waters and repairing a damaged world also got buried beneath the myth of King Yu, the supposed founder of the Xia dynasty.

The hero myth of the Great Yu (大禹) is almost certainly the most powerful in early Chinese literature. This myth is often compared with flood myths in other civilizations, such as the story of Noah's flood in the Biblical Book of Genesis. The Noah myth focuses on remaking life on earth and restoring the correct relationship between God and humans. The Yu myth, on the other hand, focuses on active control of water flow and the establishment of good government based on dynasties led by men. This became the primary system of government in China for the next 4,000 years. China's ancient myths provide insight into the origins of many of the beliefs, customs, and heroes that have been central to the way people define their own culture.

Organizing Idea

Early Chinese mythology, like that of other civilizations, has had a profound effect on the nation's history and sense of self. The stories focus on how order was established so that humans could survive and flourish.

Student Objectives

Students will:

- recognize some basic themes in early Chinese myths
- compare Chinese myths to those of other cultures
- explore how the myths may have affected Chinese history
- begin to understand how myths help people make sense of their world

Key Questions

- What are some ways in which the Chinese explained creation in ancient times?
- How do myths affect the way people think of themselves and others?
- Why did Huangdi and Yu serve as the models for how an ideal emperor should be?

Vocabulary

archetype
creation
deity
divine
hero
myth
patriarchal

Supplementary Materials

Item 6.A: Additional vocabulary from primary sources

Student Activities

❯❯ Activity 1: Defining Myth and Finding Examples

With the help of a dictionary, as a class, define "myth." Display a definition that everyone can understand somewhere prominent in the classroom. Ask the students to give examples of myths they know from their own and other cultures. If the students are not familiar with many (or any), ask them to find examples in books or online, bring them to class, and share them.

- What do these narratives appear to have in common? Why?
- How and why are they different?
- How do students think myths come to exist?

PRIMARY SOURCES *related to Activity 2*

Document 6.1: Excerpts from myths describing Nüwa (女娲), written between the 2nd century B.C.E. and 3rd century C.E.

People say that when Heaven and earth opened and unfolded, humankind did not yet exist. Nüwa kneaded yellow earth and fashioned human beings. Though she worked feverishly, she did not have enough strength to finish her task, so she drew her cord in a furrow through the mud and lifted it out to make human beings. That is why rich aristocrats are the human beings made from yellow earth, while ordinary poor commoners are the human beings made from the cord's furrow.

• Full text available on CD-ROM •

Document 6.2: Excerpts of a creation myth describing Yin (阴) and Yang (阳), written around 139 B.C.E.

Long ago, before heavens and earth existed, there were only images but no forms, and all was dark and obscure, a vast desolation, a misty expanse, and nothing knew where its own portals were. There were two gods born out of chaos who wove the skies and designed the earth. So profound were they that no one knew their lowest deeps, and so exalted were they that no one knew where they came to rest. Then they divided into Yin and Yang and separated into the eight Poles. The hard and the soft formed, and the myriad living things took shape. The dense cloudy vapor became insects, and the pure vapor became humans…

• Full text available on CD-ROM •

Document 6.4: Excerpts from myths describing Fuxi (伏羲), written between the 1st century B.C.E. and 3rd century C.E.

Long Ago, when Baoxi [another name for Fuxi] ruled the world, he looked upward and meditated on the images in the skies, and he looked downward and meditated on the patterns on the ground. He meditated on the markings of birds and beasts and the favorable lie of the land. He drew directly from his own person, and indirectly he drew upon external objects. And so it was that he created the Eight Trigrams in order to communicate with the virtue of divine intelligence and to classify the phenomena of all living things. He made knotted cord for nets and fishing pots in hunting and fishing.

• Full text available on CD-ROM •

Document 6.6: Excerpts from myths describing Huangdi (黄帝), the Yellow Emperor, written between the 2nd century B.C.E. and 4th century C.E.

When the Yellow Emperor and the Flame Emperor fought on the Wastes of Panquan, all the bears, grizzly bears, wolves, panthers, cougars, and tigers were in his [the Yellow Emperor's] vanguard, while the eagles, fighting pheasants, falcons, and kites served as his banners and flags.

• Full text available on CD-ROM •

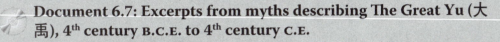

Document 6.7: Excerpts from myths describing The Great Yu (大禹), 4th century B.C.E. to 4th century C.E.

[T]he river passed above Mengmen, its waters greatly swollen and its current irregular, so that it destroyed all in its path, the hills and high mounds, and this was what was known as the Flood. Yu channeled the river and sluiced off the Great River. For ten years he did not visit his home, and no nails grew on his hands, no hair grew on his shanks. He caught an illness that made his body shrivel in half, so that when he walked he could not lift one leg past the other, and people called it "the Yu walk."

• Full text available on CD-ROM •

» Activity 2: Creative Extension—Dramatizing a Myth

Divide the five documents that tell of mythological figures among small groups (Documents 6.1, 6.2, 6.4, 6.6, and 6.7). Have each group read the documents and come to a clear understanding of the event(s) each excerpt describes. (Among the teaching resources on the CD-ROM is one that includes ideas to help students deal with the challenging language of ancient documents.)

Next, each group should plan a skit that will capture important information about the mythological figure. They will need to make clear who the central figure is in the myth and what his or her accomplishments were. Have the students perform the skits in class.

After students have learned the essence of each myth, discuss:

- What is the central theme of each myth?
- What values and concerns does each myth embody?
- How might each myth influence how people view their leaders and what they expect of them?

PRIMARY SOURCES *related to Activity 3*

Document 6.3: Symbol that represents concept of Yin (阴) and Yang (阳)

The outer circle represents the whole. The black and white areas within represent the two essential energies: yin and yang. Yin is black and yang is white.

Document 6.5: Rubbing of stone carving from Han (汉) dynasty (202 B.C.E.–220 C.E.) of Nüwa (女娲) and Fuxi (伏羲)

Cambridge University Library.

On the left, Nüwa holds her compass, and on the right Fuxi has his carpenter's square.

>> Activity 3: Creative Extension—Visual Art

Have students examine and discuss two visual images (Documents 6.3 and 6.5). One captures mythological figures, the other the concept of yin and yang. As a homework project, ask each student to choose one of the gods or heroes from China's ancient myths and to create a piece of art that captures the essence of him or her. For example, they can create a painting, a sketch, a collage, or a sculpture. For extra credit, students can do research on one of the additional figures in Chinese mythology and create a work of art on that figure instead.

>> Activity 4: Extended Research

This lesson includes only a sampling of Chinese myths. Students can use books and the Internet to research additional narratives, heroes, and heroines, among them:

- any one of China's four greatest creatures: dragon, phoenix, tiger, or tortoise
- origins of silk
- Queen Mother of the West
- Pangu (盘古) (which translates as "giant coiled antiquity") and the creation myth
- Houji (后稷), the "Sovereign Millet"
- Shun (舜), one of the three legendary kings

>> Activity 5: Closing Discussion

Discuss the key questions from the beginning of the lesson. Also consider:

- What do the myths have in common?
- How do they compare with myths from other cultures?

Further Resources for Students and Teachers

Birrell, Anne. *Chinese Mythology: An Introduction.* Baltimore: The Johns Hopkins University Press, 1993.

————. *Chinese Myths.* London: British Museum Press, 2000. (excellent short introduction)

Sanders, Tao Tao Liu. *Dragons, Gods & Spirits from Chinese Mythology.* New York: Schocken Books, 1980.

Web Sites

http://www.chinavista.com/experience/myth/myth.html

http://www.chinavista.com/experience/story/story.html

http://www.pantheon.org/areas/mythology/asia/chinese/articles.html

---

In the World Today

Sites Honoring Mythological Heroes

In China today a number of sites honor figures from ancient myths. On the top of Mount Qiaoshan north of Xi'an (西安) in Shaanxi Province (陕西), stands a mausoleum to Huangdi, the Yellow Emperor. According to legend, the yellow dragon carrying Huangdi to heaven landed here so the emperor could bid farewell to his people. On Mount Lishan (骊山), also near Xi'an, there is a Daoist temple dedicated to Nüwa. And in Shaoxing (绍兴) in Zhejiang Province (浙江), a huge memorial has been built to the Great Yu. It is said that construction of the mausoleum began in the sixth century and has been expanded over the centuries. It consists of several structures: a temple, a mausoleum, and a shrine. In 1995, a paved walkway, flanked by sculptures of divine animals, and an archway were added. The president of the People's Republic of China at the time, Jiang Zemin (江泽民) visited the site. He wrote the characters 大禹陵 (*Dayu ling*), meaning "the mausoleum of Yu the Great," that are carved on the gateway. Students can visit http://old.sx.gov.cn/english/outskirt3.htm to see photographs and read more details. Discuss why the present Chinese government might want to devote funds to maintaining, adding to, and promoting sites such as these.

草書豪情風の書画集

像子孔師先

Lesson 7 CD-ROM Contents

Primary Sources

- Document 7.1: Image of Confucius (孔子)
- Document 7.2: Photograph of statue of Confucius (孔子) in Chinatown in New York City
- Document 7.3: Excerpts from the *Analects of Confucius* (《论语》) on relationships within the family
- Document 7.4: Excerpts from the *Analects of Confucius* (《论语》) on education
- Document 7.5: Excerpts from the *Analects of Confucius* (《论语》) on behavior
- Document 7.6: Excerpts from the *Analects of Confucius* (《论语》) on government
- Document 7.7: Excerpts from the *Analects of Confucius* (《论语》) on relationships
- Document 7.8: Excerpts from the *Analects of Confucius* (《论语》) on his general observations and reflections
- Document 7.9: Excerpts from young-adult works of historical fiction

Supplementary Materials

- Item 7.A: Additional vocabulary for primary sources
- Item 7.B: An introduction to Confucius

Lesson 7
The Impact of Confucius

Lesson Contents
- Confucianism
- The civil service examinations

Confucianism permeates China's political and social fabric, particularly the family and educational systems. Confucian values underlie the respect generally accorded to parents, teachers, elders as a whole, and ancestors in particular. Although Confucianism stopped being China's official ideology at the beginning of the twentieth century, Confucian ideas continue to influence the way life is lived and business is carried out right up to the present day.

Little is known about the early years of *Kong Qiu* (孔丘), who became known in the West as Confucius. Sima Qian (司马迁), China's first historian, wrote a biography of Confucius around 91 B.C.E., 450 years after his death. Based on that, it is believed that Confucius was born in 551 B.C.E. His father died when he was a young boy, and it appears that Confucius grew up in poverty. Somehow, though, he managed to become educated.

The state of Lu (鲁), where Confucius is believed to have been born, was invaded twenty-one times between 722 and 481 B.C.E. Confucius wished to bring order and harmony to society. He traveled extensively through China's provinces, often barely able to eke out a living. He believed fervently in his mission to restore cultural integrity in a China that lacked unity. Because of his strong beliefs, he attracted followers from many walks of life. (For additional information about Confucius see Item 7B on the CD-ROM.)

Confucius (孔子) believed that in order for people to live in harmony, they should follow certain rules of behavior in private and in public. Ancient Chinese referred to this as *li* (礼). The ideal man, Confucius believed, was a cultivated or superior man, a *junzi* (君子) (loosely translated: a gentleman). In order to be considered a *junzi*, a man must be caring of others, honest, wise, trustworthy, and conduct himself correctly.

The Five Relationships

Centuries later, followers added the idea that five relationships are the key to a stable society: Ruler to Subject, Father to Son, Husband to Wife, Older Brother to Younger Brother, and Friend to Friend. All of the relationships were unequal; in four instances, the first person was superior to the second. The fifth relationship—friendship—might be somewhat more equal, but still would be subject to age and social status differences between the individuals.

Confucius saw relationships within the family as a model for relationships between a ruler and his subjects. He attached great importance to the family as the setting in which moral values could be taught and practiced. Filial piety, respect from a child to his or her parent, was the central value supporting the family. In written Chinese, the character for filial piety, *xiao* (孝), is a symbol of a son supporting his parents. Filial piety was the cornerstone of society. Family stability also depended on great respect for the father and gratitude for emotional support from the mother. Beyond the parents were the grandparents and ancestors. Continuing the century-old practice of ancestor worship (see Lessons 3 and 4), Confucius stressed that respect for ancestors was the most essential part of maintaining the social fabric. He even placed protection of the family above loyalty to the ruler.

During the short-lived dynasty of the First Emperor of Qin Shi Huangdi (秦始皇帝) (221 B.C.E.–206 B.C.E.), all that pertained to Confucius was suppressed. At the urging of his advisers, who sought to destroy any and all beliefs that might contradict their own, the emperor had all non-legalist philosophical books burned, with the exception of those on agriculture and medicine, and he had hundreds of Confucian scholars killed, reportedly by being buried alive. The First Emperor believed unequivocally in Legalism (see Lesson 8) and harsh authority. However, during the Han (汉) dynasty that followed (202 B.C.E.–220 B.C.E.), Confucianism became the national ideology. Four centuries after his death, Confucius's dream to advise rulers became a reality.

The Civil Service Examinations

Confucian teachings also became the foundation of schooling in China. Beginning in the Han dynasty, the Chinese established a system whereby government officials would ideally be appointed based on merit rather than family status and connections. Chinese governments designed a series of increasingly difficult civil service examinations—the first in the world. As a man passed each exam, he would become eligible for a position of greater authority. From the Song (宋) dynasty (960 C.E.) on, the exams were based on mastery of four key Confucian books, including the *Analects* (《论语》), and five ancient classics. They did not directly assess a person's ability to run an office; rather they tested his knowledge of literature and his moral worth. The exams were carefully supervised, but as in all human systems, abuses occurred. Men bribed officials scoring the exams or found ways to bypass the system all together. Nevertheless, for 2,000 years, the Chinese were the only people who had as their stated goal a government run by moral and literate people selected through competitive written tests.

Note: For a complete sense of the philosophies that continue to influence China today, this lesson should be studied in conjunction with Lesson 8, "Additional Chinese Belief Systems."

Organizing Idea

Confucian thought on leading a moral life permeated every level of society, defining for the Chinese people what it means to be human in a social and political environment.

Student Objectives

Students will:

- understand the basic tenets of Confucianism
- recognize that filial piety and reverence for ancestors are central values in Chinese culture and remain powerful influences today
- understand how the civil service examination system worked
- recognize the similarities and differences between religions they are familiar with and Confucian beliefs

Key Questions

- What are the most important principles of Confucianism?
- In what ways are principles similar to those of Confucius present in our lives?
- Which principles appear to be the longest lasting, based on works of contemporary historical fiction?
- What are the advantages and disadvantages of the type of civil service exam system that was in place in China for centuries?

Vocabulary

benevolent
Confucianism
enlightened
filial piety
harmony
junzi
moral
rite/ritual

Supplementary Materials

Item 7.A: Additional vocabulary for primary sources
Item 7.B: An introduction to Confucius

Student Activities

» Activity 1: Discussion—An Introduction to Confucius

Have students read the introduction to the lesson and the brief biography of Confucius (Item 7.B on the CD-ROM) or present the information in lecture form. Distribute images of Confucius (7.1 and 7.2) or show them on a screen. It may be interesting initially not to tell students where the statue stands. Ask them:

- How is Confucius depicted in this image (7.1)? Why might this be so?
- Where do they think the statue (7.2) stands?
- Why is it in New York City?
- What does it say about the strength of Confucian beliefs that it is there?

Explain to students that the statue was presented to the city by the Chinese Consolidated Benevolent Association, as a way to commemorate the U.S. bicentennial in 1976. One of Confucius's sayings is inscribed on the base. It states that a just government is one that cares for the weak and has leaders chosen for their wisdom and ability. Why might Chinese Americans have chosen to commemorate the bicentennial in this way?

PRIMARY SOURCES related to Activity 1

Document 7.1: Image of Confucius (孔子)

Document 7.2: Photograph of statue of Confucius (孔子) in Chinatown in New York City

Photo by Liz Nelson

The fifteen-foot-tall statue created by Liu Shih stands in Confucius Plaza. It faces east.

PRIMARY SOURCES *related to Activity 2*

Document 7.3: Excerpts from the *Analects of Confucius* (《论语》) on relationships within the family

2.6   When asked about being filial, Confucius replied, "The only time a dutiful son ever makes his parents worry is when he is sick."

4.18 Confucius said, "In serving your father and mother you ought to dissuade them from doing wrong in the gentlest way. If you see your advice being ignored, you should not become disobedient but should remain [respectful]. You should not complain even if you are distressed."

• *Full text available on CD-ROM* •

Document 7.4: Excerpts from the *Analects of Confucius* (《论语》) on education

2.15 Confucius said, "To study without thinking is futile. To think without studying is dangerous."

2.16 Confucius said, "I will tell you what it is to know. To say you know when you know, and to say you do not when you do not, that is knowledge."

7.22 The Master said, "Even when walking in the company of two other men, I am bound to be able to learn from them. The good points of the one I copy; the bad points of the other I correct in myself."

• *Full text available on CD-ROM* •

Document 7.5: Excerpts from the *Analects of Confucius* (《论语》) on behavior

1.8   The Master said, "Make it your guiding principle to do your best for others and to be trustworthy in what you say. Do not accept as friend anyone who is not as good as you. When you make a mistake, do not be afraid of mending your ways."

4.10 The Master said, "In his dealings with the world the gentleman is not [always] for or against anything. He is on the side of what is moral [in that particular situation]."

4.24 Confucius said, "A gentleman should be slow to speak and quick to act."

• *Full text available on CD-ROM* •

Document 7.6: Excerpts from the *Analects of Confucius* (《论语》) on government

2.3 The Master said, "Guide them by edicts, keep them in line with punishments, and the common people will stay out of trouble but will have no sense of shame. Guide them by virtue, keep them in line with the rites, and they will, besides having a sense of shame, reform themselves.

13.6 The Master said, "If a man is correct in his own person, then there will be obedience without orders being given; but if he is not correct in his own person, there will not be obedience even though orders are given."

• Full text available on CD-ROM •

 Document 7.7: Excerpts from the *Analects of Confucius* (《论语》) on relationships

1.16 The Master said, "Don't worry if people don't recognize your merits; worry that you may not recognize theirs."

5.10 (excerpt) The Master said: "There was a time when I used to listen to what people said and trusted that they would act accordingly, but now I listen to what they say and watch what they do."

13.19 Asked about humanity, the Master said: "Be courteous in private life; reverent in public life; loyal in personal relations. Even among barbarians [foreigners], do not depart from this attitude."

• Full text available on CD-ROM •

 Document 7.8: Excerpts from the *Analects of Confucius* (《论语》) on his general observations and reflections

1.6 The Master said: "At home, a young man must respect his parents; abroad, he must respect his elders. He should talk little, but with good faith; love all people, but associate with the virtuous. Having done this, if he still has energy to spare, let him study literature."

15.28 The Master said: "When everyone dislikes a man, one should investigate. When everyone likes a man, one should investigate."

17.3 The Master said, "Only the wisest and the stupidest never change."

• Full text available on CD-ROM •

⟫ Activity 2: Discussing Analects of Confucius

The six documents with excerpts from the *Analects* (7.3–7.8) are categorized by topic. The class can be divided into six groups, and, if need be, each group can be further broken down so students study just a few sayings. (See Teacher Resources for "Ways to tackle challenging reading.") The goal for each group, after studying the sayings, is to make clear to classmates what Confucius thought about the topic. Suggest to each group:

- Based on these excerpts from the *Analects*, how would you describe Confucius's thoughts on the topic?
- Discuss Confucius's beliefs in your group and have the secretary of the group record key points.

Create a five-minute vignette in which the group communicates Confucius's beliefs to the class. For example, you can set up an interview, where one member of the group becomes Confucius, and the rest are a panel of TV/radio interviewers. Or you might create a scene where Confucius is holding a discussion with his disciples.

PRIMARY SOURCE *related to Activity 3*
Document 7.9: Excerpts from works of historical fiction

In McCaughrean's Kite Rider, *the young boy Haoyou grapples with how much he should or should not obey his elders. He is having a conversation with his cousin in the excerpt.*

"Why do you talk about him that way?" asked Haoyou, refusing to laugh.

"Because I have no respect for him. Uncle Bo is mean-minded, greedy, selfish, dishonest, bombastic." But Haoyou had put his fingers in his ears. He had not really wanted to hear her reasons.

Mipeng's disrespect went against everything twelve years of life had drummed into him. Respect is everything. Without respect, the sun can fall off its hook, the stars run down out of the sky, the earth blow away. Without respect and obedience, all doors stand open to chaos and disorder.

• Full text available on CD-ROM •

≫ Activity 3: Recognizing Traditional Chinese Beliefs in Contemporary Historical Fiction

Many works of historical fiction set in China or with Chinese Americans as lead characters include examples of or references to Confucian beliefs. This lesson lends itself to having students read one of the books listed in the Teacher Resources with an eye out for examples of the beliefs they have studied. Document 7.9 includes brief excerpts from several books. Have students read the selections and identify which beliefs are reflected.

≫ Activity 4: A Look at China's Examination System through Historical Fiction

The Examination, a young-adult novel by Malcolm Bosse, is an excellent way for students to learn about civil service exams in imperial China. It is the story of two brothers traveling across the country, as the elder prepares to take the series of exams. Historically accurate and engagingly written, it gives students an introduction to two different cultural worlds, those of a young scholar and a street-smart rebel.

Students can read the novel and record in a journal what they learn from each chapter about any one of several topics: the Chinese language, beliefs, leisure activities, art and architecture, values, geography and climate, food, or interpersonal relations. When they have finished the novel, they can demonstrate their knowledge of the examination system by creating a poster, a PowerPoint presentation, or a very short video, or by writing a report.

≫ Activity 5: Extended Research

Have students research one of the topics below or a related topic and present their findings in writing, with a poster, or, working with a partner, in a short video.

- How did the teaching practices of Socrates, the Greek philosopher who lived around the same time as Confucius, compare to those of Confucius?
- Who was Mengzi (孟子) (ca. 371–289 B.C.E.), and how did he contribute to Confucianism?
- Who were Cheng Yi (程颐) and Zhu Xi (朱熹), and how did they contribute to neo-Confucianism, as it was understood during the Song dynasty (960–1279)?
- Who was Wang Yangming (王阳明) (1472–1529), and what ideas did he add to Confucianism?

Further Student and Teacher Resources

Bosse, Malcolm. *The Examination.* New York: Farrar, Strauss and Giroux, 1994.

Hoobler, Thomas and Dorothy Hoobler. *Confucianism.* New York: Facts On File, Inc., 1993.

Hong, Louis Fong Sui. *Inspiring Deeds of Dutiful Children.* New York: Acme Press, 1965.

Lau, D. C., trans. *Confucius: The Analects.* Hong Kong: The Chinese University Press, 1992.

Leys, Simon, trans. *The Analects of Confucius.* New York: W. W. Norton & Co., 1997.

Wilker, Josh. *Confucius: Philosopher and Teacher.* New York: Franklin Watts, 1999.

Web Sites

http://www.warriortours.com/intro/religion_confucianism.htm (includes pictures and information, and is easy to navigate; it has links to information on Confucianism, Daoism and Buddhism in China)

Video

Religions in China, Film for Humanities and Sciences, 2001, 60 min. (valuable overview of the major traditions in China, including the place of religion in modern-day China. It includes strong opinions by the famous German Catholic theologian Hans Küng.)

Elsewhere in the World

- **Siddhartha Gautama, Buddha lived in India 563–483 B.C.E.**

- **Socrates lived in Greece 469–399 B.C.E.**

In the World Today

Honoring Confucius

Each year, more than 3 million people, from China and abroad, visit the Mansion, Temple, and Cemetery of Confucius in Qufu, where he was supposedly born and buried. In 1994, UNESCO listed this center as a world cultural heritage site. The original temple at Qufu dates from 478 B.C.E., one year after Confucius's death. However, over the centuries, the temple has undergone expansion, reduction, and even destruction, depending on the politics of the time.

For more than 2,000 years, Confucius's birthday (on the twenty-seventh day of the eighth lunar month) had been celebrated in China. But during the Cultural Revolution (1966–76), Confucianism was repressed, and all commemorations ceased on mainland China. The Chinese in Taiwan have grand ceremonies each September 28, honoring the ancient sage. Designated a national holiday, September 28 is also Teacher's Day in Taiwan.

As of 2002, Confucius's birthday is now celebrated in style in Qufu. The Qufu International Confucius Cultural Festival lasts approximately ten days. September 28 is marked with activities honoring Confucius, such as performances of ancient Chinese music and dances, and exhibits of calligraphy.

Have students plan a (mock or real) half-day ceremony to honor Confucius. What activities would best commemorate what he held as important? Who should be invited? Who should be especially honored, besides Confucius?

Lesson 8 CD-ROM Contents

Primary Sources

- Document 8.1: Excerpts from *Daodejing* (《道德经》) on Dao, written around the 4th century B.C.E.
- Document 8.2: Excerpts from *Daodejing* (《道德经》) on personal behavior, written around the 4th century B.C.E.
- Document 8.3: Excerpts from *Daodejing* (《道德经》) on government, written around the 4th century B.C.E.
- Document 8.4: Excerpts from *Daodejing* (《道德经》), observations, written around the 4th century B.C.E.
- Document 8.5: Excerpts from *Han Feizi* (《韩非子》), explaining Legalist thought, written in the 3rd century B.C.E.
- Document 8.6: Excerpts from Wei Shou's summary of Buddhist doctrine
- Document 8.7: Excerpts describing Pure Land (净土), a form of Buddhism in China
- Document 8.8: Photographs from the Longmen Grottoes created during Tang dynasty
- Document 8.9: "The Lost Horse" (*Saiweng shi ma*, 塞翁失马), a Chinese folktale by Liu An (刘安)
- Document 8.10: "Man and Beast," a Chinese folktale by Liezi (列子)
- Document 8.11: "Three Former Lives" (*San Sheng*, 三生), a Chinese folktale by Pu Songling (蒲松龄)
- Document 8.12: "Underworld Justice" (*Xi Fangping*), a Chinese folktale by Pu Songling (蒲松龄)

Supplementary Materials

- Item 8.A: Additional vocabulary for primary sources
- Item 8.B: Graphic organizer
- Item 8.C: An introduction to Daoism
- Item 8.D: An introduction to Legalism
- Item 8.E: Additional study questions for *Han Feizi*
- Item 8.F: An introduction to Buddhism
- Item 8.G: Suggested topics and questions for "The Tea"

Lesson 8
Additional Chinese Belief Systems

Lesson Contents

- Daoism
- Legalism
- Buddhism

During the last two centuries of the weakened Zhou (周) Dynasty (ca. 1050–256 B.C.E.), various feudal states fought each other ruthlessly for dominance. Sometimes armies of more than 100,000 men would break through city fortifications and destroy everything within. This era, known as the Warring States Period (*Zhanguo shiqi,* 战国时期), finally ended in 221 B.C.E., when the Qin (秦) state overthrew its last enemies and proclaimed a unified empire. During the era of chronic instability, many schools of thought emerged on how people should live and how rulers should govern. Patricia Buckley Ebrey explains in the *Cambridge Illustrated History of China*, "Rulers searching for ways to survive or prevail were more than willing to patronize men of ideas…[A]mbitious rulers and even high officials were able to gather around them numerous advisors, assistants, teachers, strategists, and clerks. These men made proposals about what the rulers should do and rebutted each other's ideas, in the process advancing the art of oratory, the science of strategy, and the study of logic" (p. 42). The Chinese refer to the beliefs that came out of this "golden age of philosophy" as the Hundred Schools of Thought. This is not an exact tally of the number of schools of thought. It suggests that this was a period in history when many men advocated ideas on politics, ethics, and human behavior.

The principal schools of thought were Confucianism (see Lesson 7), Daoism (*Daojia*, 道家), and Legalism (*Fajia,* 法家). Although the Buddha (living in India) was a contemporary of Confucius, Buddhism (*Fojiao,* 佛教) did not spread into China until around the first century C.E.

In later centuries, the lines between Confucianism, Daoism, and Buddhism blurred. Daoists established a formal religion, with monks and nuns. Temples were built for Confucius. Matteo Ricci, a Jesuit brother who lived in China from 1583 to 1610, wrote, "The commonest opinion held here among those who consider themselves most wise is to say that all three of these sects come together as one, and that you can hold them all at once…[Such people feel] that as far as religion is concerned, the more ways of talking about religion there are, all the more benefit will that bring to the kingdom." Meanwhile Legalism continued to exert an impact through the state administrative and legal codes. In short, Confucianism, Daoism, Legalism, and Buddhism guided China's moral, spiritual, and political life for over 2,000 years.

Notes:

- This lesson is best taught together with Lesson 7, "The Impact of Confucius."
- Summaries of the basic principles of Daoism, Legalism, and Buddhism are available as Supplementary Materials on the CD-ROM. Those, together with the primary sources, make this lesson one that involves extensive reading. Refer to the Teacher Resources, "Teaching Guide for Difficult Text" (also on the CD-ROM) for suggestions on how to help students.

Organizing Idea

Chinese belief systems—Confucianism, Daoism, and Legalism—together with its own approach to Buddhism have permeated Chinese culture and traditions for centuries, and continue to through the present day.

Student Objectives

Students will:

- understand the basic tenets of Daoism, Legalism, and Buddhism
- review the essential elements of Confucianism
- compare and contrast Confucianism, Daoism, Legalism, and Buddhism in terms of key principles, approaches to government, and ultimate goal for followers
- recognize the presence of one or more of the four beliefs in traditional Chinese folk tales
- consider how elements of Chinese belief systems are present in their lives

Key Questions

- What are the most important principles of these three additional Chinese beliefs?
- In what ways are Confucianism, Daoism, Legalism, and Buddhism similar and different?

Vocabulary

Buddhism
Daoism
enlightened
harmony
karma
Legalism
nirvana
reincarnation
ritual
sage
the Way

Supplementary Materials

Item 8.A: Additional vocabulary for primary sources
Item 8.B: Graphic organizer
Item 8.C: An introduction to Daoism
Item 8.D: An introduction to Legalism
Item 8.E: Additional study questions for *Han Feizi*
Item 8.F: An introduction to Buddhism
Item 8.G: Suggested topics and questions for "The Tea"

Student Activities

» Activity 1: Constructing a Graphic Organizer for the Four Major Chinese Traditions

Briefly review the key questions from Lesson 7 on Confucianism. Then distribute copies of the Graphic Organizer (Item 8.B) and have students fill in the sections on Confucianism. As they study each of the Chinese beliefs, have them complete additional sections of the chart.

PRIMARY SOURCES related to Activity 2

 Document 8.1: Excerpts from *Daodejing* (《道德经》) on Dao, written around the 4th century B.C.E.

Chapter 34

The way is broad, reaching left as well as right.
The myriad creatures depend on it for life yet it claims no
    authority.
It accomplishes its task yet lays claim to no merit.
It clothes and feeds the myriad creatures yet lays no claim
    to being their master.
For ever free of desire, it can be called small; yet, as it lays
    no claim to being master
when the myriad creatures turn to it, it can be called great.
It is because it never attempts itself to be great that it
    succeeds in becoming great.

• *Full text available on CD-ROM* •

 Document 8.2: Excerpts from *Daodejing* (《道德经》) on personal behavior, written around the 4th century B.C.E.

Chapter 16

I do my utmost to attain emptiness;
I hold firmly to stillness.
The myriad creatures all rise together
And I watch their return.
The teaming creatures
All return to their separate roots.
Returning to one's roots is known as stillness.
That is what is meant by returning to one's destiny…

• *Full text available on CD-ROM* •

›› Activity 2: Analyzing *Daodejing*

Students should first read the introduction about Daoism (Item 8.C on the CD-ROM), or the teacher can provide students with the information. Discuss whether this approach to living reminds them of anything. (If it doesn't, that's fine. Responses will vary.) The writing in *Daodejing* is more abstract than in the Confucius *Analects*; however, students are likely to be intrigued by the ideas expressed. Divide the class into groups of three or four. Each group should work on one set of excerpts from *Daodejing* (Documents 8.1–8.4). Encourage students to put the ideas into their own words. Are there apparent contradictions in the text? How can these be explained? Ask each group to summarize in a few sentences what is written in the excerpts from *Daodejing*. After the groups report their conclusions, as a class, fill in the Graphic Organizer.

Document 8.3: Excerpts from *Daodejing* (《道德经》) on government, written around the 4th century B.C.E.

Chapter 12

> The best of all rulers is but a shadowy presence to his
>   subjects.
> Next comes the ruler they love and praise;
> Next comes one they fear;
> Next comes one with whom they take liberties.
> When there is not enough faith, there is lack of good faith.
> Hesitant, he [the ruler] does not utter words lightly.
> When his task is accomplished and his work done
> The people all say, 'It happened to us naturally.'

• Full text available on CD-ROM •

 Document 8.4: Excerpts from *Daodejing* (《道德经》), observations, written around the 4th century B.C.E.

Chapter 63

> Do that which consists in taking no action;
>   pursue that which is not meddlesome;
>   savor that which has no flavor.
> Make the small big and the few many;
>   do good to him who has done you an injury.
> Lay plans for the accomplishment of the difficult before it
>   becomes difficult;
>   make something big by starting with it when small.
> Difficult things in the world must needs have their
>   beginnings in the easy;
>   big things must needs have their beginnings in the small.
> Therefore it is because the sage never attempts to be great
>   that he succeeds in becoming great.
> One who makes promises rashly rarely keeps good faith;
>   one who is in the habit of considering things easy meets
>   with frequent difficulties.
> Therefore even the sage treats some things as difficult.
> That is why, in the end, no difficulties can get the better
>   of him.

• Full text available on CD-ROM •

PRIMARY SOURCES related to Activity 3

Document 8.5: Excerpts from *Han Feizi* (《韩非子》), explaining Legalist thought, written in the 3rd century B.C.E.

Han Feizi was born a prince in the ruling family of the state of Han around 280 B.C.E. He laid the groundwork for Legalist thought. The Qin king was interested in Han Feizi's writings and apparently gave him a position in his government. Han Feizi's essays and those of other Legalist thinkers appeared in a book in his name, Han Feizi. *Han Feizi got into a dispute with the Qin prime minister, Li Si, who had him imprisoned, and forced him to commit suicide.*

When a sage rules a state he does not count on people doing good on their own but rather takes measures to keep them from doing wrong. If he depended on people who do good of themselves, he could hardly find a few dozen in the whole realm. But if he uses methods to keep them from doing wrong, then everyone in the state can be made to act the same. In governing it is better to disregard the small minority to make use of the bulk of the population. Thus the ruler should concentrate on laws rather than on moral influence…

• *Full text available on CD-ROM* •

Document 8.6: Excerpts from Wei Shou's summary of Buddhist doctrine

Wei Shou was a Chinese historian in the 6th century. He wrote this description of Buddhism as part of a history of the Northern Wei dynasty (265-581).

The general import of [Buddhist] scriptures is that everything in this and all other lives is a result of karma. Through the three ages of the past, the present, and the future, the conscious spirit is never destroyed. Any act of good or evil will be recompensed. By gradually accumulating good deeds, purifying vulgarities, passing through many forms, and refining the spirit, one can arrive at a level at which rebirth will not recur and thus attain buddhahood. There are many steps and mental activities to take, all proceeding from the simple to the profound, the imperceptible to the manifest. Through building up one's goodness and obedience, eliminating desires, and practicing serenity, one can break through.

• *Full text available on CD-ROM* •

Document 8.7: Excerpts describing Pure Land (净土), a form of Buddhism in China

[Pure Land is] the world system of the Lord Amitabha, rich and prosperous, comfortable, fertile, delightful, and crowded with many Gods and men. And in this world system...there are no hells, no animals, no ghosts, no Asuras [demons] and none of the inauspicious places of rebirth...

[Nowhere] does one hear of anything unwholesome, nowhere of the hindrances, nowhere of the states of punishment, the states of woe and the bad destinies, nowhere of suffering. Even of feelings which are neither pleasant nor unpleasant one does not hear here, how much less of suffering! And that...is the reason why this world-system is called the "Happy Land."

• Full text available on CD-ROM •

Document 8.8: Photographs from the Longmen Grottoes created during Tang dynasty

Photos by Liz Nelson

Around the year 500, men began to carve into the cliff along the Yi River in Henan Province. Over the next 200 years, they created more than 100,000 images and statues of Buddha and his disciples. The top photograph is of the 55-foot-tall statue of Vairocana, the Buddha of Ultimate Wisdom.

>> Activity 3: Reading and Responding to Legalist Thought and Buddhism in China

Have the students read the introductions to Legalism and Buddhism (Items 8.D and 8.F on the CD-ROM) or provide students with the information. Emphasize that Buddhism is a world religion about which they are learning only a little at this time. Form six groups. (Half the groups will work on the document pertaining to Legalism; the other groups will analyze documents on Buddhism.)

Part A: Legalism
To each of three "Legalist" groups assign one of the three parts from *Han Feizi* (Document 8.5). They should

- determine what is the topic of the excerpt
- discuss in their group what main points Han Feizi made
- prepare a short explanation to the class

To help them analyze the selections, students can first answer the questions to each part in the supplementary materials (Item 8.E).

Part B: Buddhism
To the remaining three groups, distribute two writings about Buddhism in China (Documents 8.6 and 8.7) and the photographs from the Longmen Grottoes (8.8).
    For Documents 8.6 and 8.7, students should

- determine what is the topic of the excerpt
- discuss in their group what main points the writer made
- prepare a short explanation to the class

For Document 8.8, have students examine the photographs taken at the Longmen Grottoes and consider the following questions:

- How long might it have taken to carve hundreds of one-inch tall Buddha statues?
- Why might people create such grottoes and carve thousands of statues?
- What does this tell you about the importance of Buddhism during the sixth, seventh, and eighth centuries?
- What comparable monuments do other religions have?

After students share their findings, have them fill in their Graphic Organizers. Discuss what the most important differences are between the three schools of thought. Then discuss how Buddhism fits in with the schools of thought. Would it be possible to combine the traditions? Which aspects of each do the students find most engaging?

PRIMARY SOURCES *related to Activity 4*

Document 8.9: "The Lost Horse" (*Saiweng shi ma*, 塞翁失马), a Chinese folktale by Liu An (刘安)

A man who lived on the northern frontier of China was skilled in interpreting events. One day for no reason, his horse ran away to the nomads across the border. Everyone tried to console him, but his father said, "What makes you so sure this isn't a blessing?" Some months later his horse returned, bringing a splendid nomad stallion. Everyone congratulated him, but his father said, "What makes you so sure this isn't a disaster?" Their household was richer by a fine horse, which the son loved to ride. One day he fell and broke his hip. Everyone tried to console him, but his father said, "What makes you so sure this isn't a blessing?"

A year later the nomads came in force across the border, and every able-bodied man took his bow and went into battle. The Chinese frontiersmen lost nine of every ten men. Only because the son was lame did father and son survive to take care of each other. Truly, blessing turns to disaster, and disaster to blessing: the changes have no end, nor can the mystery be fathomed.

Document 8.10: "Man and Beast," a Chinese folktale by Liezi (列子)

The leader of the Tian clan was preparing a grand feast for a thousand guests. At the place of honor someone presented an offering of fish and wild geese. The clan leader examined the offering and sighed, "How generous heaven is to the people, growing the five grains and breeding fish and fowl for us to use." The whole assembly echoed their leader's praise.

A boy of twelve, a son of the Bao clan who was present in the ranks, stepped forward and said, "Not at all! Heaven and earth and the ten thousand things between are born as one with us, alike in kind to us. There is no high and low among the kinds. It is merely that one kind dominates another by virtue of size or strength or wit. And so one devours the other and is devoured in turn. But heaven did not create things for each other. Man eats whatever he can, but did heaven breed what man eats specifically for man? The mosquito and the gnat bite man's skin, the tiger and the wolf feed on flesh. Has heaven created man for the mosquito, or flesh for the tiger and the wolf?"

Document 8.11: "Three Former Lives" (*San Sheng,* 三生), a Chinese folktale by Pu Songling (蒲松龄)

After a while the king looked up Mr. Liu's record of misdeeds in life and angrily ordered a group of ghosts to remove him. The king punished him by reincarnation as a horse, and some fierce ghosts marched him off. He found himself before a house with a threshold too high for him to cross. He balked, but the hosts lashed him. In great pain he stumbled forward. Then he was in a stable and heard a voice saying, "The black mare has given birth to a colt. A male!" He understood the words but could not speak. Too hungry to do anything else he went to the mare and suckled...

• *Full text available on CD-ROM* •

Document 8.12: "Underworld Justice" (*Xi Fangping*), a Chinese folktale by Pu Songling (蒲松龄)

As the axe strikes the wedge and the wedge cuts the wood, our conduct starts a chain reaction that eventually sucks the blood out of women and children. As the whale devours the fish and the fish devours the shrimp, so the life of the lowly is miserable. . . .

As for the city god and the governor, in behalf of the Highest they serve the common people as parent-officials, pastors of the human flock. Though they are offices of lower rank, a true office-seeker will not disdain them. Even if they are pressured by higher officials, they should resist. But you two brandish your hawklike claws, giving no thought to the poverty of the people. You have worked with the cunning of a monkey, indifferent to the plight of the dead. Taking bribes to pervert the law, you hid a bestial heart behind a human face! You shall have the marrow scooped from your bones and the hair plucked from your hides. You shall suffer death even in the realm of the dead and be reborn beasts, not men...

• *Full text available on CD-ROM* •

≫ Activity 4: Recognizing Chinese Beliefs in Folk Tales

Divide the class into small groups and distribute the four folk tales (Documents 8.9–8.12). The four folk tales are of varying lengths. Teachers may wish to give the two very short tales "The Lost Horse" and "Man and Beast" to one group. The first time students read the story, they should read it through simply for pleasure. On the second reading, have students determine which Chinese belief(s) are reflected in the story. They can mark passages with Post-it notes. They should refer to excerpts of Confucian, Daoist, Legalist, and Buddhist thought and explain their reasoning.

For "Underworld Justice" (Document 8.12) students should also

- Describe the justice system in the world of the dead.
- Consider how much the world of the dead might mirror life on earth.
- Determine what Confucian ideal Xi Fangping follows.
- Determine what Confucian ideals the god Er Lang follows.
- Decide whether Xi Fangping sees justice served.

≫ Activity 5: Creative Extentions

Ideas for having students demonstrate their understanding of Chinese beliefs are virtually limitless. Some options:

1) "The Tea" (will need tea, cookies, and adult volunteers): Students choose to be the representative for one of the schools of thought. At the tea, each cluster of students will include a representative from each of the four beliefs and an adult, who has a basic idea of the material in this lesson. The "thinkers/philosophers" discuss current issues of the day from their chosen perspective, while eating cookies and drinking tea. (A suggested list of topics can be found in Item 8.G.)

2) Students choose one saying from the *Analects* or one chapter from *Daodejing* and create an illustration for it or a four- to five-frame comic strip. Conversations between characters should be in the students' own words.

3) Students write a composition in which they give an example of a time they witnessed or experienced in their lives something related to Confucian, Daoist, or Legalist thought. Describe the event and explain how it fits the ancient belief.

4) Each student writes a letter explaining a problem for which he or she needs advice. Students should choose a Chinese name (see Lesson 5) and use that to sign the letter. Randomly distribute the letters, and ask the students to respond to the problem from the perspective of one of the schools of thought or religions. Ask them to use quotes from their primary sources. Return the responses and ask students to identify which belief the response reflects.

5) "Create the Perfect School": Students will work in groups of four. Each group represents one school of thought/religion. Group members assume the positions of leader, timekeeper, secretary, and architect. Using notes, primary sources, and supplementary materials, create a school. Students must determine:

- the major curriculum focus for the school. What subjects will be offered and why?

- the hierarchical structure of the school. What is the relationship between the teachers and students? What is the relationship between the teachers and the principal, and the school personnel and the community?
- six most important rules for the school and give a philosophical justification for each.
- the school's mission.
- how the school will be designed physically. Draw a diagram of the structural layout of the school and give a detailed account of why these choices have been made.

Once each school has been created, students prepare a presentation to the class. Each group must ask at least one question of each other group.

≫ Activity 8: Extended Research

Have students research one of the topics below or a related topic and present their findings in writing, with a poster, or, working with a partner, in a short video.

- Who was Zhuangzi (庄子) (369–286 B.C.E.), and how did he contribute to Daoism?
- When and how did Daoism emerge as a religion?
- Who was Xuanzang (玄奘), and what was his role in spreading Buddhism in China?
- Who is the mythical Monkey King, what relation did he have to Xuanzang, and what role has the Monkey King had in Chinese folklore?
- How have the discoveries at Dunhuang (敦煌) contributed to our knowledge of Buddhism in China?
- What is the significance of the Yungang Caves (*Yungang shiku*, 云冈石窟) in Datong, Shanxi Province?
- The Bodhisattva of Compassion is always depicted as a woman. Her name is Guanyin (观音). What are Bodhisattvas and what is their role in Buddhism?

Further Student and Teacher Resources

Boisselier, Jean. *Wisdom of Buddha*. New York: Harry N. Abrams, Inc. Publishers, 1993.

Dawson, Raymond. *Legacy of China*. Boston: Cheng & Tsui Co., 1998.

Esposito, John L., Darrell J. Fasching, and Todd Lewis. *World Religions Today*. Oxford: Oxford University Press, 2002.

Moss, Roberts, ed. and trans. *Chinese Fairy Tales and Fantasies*. New York: Pantheon Books, 1979. (excellent source for additional folk tales)

Overmyer, Daniel L. *Religions of China*. Prospect Heights, Illinois: Waveland Press, Inc., 1986.

Rickett, W. Allyn. *Guanzi 1: Political, Economic, and Philosophical Essays from Early China*. Boston: Cheng & Tsui Co., 1999.

Tu, Wei-Ming. *Humanity and Self-Cultivation: Essays in Confucian Thought*. Boston: Cheng & Tsui Co., 1999.

Wriggins, Sally Hovey. *Xuanzang: A Buddhist Pilgrim on the Silk Road*. Boulder, CO: Westview Press, 1996.

Web Sites

http://www.warriortours.com/intro/religion_confucianism.htm (includes pictures and information and is easy to navigate; links to information on Confucianism, Daoism and Buddhism in China)

http://www.buddhanet.net/e-learning/buddhistworld/china-txt.htm (focuses on the spread of Buddhism among the Chinese)

http://members.aol.com/Donnclass/Chinalife.html (section called "Daily life in ancient China" gives a brief overview of Confucianism, "Daoism & Winnie the Pooh," and Daoism)

http://depts.washington.edu/chinaciv/bud/5temmain.htm (excellent information on and images of Buddhism in China)

Video

Religions in China, Film for Humanities and Sciences, 2001, 60 min. (valuable overview of the major traditions in China, including the place of religion in modern-day China. It includes strong opinions by theologian Hans Küng.)

Elsewhere in the World

- **Siddhartha Gautama, Buddha lived in India 563–483 B.C.E.**
- **Socrates lived in Greece 469–399 B.C.E.**
- **The Peloponnesian War 431–404 B.C.E.**
- **Alexander the Great conquered Egypt 332 B.C.E.**
- **Early Mayan cities and states formed ca. 350 B.C.E.**
- **Rome conquered all of peninsular Italy 272 B.C.E.**
- **Earliest known Celtic coinage ca. 225 B.C.E.**
- **Iron working practiced in East Africa 400–300 B.C.E.**

In the World Today

Buddhism Today

An estimated 350 million people practice Buddhism, making it the fourth largest world religion. Centuries ago, it spread throughout Asia either directly from India or via the Silk Routes to China and then on to Korea and Japan. Almost all Buddhists—98 percent—live in Asia. In Sri Lanka, Burma (also known as Myanmar), Thailand, Laos, Cambodia, Vietnam, and Japan, as well as Tibet, an overwhelming majority of the population is Buddhist. In the twentieth century, European and American converts established Buddhist centers in the West. Zen Buddhism is especially attractive to Western practitioners, who focus on the benefits of meditation. The ways people practice Buddhism vary significantly, but all sects value the central tenets: compassion, nonviolence, selflessness, interdependence, and detachment.

Students can find out about local Buddhist education centers, explore Buddhist art, or learn about organizations such as the International Network of Engaged Buddhists, which links Buddhists worldwide to work on spiritual training, gender issues, human rights, and ecology (http://www.sulak-sivaraksa.org/network22.php).

春眠不覺曉
處處聞啼鳥
夜來風雨聲
花落知多少

Lesson 9 CD-ROM Contents

Primary Sources

- Document 9.1: Excerpt from *The Good Earth* by Pearl S. Buck, describing New Year traditions

- Document 9.2: Excerpt from *River Town: Two Years on the Yangtze* by Peter Hessler, describing New Year traditions in Sichuan Province in 1996

- Document 9.3: Image of *Zaojun* (灶君) "God of the Hearth"

- Document 9.5: Excerpt from *River Town: Two Years on the Yangtze* by Peter Hessler, describing *Qingmingjie* (清明节) celebration in Sichuan Province in 1996

- Document 9.7: Excerpts from *"Wuling jingdu lüe"* (《武陵竞渡略》) by Yang Sichang (杨嗣昌), describing a dragon boat race, early 1600s

Supplementary Materials

- Item 9.A: Additional vocabulary for primary sources
- Item 9.B: The legend of the zodiac animals
- Item 9.C: Chart of Chinese festivals

Lesson 9
Festivals

Lesson Contents

Chinese tradition credits the legendary Yellow Emperor (*Huangdi*, 黄帝) with having created the Chinese lunar calendar—based on the phases of the moon—in 2637 B.C.E. Artifacts from the Shang (商) dynasty (ca. 1600—ca. 1050 B.C.E.) unearthed by archaeologists, show that a group of mathematicians prepared the annual calendar, proving that the Chinese calendar dates back at least 3,000 years. A lunar year has twelve months of twenty-nine or thirty days each. However, because a lunar calendar does not match a solar calendar, which is based on the length of time it takes for the earth to circle the sun, periodically the Chinese would have to add an extra month (similar to the way our calendar adds an extra day on leap years).

Chinese Zodiac Calendar

Each year of the Chinese calendar is associated with an animal. In order, they are rat (*shu*, 鼠), ox (*niu*, 牛), tiger (*hu*, 虎), rabbit (*tu*, 兔), dragon (*long*, 龙), snake (*she*, 蛇), horse (*ma*, 马), ram (*yang*, 羊), monkey (*hou*, 猴), rooster (*ji*, 鸡), dog (*gou*, 狗), and pig (*zhu*, 猪). Every twelve years, the cycle begins again. The year 2006—which is the year 4704 in the Chinese calendar—is the year of the dog, and 2007 the year of the pig. Many Chinese believe that an individual shares the characteristics of the zodiac animal for the lunar year of his or her birth.

Holidays and Festivals

The Chinese now use the Western solar calendar for everyday activities, but for holidays and festivals they refer to the lunar calendar. For example, *Chunjie* (春节), the Chinese New Year, also called Spring Festival, occurs on the eve of the second new moon following the winter solstice. This begins a new year. *Qingmingjie* (清明节), Clear Brightness Festival, honoring the dead, occurs on the 106th day after the winter solstice, and *Duanwujie* (端午节), the Dragon Boat Festival in memory of poet Qu Yuan (屈原), takes place on the fifth day of the fifth lunar month, and the Autumn Moon Festival, *Zhongqiujie* (中秋节) on the fifteenth day of the eighth month.

Organizing Idea

Chinese festivals date back centuries and embody China's rich and varied traditions. Chinese people on mainland China, in Taiwan, elsewhere in Asia, and in cities around the world continue the celebrations.

Student Objectives

Students will:
- understand the Chinese lunar calendar
- understand the legend of the zodiac and identify personality traits of individual zodiac signs
- know the key traditions associated with five major Chinese celebrations: New Year (*Chunjie*), Lantern Festival (*Yuanxiaojie*), Clear Brightness Festival (*Qingmingjie*), Dragon Boat Festival (*Duanwujie*), and Mid-Autumn Moon Festival (*Zhongqiujie*)
- create objects and make food associated with Chinese festivals
- consider how festivals and traditions create cultural continuity
- explore how the festivals are celebrated outside of mainland China

Key Questions

- How is a lunar calendar different from a solar calendar?
- What are the important traditions associated with the five Chinese festivals noted above?
- What food is associated with each festival?
- What legends are associated with the festivals?
- Why do festivals such as these endure?

Vocabulary

dragon boat
festival
lunar
mooncake
solar
tradition
zodiac

Supplementary Materials

Item 9.A: Additional vocabulary for primary sources
Item 9.B: The legend of the zodiac animals
Item 9.C: Chart of Chinese festivals

Student Activities

›› Activity 1: Understanding the Lunar Calendar and Zodiac Symbols

Have students read the introduction to the lesson and the legend of how the zodiac animals were named (Item 9.B on the CD-ROM). On a class calendar, mark off the months of the year based on a Chinese lunar calendar. (The New Year begins on the eve of the second new moon following the winter solstice.) Add the dates for all the festivals as they are discussed. Students in the class were likely born within eighteen months of each other. (1992: Year of the Monkey, 1993 Year of the Rooster, etc.) Have students determine under which animal they were born and then find the characteristics for individuals born that year. (http://www.c-c-c.org/chineseculture/zodiac/zodiac.html has good summaries.) How does this zodiac calendar compare with the one often used in Western societies? For example, if someone is a Scorpio born in the Year of the Snake, how do the characteristics compare? What do students think of describing everyone born in the same year with the same characteristics?

›› Activity 2: Family Traditions

Ask the students to describe traditions/festivals their families observe.

- Who participates?
- What do they do?
- Are there special foods involved?
- Are there particular decorations associated with the tradition/festival?
- Why do people have traditions and festivals that they celebrate each year?
- Of the ones students described, which are from the country where students live and which are from another culture?
- Why do people continue to celebrate their native traditions after they move to another country?

PRIMARY SOURCES related to Activity 3

Document 9.1: Excerpt from *The Good Earth* by Pearl S. Buck, describing New Year traditions

The New Year approached and in every house in the village there were preparations. Wang Lung went into the town to the candlemaker's shop and he bought squares of red paper on which were brushed in gilt ink the letter for happiness and some with the letter for riches, and these squares he pasted upon his farm utensils to bring him luck in the New Year. Upon his plow and upon the ox's yoke and upon the two buckets in which he carried his fertilizer and his water, upon each of these he pasted a square. And then upon the doors of his house he pasted long strips of red paper brushed with mottoes of good luck, and over his doorway he pasted a fringe of red paper cunningly cut into a flower pattern and very finely cut.

• Full text available on CD-ROM •

Document 9.2: Excerpt from *River Town: Two Years on the Yangtze* by Peter Hessler, describing New Year traditions in Sichuan Province in 1996

Traditionally, on New Year's Day you didn't wear anything old, and especially the children were dressed brightly. Many of the little girls wore makeup; all of the boys carried guns. That seemed to be another holiday tradition: plastic pellet guns were for sale everywhere on special streetside stands, and every male child had a rifle or a pistol, or both. The guns were accurate and powerful, and in America you could sell perhaps two of them before you were sued. In America there was also a chance that a child would use the guns to shoot at birds, dogs, or cats; in Fuling there were very few animals but plenty of people. All around town boys chased after each other, shouting and firing their weapons.

≫ Activity 3: Reading about the Chinese New Year

Divide the class into three groups. Have a third of the students read the excerpt from *The Good Earth* (9.1), another third read the excerpt from *River Town* (9.2), and the last third examine the image of *Zaojun*, the "God of the Hearth"—also known as Kitchen God or Stove God—(9.3) and read the excerpt from *Dragonwings* (9.4). From the documents they examine, what do the students learn about traditions associated with New Year? Have students fill in their charts on Chinese Festivals (Item 9.C on the CD-ROM). Members of each group report to the rest of the class, and as they do, students should add information to their charts. Explain to students that they will be learning more about the Chinese New Year celebrations later in the unit.

Document 9.3: Image of *Zaojun* (灶君) "God of the Hearth"

"God of the Hearth" is also known as the Kitchen God and Stove King. Many Chinese have an image such as this one hanging in their kitchens.

Document 9.4: Excerpt from *Dragonwings* by Laurence Yep, describing the tradition of "God of the Hearth"

God of the Hearth is also known as the Kitchen God or Stove King. In this excerpt, Moon Shadow, who has recently joined his father in San Francisco, is sharing the tradition with an American girl his age. Many Chinese consider the Tang (唐) dynasty (618–907) as the high point of Chinese civilization and in the past would refer to themselves the way Moon Shadow does, as "Tang people," meaning Chinese.

We took the old picture of the Stove King and smeared some honey on it before we burned it in the stove. Later that evening we would hang up a new picture of the Stove King that we had bought in the Tang people's town [China-town]. That was a sign the Stove King had returned to his place above our stove. After we had finished burning the old picture, we sat down to a lunch of meat pastries and dumplings…

PRIMARY SOURCES related to Activity 4

Document 9.5: Excerpt from *River Town: Two Years on the Yangtze* by Peter Hessler, describing *Qingmingjie* (清明节) celebration in Sichuan Province in 1996

He Zhonggui's father and uncle are buried side by side, a pair of solid limestone tombs facing south and east toward the Yangtze and the world beyond. The visitors have walked single-file through wheat fields to the graves, careful not to trample the young green stalks, and now they light fat red candles and burn piles of paper money.

The bills, which are in denominations of $800 million, say "Bank of Heaven" on the front. They are legal tender in the next world. The money crumples into black balls of ash as the fire flickers and gasps. The candles dance in the Yangtze wind. Waves of heat come and go as the flames rise and fall.

The old women kowtow and pray before the burning of money. After they finish, the children take their turns, urged on by their elders. They giggle and sloppily kowtow three times, kneeling on strips of paper so their trousers and dresses won't get dirty, and then they close their eyes and pray, sometimes aloud. "Please help me do well on my examinations," murmurs Dai Mei's cousin, a sixteen-year-old boy in glasses.

• Full text available on CD-ROM •

Document 9.6: Excerpt from *Dragonwings* by Laurence Yep, describing *Qingmingjie* (清明节)

Moon Shadow has recently joined his father in San Francisco. He is the narrator in the book, and here he describes the Feast of Pure Brightness—Qingmingjie. Many Chinese consider the Tang (唐) dynasty (618–907) as the high point of Chinese civilization and in the past would refer to themselves as "Tang people," meaning Chinese.

[N]ear the time of the Feast of Pure Brightness,…we go out to the graves and make offerings to the dead. It's not nearly as somber as it sounds. It is really the major festival for the springtime. We go out to the graves and sweep them and clean them and tell the dead about some of the things that have happened. Then we make them offerings of food, only we don't give all of it to them. After all, it's a banquet where we all share. So we take home some of the better things to eat, knowing the hungry dead will be happy. Unlike the other holidays, it is determined by a solar calendar like that of the demons, and so it is always on April 5.

The Tang people's cemetery at the time was not a permanent one. All Tang people wanted to be buried finally in their homeland. But there were often delays of several years between when a man died and when his body got shipped home. So there was a cemetery where the coffins were temporarily buried.

PRIMARY SOURCE *related to Activity 5*

Document 9.7: Excerpts from *"Wuling jingdu lüe"* (《武陵竞渡略》)
by Yang Sichang (杨嗣昌), **describing a dragon boat race, early**
1600s

The people watch the boat races from the shore. Along the northern shore from Qingpingmen to Shigui, about five or six li, are buildings of three or four stories in which space can be reserved by paying an advance fee of up to several hundred cash. On the day of the races, the people, carrying wine bottles and food boxes, ride on carts and horses or walk along the roads to get there by mid-morning. Tables are covered with fruit and food for sale. The best fruits are the "plums from the Han family" and the "wheat-yellow peaches"; the food includes shad [fish] and vegetables. When the start of the race is announced, everyone stops talking, laughing, or leaning against the balustrades. Attentively they watch, wondering which is their boat and whether it will meet victory or defeat. All too quickly victory is decided. Then some are so proud it seems as if their spirits could break the ceiling, and some have faces so pale as death and seem not to know how to go down the stairs...

• *Full text available on CD-ROM* •

≫ Activity 4: An Introduction to Clear Brightness Festival

Ask students to read Documents 9.5 and 9.6, excerpts from the books, and with a partner to add details about *Qingmingjie* to their Festival Charts. What do they learn about this festival?

≫ Activity 5: Reading and Illustrating an Ancient Account of a Dragon Boat Race

The excerpt by Yang Sichang, describing a race (9.7) can be divided into four sections so that a group of students is only responsible for one segment. (Part 1 ends with "shore." Part 2 begins with "Priests" and ends with "purification." Part 3 begins with "The boatmen" and ends with "stairs." Part 4 begins with "The victorious boat.") After students have read and discussed their assigned sections, they report on the content to their classmates. Next, ask each group to decide how many illustrations they will need to create to visually represent what Yang Sichang describes. Have them divide the work and create illustrations. Each illustration should include two to three sentences of text. When all illustrations are finished, compile them in a booklet or display them on the wall.

≫ Activity 6: Independent Research—Filling in the Pieces

Note: This activity involves extensive cooperative work in groups. Students need to assign/choose subtopics/tasks and plan engaging, coherent presentations.

The students will work in pairs to find more information about five major Chinese festivals. Each pair is responsible for one subtopic. When all the information is gathered, the group working on various aspects of one festival will gather to decide how best to present all of the information about the festival to the class. Each presentation must include brief written pieces, which will be presented orally; visual materials; and food, where appropriate. Students may wish to perform a short skit, too. After each group finishes its presentation, students should take time to fill in their Festival Charts. If there are boxes without information on the chart, students should ask the group responsible to help them fill it in. (Not every box will necessarily be filled, but almost all will.) Alternatively, the class could stage a "festival of festivals" and invite guests to see their displays and learn about Chinese festivals.

The New Year or Spring Festival is the biggest of the year; so more students should be assigned to work on this. To help address the subtopics on the chart, the group presentation should include information about

- preparations for the New Year
- legend of *Zaojun*, the God of the Hearth (also known as the Kitchen God or Stove God)
- *laise* (in Cantonese) or *hongbao* (red envelopes) (红包)
- how individuals are to behave on Day 1
- do's and don't's/superstitions
- the lion dance
- what happens on Day 7 of the celebration

Also:
One or two pairs should create scrolls with good wishes written in Chinese characters.

The Lantern Festival presentation should include information about the subtopics as well as:

- the origins of the festival, story of Yuan Xiao (元宵)
- lantern riddles

Also:

- Two or three pairs should make lanterns.
- One or two pairs should make traditional food (*tangyuan*, 汤圆).

The Clear Brightness Festival presentation should include information about the subtopics as well as:

- the origins of the festival
- description of sacrifices
- role of kites

Some students may wish to make their own kites.

The Dragon Boat Festival should include information about the subtopics as well as:

- the story of Qu Yuan (屈原)
- samples of his poetry
- story of Zhong Kui (钟馗), the demon-slayer (see Document 11.11)

Also:

- One or two pairs should make traditional food (*zongzi*, 粽子).
- A pair may even wish to make a model of a dragon boat.

The Mid-Autumn Moon Festival should include information about the subtopics as well as:

- story of its origin, Hou Yi (后羿) and Chang E (嫦娥)
- Liu Bowen's (刘伯温) resistance to Mongol rule with the help of mooncakes (*yuebing*, 月饼)

Also:

- Two or three pairs can make traditional food (mooncakes).

›› Activity 7: Discussion of Ancient Traditions Continued

Students have read excerpts from *River Town*, a book set in 1996–98, and have looked at photographs on the Internet of festivals celebrated in China. What do these primary sources tell the students about how the Chinese celebrate festivals in the present day? Two additional primary sources are from *Dragonwings*, a historical fiction book set in San Francisco. Together with information they have learned in their independent research, what have students learned about how Chinese people continue their traditions after they move from China? What purpose do traditions and festivals serve? Ask the question posed at the beginning of the unit: Why do people continue to celebrate their native traditions after they move to another country?

Further Resources for Students and Teachers

Chan, Arlene. *Awakening the Dragon: The Dragon Boat Festival*. Toronto, Canada: Tundra Books, 2004.

Simonds, Nina, Leslie Swartz, and The Children's Museum, Boston. *Moonbeams, Dumplings & Dragon Boats: A Treasury of Chinese Holiday Tales, Activities & Recipes*. New York: Gulliver Books, 2002.

Thompson, Stuart and Angela Dennington. *Chinese Festivals Cookbook*. New York: Raintree Steck-Vaughn Publishers, 2001.

Williams, C.A.S. *Outlines of Chinese Symbolism and Art Motives*. New York: Dover Publication, Inc., 1976.

Young, Ed. *Cat and Rat: The Legend of the Chinese Zodiac*. New York: Henry Holt and Co., 1995.

Web Sites

http://www.c-c-c.org/chineseculture/zodiac/zodiac.html (Chinese Culture Center of San Francisco gives detailed information about zodiac signs and descriptions of festivals, both traditional and in San Francisco in the twenty-first century.)

http://explanation-guide.info/meaning/Chinese-calendar.html (for information about the calendar)

For information about festivals:

http://chineseculture.about.com/library/weekly/topicsub_festival.htm

http://www.chinatown-online.co.uk/pages/culture/festivals.html

http://www.chinapage.org

http://www.iub.edu/~easc/holidays/china/china.html

In the World Today

Dragon Boat Races Around the World

Chinese festivals continue to be celebrated on mainland China, Taiwan, and by people of Chinese heritage around the world. Dragon boat races not only play a vital part in the Dragon Boat Festivals in China, they have become popular worldwide, from Cape Town, South Africa, to Boston in the United States.

The world over, the colorful and exciting races draw thousands of spectators. In New Zealand and the United Kingdom, crews are largely from corporations, who see the activity as a team-building experience. The races also generate huge donations to charities. In July 2004, Racine, Wisconsin, hosted its first Great Midwest Dragon Boat Festival. Heart Lake Conservation Area sponsors near Toronto, Canada, welcomed paddlers and crowds to their "boisterous celebration...a symbol of Chinese culture and spirit." In San Francisco, the Northern California International Dragon Boat Championships and Festival draws ninety teams every year from all over the United States and Canada. The Dragon Boat Festival in Sydney, Australia, held at the rowing site of the 2000 Olympic Games, brings more than 2,000 paddlers to compete.

The boats feature a sculpted dragonhead at the bow and a tail at the stern. A drummer on board sets the rhythm as dragon boat crews race for the finish line. Students can learn about dragon boat races near them and around the world by entering "dragon boat race" or "festival" in a search engine and comparing their findings. Discuss why this particular Chinese tradition has become so popular. How does the spread of a tradition such as this one affect relationships between people of various nations?

Lesson 10 CD-ROM Contents

Primary Sources

- Document 10.1: Excerpts from *The Book of Rites* (*Liji*, 《礼记》), compiled during the Han (汉) dynasty (202 B.C.E.–220 C.E.), regarding the relationship between husband and wife

- Document 10.2: Excerpts from *Biographies of Virtuous Women* (*Lienü zhuan*, 《烈女传》) by Liu Xiang (刘向), 1st century B.C.E.

- Document 10.3: Excerpts from Ban Zhao's (班昭) *Admonitions for Women* (*Nüjie*, 《女诫》), 1st century B.C.E.

- Document 10.4: Excerpts from *Analects for Women* (《女论语》) by Song Ruozhao (宋若昭), Tang (唐) dynasty (618–907)

- Document 10.5: Pottery figures of women on horseback, Tang (唐) dynasty (618–907)

- Document 10.6: Excerpt from *Taoan mengui*, describing sale of a concubine

- Document 10.7: "A Cure for Jealousy" (*Yi ji*, 医嫉), a folktale by Yuan Mei (袁枚), 18th century

- Document 10.8: Excerpts from *The Book of Rites* (*Liji*, 《礼记》), compiled during the Han (汉) dynasty (202 B.C.E.–220 C.E.), pertaining to bringing up children

- Document 10.9: Excerpts from the *Analects of Confucius* (《论语》) on relationships within the family

- Document 10.10: Excerpts from *Family Instructions of Mr. Yan* (*Yanshi Jiaxun*, 《颜氏家训》) by Yan Zhitui (颜之推), 6th century

- Document 10.11: Excerpts from "Instructing Sons and Daughters" from *Analects for Women* (《女论语》) by Song Ruozhao (宋若昭), Tang (唐) dynasty (618–907)

- Document 10.12: Excerpt from *Wild Swans: Three Daughters of China* by Jung Chang, describing how the author's grandmother had her feet bound

- Document 10.13a–e: Segments of scroll painting "The Spring Festival Along the River" ("*Qingming Shanghe Tu*," 《清明上河图》), by Zhang Zeduan (张择端), 12th century

Supplementary Materials

- Item 10.A: Additional vocabulary for primary sources
- Item 10.B: Questions for Activity 5, folktale "A Cure for Jealousy"
- Item 10.C: Questions for Activity 6, Documents 10.8–10.11
- Item 10.D: Notes for Document 10.13a-e

Lesson 10
Family Life

Lesson Contents
- The family in ancient China
- The role of women
- Children in China
- Foot binding
- Concubines

Based on beliefs about ancestor worship, ancient texts such as the *Book of Rites* (*Liji*, 《礼记》), and the influence of Confucians, the family was central in Chinese society for millennia. To illustrate the importance of family, the Chinese character for peace or contentment (*an*, 安) is a combination of the character for woman (*nü*, 女) beneath the top part of the character for house (*shi*, 室). And *hao* (好), meaning good, right, or excellent, is written as a combination of the character for woman (*nü*, 女) and son (*zi*, 子).

Relationships Within the Family

Within the family, each member's role was clearly defined. The way individuals addressed each other is one indication of this. Rather than use first names, siblings in a family would call each other oldest brother (*dage*, 大哥), number two brother (*erge*, 二哥), younger brother (*didi*, 弟弟), big sister (*dajie*, 大姐), and so on. The oldest male was the formal head of the family. He had almost total power over its members. Under extreme economic stress, such as that caused by a famine, he could sell a daughter into permanent servitude similar to slavery.

Marriages between boys and girls were arranged by the parents and were considered legal contracts between the heads of the families. "Love and happiness were not expected from marriage," writes Olga Lang, "continuation of family was the goal" (*Chinese Family and Society* p. 49). When a young woman married, she left her home and moved in with her husband's parents. Her responsibility was to them, not to her own parents or siblings. As a result, couples had a strong preference for male offspring, who by tradition would take care of the older generation. In Chinese, the character for infant is the same as that for son. "Grain is stored against famine; sons are brought up against old age" is a traditional Chinese saying. Others like "It is more profitable to raise geese than daughters" or "Girls are goods on whom one loses money" make clear that many saw girls as being of little use.

The Role of Women

The *Analects* (《论语》) of Confucius, written down by his followers, mention women only once: "The Master said, 'Women and underlings are especially difficult to handle; be friendly and they become familiar; be distant, and they resent it.'" The absence of any further reference to women is significant as well. For centuries in ancient China, women had no property rights. An inheritance was divided among males, and only if there was no possible male heir did a woman receive anything. Women could choose among very few occupations. Life as a servant, prostitute, spiritual medium, midwife, Buddhist nun, or courtesan were options (*An Introduction to Chinese Culture Through the Family*, "Women and Gender," p. 92). Very few girls received any formal education. Only in wealthy families might a girl be literate. There were a few female scholars, artists, and writers, but almost none of them earned an income from their work. The vast majority of women led lives as wives and mothers. Within the family, especially if she gave birth to sons, a woman did have a significant role. In addition, older women—grandmothers—were greatly respected.

It is useful to compare the lives of men and women in ancient China to other ancient cultures. In ancient Greece, for example, a father had the right to have a daughter put to death if she refused his orders. What is interesting in China is that prior to the twentieth century the position of women appears to have got worse over time rather than better. One example is the increasing use of foot binding (*guo zu*, 裹足), a practice unique to China that lasted from the tenth century until it was banned by the new Chinese republic in 1911. Bound feet were seen as sexually appealing, but it is also clear that by crippling girls and women in this way, society restricted the world in which they could move. Women with bound feet literally could not leave their homes on foot.

Although recent scholarship is beginning to shed more light on the subject, it is unlikely that we will ever get a clear picture of life within Chinese families in centuries past. There is little information about the lives of peasants and artisans other than novels and stories written by those of a different social class. The literacy rate among the vast masses was very low, as it was elsewhere in the world. The texts that exist are mostly written by men, and generally describe what the authors saw as the ideal behavior for men, women, and children. We have no idea how much people conformed to the rules. We don't have primary sources such as letters or diaries, which might give us a look at what really went on in families of ancient China. It may be helpful to keep in mind that the Chinese have always valued harmony and compromise. "Harmony makes both a family and a nation prosperous" a Chinese saying tells us. Even though their marriages were arranged, often husbands and wives developed deep affection for each other. It is also likely that in the privacy of their homes, many families found ways to adapt the ideals to their personalities and needs.

Organizing Idea

Written records from ancient China indicate that for millennia the family in China was patriarchal in structure. The hierarchy within families was determined by generation, age, and gender. Outside the home, and often within it, women had few rights and opportunities. Behavior for men, women, and children was dictated by rigid rules.

Student Objectives

Students will:

- understand the ideal role a Chinese woman was supposed to play in families of ancient China
- understand the difference between how boys and girls were brought up
- explore reasons why the family structure and rigid gender roles endured for so many centuries
- begin to understand the role of marriage in society
- explain the difference between yin and yang and understand how those beliefs influenced ancient Chinese attitudes toward gender roles

Key Questions

In traditional Chinese families,

- For a woman, what were the "three dependencies"?
- How should a woman behave?
- What work did women perform?
- What role did men have in the family?
- What was a concubine?
- What advice did parents get for raising children?
- Why did mothers bind their daughters' feet?
- What similarities are there between traditional Chinese families and the families you know?

Vocabulary

ancestor
concubine
duty
filial
moral
patriarchal
propriety
rite
submit/submission
virtue
yang
yin

Supplementary Materials

Item 10.A: Additional vocabulary for primary sources
Item 10.B: Questions for Activity 5, folktale "A Cure for Jealousy"
Item 10.C: Questions for Activity 6, Documents 10.8–10.11
Item 10.D: Notes for Document 10.13a-e

Student Activities

Note: This lesson lends itself to having students read historical fiction set in China or with characters who are Chinese. Through the narratives, students will increase their understanding of familial relationships in traditional Chinese society. An annotated list of books is included in the Teacher Resources on the CD-ROM.

›› Activity 1: Defining a Family in the Student's Country

Divide students into small groups and ask each group to imagine they will be speaking to someone who knows absolutely nothing about their country. Students are responsible for helping this person understand what a family is like here. List ten characteristics that define a family. After fifteen or twenty minutes ask each group to write its list on the board. What similarities and what differences are there in the lists? How difficult was it for students to agree on a list of ten? Why? As students begin to explore the family in ancient China, it will be useful for them to keep in mind how difficult it is to describe family. Certain characteristics in traditional Chinese families endured for centuries (and continue to endure), but outside the generalities it is important to remember there were many, many exceptions.

PRIMARY SOURCES related to Activity 2

Document 10.1: Excerpts from *The Book of Rites* (*Liji*, 《礼记》), compiled during the Han (汉) dynasty (202 B.C.E.–220 C.E.), regarding the relationship between husband and wife

The men should not speak of what belongs to the inside (of the house), nor the women of what belongs to the outside. Except at sacrifices and funeral rites, they should not hand vessels [containers] to one another…Outside or inside, they should not go to the same well, nor to, the same bathing-house. They should not share the same mat in lying down; they should not ask or borrow anything from one another; they should not wear similar upper or lower garments…When a woman goes out at the door, she must keep her face covered. She should walk at night (only) with a light; and if she have no light, she should not stir. On the road, a man should take the right side, and a woman the left.

• *Full text available on CD-ROM* •

Document 10.2: Excerpts from *Biographies of Virtuous Women* (*Lienü zhuan*, 《烈女传》) by Liu Xiang (刘向), 1st century B.C.E.

Mencius (孟子) (ca. 372–289 B.C.E.) was among the most important Confucianists, second only to Confucius himself. To the basic tenets established by Confucius, he added the concept of "righteousness" (yi, 义). This includes emphasis on an individual acting based on a strong sense of duty. This excerpt is about his mother.

[Mencius's] mother answered, "A woman's duties are to cook the five grains, heat the wine, look after her parents-in-law, make clothes, and that is all! Therefore, she cultivates the skills required in the women's quarters [area] and has no ambition to manage affairs outside of the house. *The Book of Changes* says, 'In her central place, she attends to the preparation of the food.'…This means that a woman's duty is not to control or to take charge. Instead she must follow the 'three submissions.' When she is young she must submit to her parents. After her marriage, she must submit to her husband. When she is widowed, she must submit to her son. These are the rules of propriety."

• *Full text available on CD-ROM* •

Document 10.3: Excerpts from Ban Zhao's (班昭) *Admonitions for Women (Nüjie,《女诫》),* **1st century B.C.E.**

Respect and Compliance

As yin and yang are not of the same nature, so man and woman differ in behavior. The virtue of yang is firmness; yin is manifested in yielding. Man is honored for strength; a woman is beautiful on account of her gentleness…

Now for self-cultivation there is nothing like respectfulness. To avert harshness there is nothing like compliance. Consequently it can be said that the Way of respect and compliance is for women the most important element in ritual decorum…

The correct relationship between husband and wife is based upon harmony and intimacy, and [conjugal] love is grounded in proper union.

• Full text available on CD-ROM •

»» Activity 2: Examining Rules for Correct Behavior

Documents 10.1–10.3 were either compiled or written during the Han dynasty (202 B.C.E.–220 C.E.). It is during this dynasty that Confucianism became, in effect, a state doctrine (see Lesson 7). Over a period of centuries, scholars recorded information about behavior that they believed would result in a stable, orderly society that Confucius advocated. Small groups of students can work on a complete document or a section of a document. Ask students to answer the questions that follow:

- What specific instructions are given for the behavior of men and/or women?
- What unequal relationship(s) does the document address?
- Were husband and wife seen as equals? Why yes or no?
- What surprised you about this document?
- Then ask students to prepare a brief summary of the section they studied for the class and explain what they learned about the topic at hand (relationship between husband and wife, purpose of marriage, a wife's responsibilities, etc.).
- Discuss the findings as a class. During the Han dynasty, according to the ideal, how did men and women relate with each other?
- How were older men and women treated by adult sons and their wives?
- What were the characteristics of ideal behavior for a man or a woman?

Refer to Lesson 6 on Ancient Mythology to review the concepts of yin and yang. How do these ancient beliefs fit with the expected roles of men and women?

PRIMARY SOURCES related to Activity 3

Document 10.4: Excerpts from *Analects for Women* (《女论语》), by Song Ruozhao (宋若昭), Tang (唐) dynasty (618–907)

Establishing Oneself as a Person

To be a woman, you must first learn to establish yourself as a person. The way to do this is simply by working hard to establish one's purity and chastity. By purity, one keeps one's self undefiled; by chastity, one preserves one's honor.

When walking, don't turn your head; when talking, don't open your mouth wide; when sitting, don't move your knees; when standing, don't rustle your skirts; when happy, don't exult with loud laughter; when angry, don't raise your voice. The inner and outer quarters are each distinct; the sexes should be segregated. Don't peer over the outer wall or go beyond the outer courtyard. If you have to go outside, cover your face; if you peep outside, conceal yourself as much as possible. Do not be on familiar terms with men outside the family; have nothing to do with women of bad character. Establish your proper self so as to become a [true] human being.

• *Full text available on CD-ROM* •

Document 10.5: Pottery figures of women on horseback, Tang (唐) dynasty (618–907)

Courtesy of Palace Museum, Beijing

» Activity 3: Creative Extensions—Illustrating Descriptions of Women in the Tang Dynasty

Have students work in small groups reading a section of Document 10.4 or examining the photograph of the statues in Document 10.5. After students have read, understood, and discussed Document 10.4, ask them to select one directive given to women and to illustrate it. The statues may puzzle students. Though students may not guess that the women are playing polo, it is clear that they are in active but not work-related stances on their horses. Students who looked at the statues should plan how to illustrate what they learned, too.

Explain that many scholars see the Tang dynasty as a golden age for China (see Lessons 13–15 on the arts). This flourishing culture included women, as well. They were able to take a more active role in social life, to walk freely on streets, and to ride horses. At one time, led by ladies of the court, women took to wearing men's clothes. Yet at the same time, two of the most famous guides on female behavior were written: *Classic of Filiality for Women* and *Analects for Women*. Discuss as a class:

- Are there differences between what was being written more than 500 years earlier (Documents 10.1–10.3) and this period?
- What additional information have these documents contributed to their knowledge of the role of Chinese women?
- Why, if life was becoming less restricted, was this also the period in which the two guides on women's behavior became popular?

Finally, ask the class to create a collage or mural showing the range of behavior for women during the Tang dynasty.

» Activity 4: Discussion about Concubines

The notion of concubines will be foreign to many students. However, the practice of having concubines was widespread across East Asia up to the 20th century and still continues. Document 10.6 is likely to elicit strong reactions from boys and girls. Ask them to express what disturbs them about the excerpt. Is it the practice itself? The way the young woman had to behave? Is it similar to anything they've read about or heard about (a slave auction block, for example)? Ask students to imagine themselves in the 17th or 18th century and have them write a letter to government officials expressing their thoughts and requesting changes if they wish.

PRIMARY SOURCE *related to Activity 4*

Document 10.6: Excerpt from *Taoan mengui*, describing sale of a concubine

In her introduction, editor Patricia Ebrey explains that most girls being offered for sale as concubines would have been sold to a broker by their parents.

The customer is then served tea and seated to wait for the women. The broker leads out each of them, who do what the matchmaker tells them to do. After each of her short commands, the woman bows to the customer, walks forward, turns toward the light so the customer can see her face clearly, draws back her sleeves to show him her hands, glances shyly at him to show her eyes, says her age so he can hear her voice, and finally lifts her skirt to reveal whether her feet are bound. An experienced customer could figure out the size of her feet by listening to the noise she made as she entered the room. If her skirt made noise when she walked in, she had to have a pair of big feet under her skirt. As one woman finishes, another comes out, each house having at least five or six. If the customer finds a woman to his liking, he puts a gold hairpin in her hair at the temple, a procedure called "inserting the ornament." If no one satisfies him, he gives a few hundred cash to the broker or the servants…

PRIMARY SOURCE *related to Activity 5*

Document 10.7: "A Cure for Jealousy" (*Yi ji*, 医嫉), a folktale by Yuan Mei (袁枚), 18th century

The young scholar Xianyuan of Changzhou was childless at thirty. His wife, a woman of the Chang clan, was abnormally jealous, and Xianyuan was too afraid of her to take a second wife who might bear him the sons he wanted. Chancellor Ma of the Grand Secretariat, the presiding official at Xianyuan's degree examination, felt sorry for the young man and presented him with a concubine. First Wife Chang was furious for this intrusion into her family affairs and swore to repay Chancellor Ma in kind.

It happened around then that Chancellor Ma lost his own wife. So Lady Chang found a country woman widely known for her bad temper and bribed a go-between to persuade Ma to make the shrew his new first wife. The Chancellor saw through Chang's scheme but proceeded with the betrothal. On the wedding day the trousseau included a five-colored club for the purpose of beating husbands. It was an heirloom that had been in the country woman's family for three generations…

• **Full text available on CD-ROM** •

» Activity 5: Reading a Folktale

Distribute the questions for "A Cure for Jealousy" (Item 10.B). Read the folktale aloud to the class (Document 10.7). Stop periodically so students can address the questions. When the story is finished, have the students consider: From this folktale, what do we learn about the following?

- women in traditional Chinese society
- the role of concubines
- what was considered correct behavior for women
- what was acceptable behavior for men
- the lesson this folktale teaches

Discuss how folktales do or do not reflect cultural norms. What are popular folktales in our culture, and what lessons do they teach?

PRIMARY SOURCES related to Activity 6

Document 10.8: Excerpts from *The Book of Rites* (*Liji*, 《礼记》), compiled during the Han (汉) dynasty (202 B.C.E.–220 C.E.), pertaining to bringing up children

32. When the child was able to take its own food, it was taught to use the right hand. When it was able to speak, a boy [was taught to] respond boldly and clearly; a girl, submissively and low…

33. At six years, they were taught the numbers and the names of the cardinal points; at the age of seven, boys and girls did not occupy the same mat nor eat together; at eight, when going out or coming in at a gate or door, and going to their mats to eat and drink, they were required to follow their elders:—the teaching of yielding to others was now begun; at nine, they were taught how to number the days.

• Full text available on CD-ROM •

Document 10.9: Excerpts from the *Analects of Confucius* (《论语》) on relationships within the family

2.6 When asked about being filial, Confucius replied, "The only time a dutiful son ever makes his parents worry is when he is sick."

2.7 Nowadays people think they are dutiful sons when they feed their parents. Yet they also feed their dogs and horses. Unless there is respect, where is the difference?

• Full text available on CD-ROM •

Document 10.10: Excerpts from *Family Instructions of Mr. Yan* (*Yanshi Jiaxun*, 《颜氏家训》) by Yan Zhitui (颜之推), 6th century

[A]s soon as a baby can recognize facial expressions and understand approval and disapproval, training should be begun so that he will do what he is told to do and stop when so ordered. After a few years of this, punishment with the bamboo can be minimized, as parental strictness and dignity mingled with parental love will lead the boys and girls to a feeling of respect and caution and give rise to filial piety. I have noticed about me that where there is merely love without training this result is never achieved. Children eat, drink, speak, and act as they please...

• Full text available on CD-ROM •

Document 10.11: Excerpts from "Instructing Sons and Daughters" from *Analects for Women* (《女论语》) by Song Ruozhao (宋若昭), Tang (唐) dynasty (618–907)

Instructing Sons and Daughters

Most all families have sons and daughters. As they grow and develop, there should be a definite sequence and order in their education. But the authority/responsibility to instruct them rests solely with the mother...

Daughters remain behind in the women's quarters and should not be allowed to go out very often...Teach them sewing, cooking, and etiquette...don't allow them to be indulged, lest they throw tantrums to get their own way...

• Full text available on CD-ROM •

❯❯ Activity 6: Examining How Children Were Raised

Divide Documents 10.8–10.11 among students. Remind the students they will be examining documents dating from several centuries B.C.E. to ones from the sixth and seventh centuries, in other words, spanning more than a thousand years. Ask students to answer the questions pertaining to their document. (See Item 10.C.) After students report to the class on their readings, discuss:

- Did the approach to child rearing change over time? How?
- In the families you know, are there differences between how boys and girls are raised? Does it vary from family to family? Why? How? Should boys and girls be raised identically?
- Are there similarities between how children were raised in ancient China and child rearing practices today? Describe them.

›› Activity 7: Creative Writing Extensions

"You Set the Rules"
Students can choose to write 1) Six Rules by Which to Raise Children, 2) Six Rules by Which to Raise Girls, 3) Six Rules by Which to Raise Boys, or 4) a description of a perfect relationship between parent and child.

"Three Days in My Life"
Alternatively, ask students to imagine themselves living in one of the periods when the documents were written and then to write diary entries for three days. They should include details about their activities, the individuals with whom they have contact, their surroundings, and so on.

PRIMARY SOURCE related to Activity 8

Document 10.12: Excerpt from *Wild Swans: Three Daughters of China* by Jung Chang, describing how the author's grandmother had her feet bound

My grandmother's feet had been bound when she was two years old. Her mother, who herself had bound feet, first wound a piece of white cloth about twenty feet long round her feet, bending all the toes except the big toe inward and under the sole. Then she placed a large stone on top to crush the arch. My grandmother screamed in agony and begged her to stop. Her mother had to stick a cloth into her mouth to gag her. My grandmother passed out repeatedly from the pain.

The process lasted several years. Even after the bones had been broken, the feet had to be bound day and night in thick cloth because the moment they were released they would try to recover. For years my grandmother lived in relentless, excruciating pain. When she pleaded with her mother to untie the bindings, her mother would weep and tell her that unbound feet would ruin her entire life, and that she was doing it for her own future happiness.

• Full text available on CD-ROM •

» Activity 8: A Discussion on Foot Binding

The subject of foot binding is likely to evoke strong reactions among students. The mutilation was so extreme. Teachers may wish to refer to books on the resource list to become more familiar with the practice. To open the discussion, ask the students what present or past customs they know of which change a person's appearance. (Consider: face lifts, body-building, tattooing, body piercing, corsets, stiletto heels, facial scarring, neck elongation, and so on.) Why do men and especially women make changes such as these to their bodies? Have the students read the excerpt from *Wild Swans* (Document 10.12). Discuss why a tradition such as this not only lasted about 1,000 years, but increased in popularity. To further student understanding have them conduct research online to learn about other cultural practices. Ask them to write guidelines for what physical changes individuals should and should not make and to explain their reasoning. The young-adult historical fiction *Ties That Bind, Ties That Break* by Lensey Namioka gives students an excellent introduction to the role of foot binding.

PRIMARY SOURCES *related to Activity 9*

Document 10.13a–e: Segments of scroll painting "The Spring Festival Along the River" ("*Qingming Shanghe Tu*," 《清明上河图》) by Zhang Zeduan (张择端), 12th century

The full length of the scroll is seventeen feet. One of the most famous of Chinese paintings, it depicts Kaifeng, the capital of the Northern Song (北宋) dynasty (960–1127).

• *Additional images of the scroll painting are on the CD-ROM* •

» Activity 9: Learning about Men, Women, and Children from an Early 12th-century Painting

This 12th-century scroll painting by Zhang Zeduan is one of the most famous in Chinese history. Working in pairs, ask students to examine one of the five segments, Documents 9.13a–9.13e. After getting a general impression of the painting, have them divide the image into quarters so they can examine the details. (Item 10.D notes details of the scroll that students should find.) Students should write notes in answer to the following questions:

- Whom do you see most of? Men, women, or children? If they are not "here" outside in the busy city, where might the "missing" people be?
- What are men doing?
- What are women doing?
- If there are children present, what are they doing? What can you tell about the relationship between adults and children from this painting?
- What new information have you learned about the lives of men, women, and children in ancient China?
- What questions do you have after examining this painting? Where might you find answers?

» Activity 10: Extended Research—Celebrated Chinese Women

The history of ancient China includes stories of dozens of remarkable women. To gain a broader understanding of the range of roles women played, students should research:

- Fu Hao (妇好), wife of King Wuding of the Shang dynasty (ca. 1600 B.C.E.–ca. 1050 B.C.E.)
- Wang Zhaojun (王昭君), wed to chieftain of Xiongnu to maintain peaceful relations, Han dynasty (202 B.C.E.–220 C.E.)
- Ban Zhao (班昭), historian and author, Han dynasty
- Hua Mulan (花木兰), female warrior, some time between 581 and 960
- Wen Cheng (文成), wed to Tibetan king to maintain peaceful relations, Tang dynasty (618–907 C.E.)
- Empress Wu Zetian (武则天女皇), the only female to assume the role, Tang dynasty
- Yang Guifei (杨贵妃), famous concubine of the emperor Xuanzong, first half 8th century
- Li Qingzhao (李清照), famous female poet, Song dynasty (960–1279)
- Empress Ma (马皇后), wife of founder of Ming dynasty (1368–1644)
- Empress Xu (徐皇后), wife of third Ming emperor, writer

Further Resources for Students and Teachers

Giskin, Howard and Bettye S. Walsh, eds. *An Introduction to Chinese Culture Through the Family*. "Women and Gender," by Mary Gallagher. Albany: State University of New York Press, 2001.

Jackson, Beverley. *Splendid Slippers: A Thousand Years of an Erotic Tradition*. Berkeley, Calif.: Ten Speed Press, 2000.

Lang, Olga. *Chinese Family & Society*. New Haven: Yale University Press, 1946. (based on field work done in China 1935–37)

Lip, Evelyn. *Out of China: Culture and Traditions*. Wokingham, England: Addison-Wesley Publishing, Co., 1993.

Namioka, Lensey. *Ties That Bind, Ties That Break*. New York: Delacorte Press, 1999.

O'Hara, Albert. *The Position of Woman in Early China*. Taipei: Mei Ya Publications, 1971.

Ping, Wang. *Aching for Beauty: Footbinding in China*. New York: Anchor Books, 2000.

Spence, Jonathan. *The Death of Woman Wang*. New York: Viking Press, 1978. (an excellent recreation of the life of a poor widow in the 17th century)

Women of the Tang Dynasty. Hong Kong: Airphoto International Ltd., 1999. (Original Chinese text by Li Wei, Yan Xinzhi, and Shen Qinyan; translated by Wu Qi; rewritten by May Holdsworth)

Yu, Lu. *Chinese Women in History and Legend, Volumes 1 & 2*. New York: A.R.T.S. Inc., 1981.

Zhuozhi, Cai. *100 Celebrated Chinese Women*. Singapore: Asiapac Books Pte Ltd., 1995. (translated by Kate Foster)

Web Sites

http://depts.washington.edu/chinaciv/painting/4ptgdoms.htm and

http://afe.easia.columbia.edu/song/main/main_b.htm (include information about the 12th century scroll painting by Zhang Zeduan and explores domestic life in various paintings from imperial China)

Video

King of Masks, 100 min. Mandarin with English subtitles. Directed by Wu Tianming. 1999. (set in Sichuan Province in the 1930s, poignantly captures the plight of a little girl and her relationship with her adopted grandfather)

In the World Today

Working to Improve the Lives of Women and Children

"Women are the backbones of their families, caregivers of young and old," notes a key United Nations agency, UNFPA (the United Nations Population Fund). "Yet, discrimination against women and girls is the most pervasive and persistent form of inequality." Many experts believe that only when we improve the lives of women will we be able to reduce poverty. "When women are educated and healthy, their families, communities, and countries benefit." UNFPA also emphasizes how important it is to provide universal primary education and to invest in programs that provide children with health care and life skills. Another UN organization that works to better the lives of children is UNICEF (the United Nations Children's Fund). Among its top priorities, UNICEF has programs in early childhood and in girls' education. Students can learn more about the work of the two funds by visiting www.UNFPA.org and www. UNICEF.org. In a classroom activity, have them work in small groups to draw up a universal set of basic rights for all children—boys and girls. Direct them to think about fundamental needs. Then, for homework, ask them to reflect on why discrimination against girls and women continues to be so widespread and to suggest at least two concrete ways in which the situation could be improved.

Lesson 11 CD-ROM Contents

Primary Sources

- Document 11.1: Photograph of Xi'an's (西安) extant city wall
- Document 11.2: Image of rubbing from stone tablet of map of Pingjiang Prefecture, early 13th century
- Document 11.3: Segment of a map painted on silk, 18th century
- Document 11.4: Images of *hangtu* (夯土), tamped earth construction, from 4th and 20th centuries
- Document 11.5: Photograph of peasant home in southeastern province of Zhejiang (浙江), 1987
- Document 11.6: Model of a courtyard home found in tomb from Eastern Han (东汉) dynasty (25–220)
- Document 11.7: Image of scene of courtyard house impressed on a brick in a tomb from 2nd century C.E.
- Document 11.9: Excerpt from *Ties That Bind, Ties That Break*, describing courtyard home in early 20th century
- Document 11.10: Woodblock print showing geomancer and his assistants choosing a building site
- Document 11.11: Woodblock print of Zhong Kui (钟馗), demon-chaser
- Document 11.12: Ceramic ornamentation, featuring lotus plants, on the wall of the Palace of Kindness and Tranquility; Forbidden City (紫禁城), Beijing (北京)
- Document 11.13: Wooden lattice work in one of the buildings of Yuyuan (豫园) in Shanghai (上海)
- Document 11.14: Good fortune banner made of red paper
- Document 11.15: Door hanging with traditional symbols of good fortune, Pangliu (庞留) village, Shaanxi (陕西) Province, 2004
- Document 11.16: Front of a home with New Year's signs, Shanghai (上海), 2004
- Document 11.17: Images of door gods hung to the left and right of a door, Pangliu (庞留) village, Shaanxi (陕西) Province, 2004

Supplementary Materials

- Item 11.A: Characters for *shuangxi* (双喜, double happiness) and *fu* (福, good fortune)
- Item 11.B: Questions for Activity 7, Documents 11.12–11.18
- Item 11.C: Answer key for Activity 7

Lesson 11
Cities and Dwellings

Archaeologists and historians view the building of cities as a major shift in a culture. Some scholars see this change, together with others, as the beginning of a civilization; others prefer to identify the period as a time when a state-level society emerged (see Lesson 3). In China, one of the earliest examples of a city is near Anyang (安阳) in Henan Province (河南). It is the site of Yin (殷), the last capital of the Shang (商) dynasty (ca. 1600–ca. 1050 B.C.E.) Extensive excavations that began in 1928 have revealed ruins of fifty-three palaces, thirteen temples, and eleven tombs. The site includes workshops, where men worked with stone and jade, bronze foundries and workshops, and houses for staff and servants.

Chang'an (present day Xi'an 西安) became the capital of China soon after the Zhou (周) dynasty (ca. 1050–256 B.C.E.) ousted the Shang rulers. Off and on, for more than 1,000 years, spanning eleven dynasties, the city served as the center of the Middle Kingdom (中国). It reached its peak during the Tang (唐) dynasty (618–907), when it was the largest and most cosmopolitan city in the world. It attracted craftsmen, traders, pilgrims, writers, and artists, and was home to people of various religions.

The emphasis on balance and symmetry and on rules of hierarchy that went into planning ancient Chinese cities can be seen in Chinese homes—from the simplest peasant home in the countryside to the elaborate *siheyuan* (四合院) or courtyard dwellings found in China's old cities. "Chinese dwellings are typically inward-looking, framed by balanced structures, hierarchically organized, and ritually centered—like the family units occupying them and the imperial state writ large" (Knapp, *China's Living Houses*, p. 10–11). Regional differences exist largely because of variations in climate, but at the same time, there continue to be certain consistent traditions. *Jia* (家) in Chinese means house, home, and family. The ways Chinese homes have been designed reflect the values of the people (Knapp and Lo, *House Home Family: Living and Being Chinese*).

Farmers' Homes

The homes of the poorest peasants may have only one room, but many Chinese families live in homes of three rooms. In traditional homes, still evident in rural areas, the center room is a common area and is open in the front. It is a multi-purpose room used for eating, entertaining, children's play, and storing farm equipment. It also has important ritual functions. The room has a high table with ancestral tablets. Images of gods and goddesses hang nearby. This is where the family honors their ancestors with offerings of food and by burning incense. The central room is symbolically the place where all generations of the family are present. The room to the left is often the parents' bedroom. The room to the right is where the children sleep.

Siheyuan, Courtyard Dwellings

During China's imperial period, courtyard dwellings—*siheyuan*—were the homes of well-to-do families. The design concepts can also be found in the layout of Buddhist temples and imperial palaces, such as the Forbidden City (紫禁城) in Beijing (北京). *Siheyuan* emphasized an inward focus. A high wall separated the family from the outside world. Few windows looked out; instead rooms opened onto the inner courtyard(s). This type of design dates back approximately 3,000 years. The more elaborate dwellings had multiple courtyards. Who slept where depended on the person's position in the family. For example, the oldest generation lived in the south-facing rooms farthest away from the main entry—the best rooms. Courtyards were used for work, play, and socializing.

Fengshui

Traditionally, the building of a dwelling in China was a careful, painstaking affair. Fengshui (风水) practices had been used for centuries to determine the best place for a burial site, for the setting of a city, and for the placement of a home. Fengshui literally means "wind and water" and is often translated as geomancy. Simply put, fengshui seeks harmony between structures and the physical environment. Ideally, dwellings should face south or southeast. If water flows nearby and a mountain ridge lies a distance behind the house for protection, the house site is close to perfect.

Home Ornamentation

In addition, Chinese people pay a lot of attention to decorative features in their homes. Almost everything has symbolic meaning. A mirror hung over a doorway can deflect bad influences. The Chinese invite *fu* (福)—good fortune—or *shuangxi* (双喜)—doubled happiness—by hanging the characters or symbolic good luck images on the doors to their homes. Pairs of magpies signify wishes for a happy marriage. Evergreen trees, rocks, tortoises, and cranes express a hope for a long life. Chinese homes reflect centuries of tradition and folk practices.

Organizing Idea

Excavations and plans of ancient Chinese cities demonstrate very sophisticated city planning and certain consistent features. Chinese homes, while allowing for regional differences, share layout and decorative features that embody the people's beliefs and values.

Student Objectives

Students will:

- recognize key features of traditional Chinese city planning
- understand the concepts that inform design of Chinese dwellings
- recognize the typical design of a simple Chinese home
- understand the design of *siheyuan*, a courtyard dwelling
- gain a basic understanding of the principles of fengshui
- recognize popular Chinese figures and symbols that ward off evil or invite good fortune

Key Questions

- How are Chinese beliefs and values reflected in the design of their homes?
- What roles has fengshui played in Chinese life?
- What is *qi*?
- In traditional times, and to a lesser degree in China today, what did people believe about good and evil forces?

Vocabulary

ancestral tablet
courtyard dwelling
fengshui
fu
geomancy
hangtu
hierarchy
manor
moat
qi
symbol
tomb

Supplementary Materials

Item 11.A: Characters for *shuangxi* (双喜, double happiness) and *fu* (福, good fortune)
Item 11.B: Questions for Activity 7, Documents 11.12–11.18
Item 11.C: Answer key for Activity 7

Student Activities

›› Activity 1: Discussion: The Purpose of Walls

Cheng is the Chinese word for both city or town *and* wall. "Walls are a particularly Chinese pre-occupation," Ronald Knapp writes in *China's Walled Cities* (p. 1). They were built to define the boundaries of provinces and the country. They enclosed cities and individual homes.

- Why is it significant that the Chinese word is the same for city and wall?
- Ask the students to speculate what the advantages and disadvantages of walls may have been in ancient China.
- Discuss the ways we define territories, separate a home or yard from a neighbor's.
- Why do humans create boundaries with fences, walls, or hedges? What are the advantages and disadvantages?

Examine the photograph of Xi'an's extant city wall (11.1). It is among only a few complete city walls still seen today in China. What purpose did it likely serve? What obstacles would invading people have needed to overcome?

PRIMARY SOURCE related to Activity 1

Document 11.1: Photograph of Xi'an's (西安) extant city wall

First built of earth during the Tang (唐) dynasty (618–907), the wall was covered in brick early in the Ming (明) dynasty (1368–1644). The wall is twelve meters high and twelve to fourteen meters wide on top. Fourteen kilometers long, it is among the few intact city walls in China.

» Activity 2: Analyzing Features of Ancient Chinese Cities

Students should read the first two paragraphs of the introduction. Then have them examine documents 11.2 and 11.3. Ask the students to

- Look on a map to see what the setting is for Suzhou? Why might people have built a city in this location?
- What is most striking about the map of the region near the Grand Canal?
- Where are cities and towns situated on the map (11.3)?
- What do the two images have in common?
- Can you tell what the orientation of each city was?

Students can study both images, or the class can be divided into pairs or small groups. Each group examines one image and students share their findings at the end of the activity. Have students identify as many details on the assigned document as they can (rivers, markets, palaces, monasteries, etc.).

Have students find online or in guidebooks maps of cities in China today (for example, Beijing, Nanjing, Shanghai, Chengdu). Compare and contrast the layout of the cities as seen today to the images of maps from centuries ago. They can also examine satellite images of Beijing on NASA's Web site (http://eol.jsc.nasa.gov/sseop/images/EO/lowres/STS090/STS090-714-42.jpg and http://edcwww.cr.usgs.gov/earthshots/slow/Beijing/Beijing).

To summarize:

- list consistent features in Chinese cities of the past
- note the features that are present in modern Chinese cities
- speculate on why some features remain and why others have been discarded

PRIMARY SOURCES *for Activity 2*

Document 11.2: Image of rubbing from stone tablet of map of Pingjiang Prefecture, early 13th century

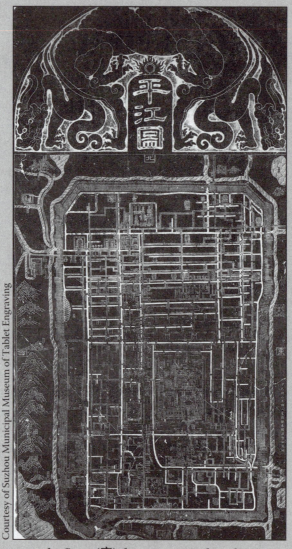

Courtesy of Suzhou Municipal Museum of Tablet Engraving

Pingjiang was the Song (宋) dynasty name for what is now Suzhou (苏州) in Jiangsu (江苏) Province. It was typical of some of the small cities that developed during that dynasty (960–1279). It was shaped as a rectangle, four kilometers north to south and three kilometers east to west. Four rivers flowed north to south and three flowed west to east. A moat surrounded the entire city.

Document 11.3: Segment of a map painted on silk, 18ᵗʰ century

The full map measures 78 cm by 1,780 cm and depicts a section of the Grand Canal (大运河) between Beijing (北京) and Hangzhou (杭州) and the area surrounding the canal.

PRIMARY SOURCE *related to Activity 3*

Document 11.4: Images of *hangtu* (夯土), tamped earth construction, from 4th and 20th centuries

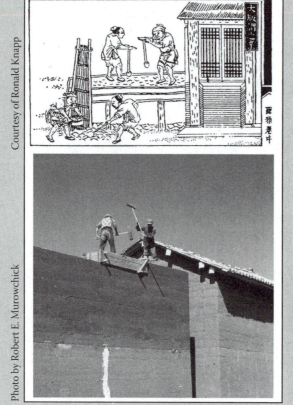

Courtesy of Ronald Knapp

Photo by Robert E. Murowchick

In the past, pounded earth walls was the way to construct city walls and the Great Wall (长城), as well as the walls of dwellings and other buildings. Presently, about 40 percent of the homes in China are built using the method.

≫ Activity 3: Examining Building Methods

Students should look at Document 11.4 of a 4th-century illustration and a 20th-century photograph. Discuss:

- What is each man doing in the 4th-century illustration?
- What keeps the soil from falling off to the side?
- What are the men doing in the photograph?
- Compare and contrast the two images.
- Why was *hangtu*, tamped earth construction, used so extensively in ancient China, and why does it continue to be used today?

Tell students that bricks also can be made using this same tamped earth method. What building techniques do you know of that are similar? (adobe, for example)

›› Activity 4: Understanding Basic Principles of Homes in Ancient China

Students should read the rest of the introduction to the lesson, or the teacher can present the information in an alternate manner. Chinese homes, simple or elaborate, reflect the values of the people. Discuss:

- Just as *cheng* (城) means both city and wall, how is it significant that in Chinese, *jia* (家) means house, home, and family?
- What was important to traditional Chinese families? How did their homes reflect these values? (Consider, especially how the individual was seen versus the family unit.)
- What are important values in the students' families? How do homes in their area reflect these values?
- Chinese dwellings are set up in a hierarchical structure. Are homes in other countries designed this way, too? (Consider the term used in the United States, master bedroom, and how the size of a master bedroom compares to the other bedrooms. How are additional bedrooms assigned and/or shared among siblings?)

As a follow-up activity, ask students to write a description (or draw a floor plan) of their home, focusing on how the layout and use of space reflects the values of the family and society at large.

PRIMARY SOURCES *related to Activity 5*

Document 11.5: Photograph of peasant home in southeastern province of Zhejiang (浙江), 1987

Photo by Ronald Knapp

This fairly typical farmer's home has three areas, *jian*, in the center and an additional room on each end.

Document 11.6: Model of a courtyard home found in tomb from Eastern Han (东汉) dynasty (25–220)

Courtesy of National Museum of China, Beijing

This model of a courtyard home was unearthed in Chengdu (成都), Sichuan Province (四川) in 1954. Together with other artifacts, a model of a home might be buried with an individual in the belief that he or she would need it in the life that followed.

Document 11.7: Image of scene of courtyard house impressed on a brick in a tomb from 2nd century C.E.

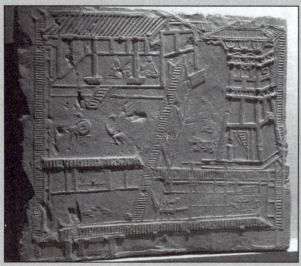

Courtesy of National Museum of China, Beijing

As an alternative to burying a model of a home with the deceased, images of the house were left in the tomb. In this case, the picture of the courtyard house was pressed into a brick that lined a tomb in Sichuan Province (四川).

≫ Activity 5: Examining Traditions in Chinese Home Design

Distribute copies of Documents 11.5, 11.6, and 11.7 or display them on a classroom screen. Discuss:

Document 11.5

- How does this farmer's home reflect a typical design?

Document 11.6

- Describe the design of this home. What are the structures on the four corners? Where is the entrance?
- How does this model from around the 2nd century compare to what you've learned about courtyard homes?
- Speculate on the use of the structures inside the wall.

Document 11.7

This remarkable brick from inside a tomb shows some of the activities that took place within a *siheyuan*.

- What is the overall layout of this courtyard home? How does it compare to the model (11.6)?
- What animals do you see?
- Describe what the people are doing.

Now have the students read the excerpts from *Dragonwings* (11.8) and *Ties That Bind, Ties That Break* (11.9).

- What additional information do the authors provide about courtyard homes?
- How do the characters in the books view Western-style structures?

As a follow-up activity, ask students to design a courtyard home where they would love to live. Students who may not have extended families can design living quarters within their compounds for close family friends, instead. The designs should include landscape features. Alternatively, students can work in small groups to design a school based on a courtyard concept. Again, the design should include landscape features.

Additional Primary Sources

Document 11.8: Excerpt from *Dragonwings* by Laurence Yep, comparing houses

Moon Shadow has just arrived from China to join his father, who is living in San Francisco. The Chinese often referred to all foreigners as "demons," but they were especially fearful of Americans when they came to the United States.

> And all the demon houses looked so strange. They were boxlike in shape, with no courtyards inside them, as if the demons hated fresh air but liked being shut up in something like a trunk. The houses had almost no ornamentation and were painted in dull colors—when they were painted at all. The little boxlike houses seemed so drab to me that I even felt sorry for the demons who lived in them, for they lived like prisoners without knowing they were in a prison.

 ## Document 11.9: Excerpt from *Ties That Bind, Ties That Break*, describing courtyard home in early 20th century

> Our family, the Taos, lived in a compound with more than fifty rooms, all surrounded by a wall. Grandfather was head of the family, and he had two sons, Big Uncle and my father. Both of them lived there with their wives and children and their own servants. Each family had a set of rooms grouped around a courtyard. Although I spent most of the time in our own rooms with my parents, my two elder sisters, and my little brother, I often visited other courtyards…

Later in the book, the main character, Ailin, describes her impression on seeing the school run by Americans.

> On examination day we arrived at the school building, which was very different from the houses in our family compound. At home our compound consisted of small one- or two-room buildings grouped around courtyards. The school occupied just one huge building but had dozens of rooms. I couldn't imagine how people could walk around inside without getting lost.

PRIMARY SOURCE *related to Activity 6*

Document 11.10: Woodblock print showing geomancer and his assistants choosing a building site

While this woodblock print dates from the Qing (清) dynasty (1644–1911), the practice of placing a home in the best place possible goes far back in Chinese history. It was a job that could only be done by professionals.

›› Activity 6: An Introduction to Fengshui

Students should examine the woodcut from the Qing dynasty (11.10).

- What landscape features are shown and why are they important?
- What is each figure doing?
- Based on what you've learned about fengshui would this site be appropriate for a home? Why?
- Are there common practices in the country where students live, regarding the siting of a home? How do these compare with some of the principles of fengshui?

Students should explore Web sites listed at the end of the lesson to learn more about fengshui principles regarding the placement of a building. Then create a plan showing what would be an ideal location for a home or school. The drawing should include a key, describing each feature and explaining its importance.

PRIMARY SOURCES *related to Activity 7*

Document 11.11: Woodblock print of Zhong Kui (钟馗), demon-chaser

Courtesy of Ronald Knapp

Woodblock prints of Zhong Kui have guarded Chinese homes for more than 1,000 years. It is said that after his death, Zhong Kui appeared in a dream to the famous Tang (唐) emperor Xuanzong (唐玄宗), at a time when the emperor was suffering from a severe fever that could not be cured. Zhong Kui destroyed a demon who was stealing all the emperor's possessions. When the emperor asked who he was, he answered "I am your servant Zhong Kui, and I promise to protect you from demons." The emperor quickly recovered, and since that time many people have believed that Zhong Kui protects against evil spirits. People put up a picture of him at the time of New Year and usually replace it at least once during the year, most likely at the summer solstice.

Document 11.12: Ceramic ornamentation, featuring lotus plants, on the wall of the Palace of Kindness and Tranquility; Forbidden City (紫禁城), Beijing (北京)

Photo by Liz Nelson

For 500 years beginning with Emperor Chengzu (明成祖) in the early 1400s, the Forbidden City was the home of the emperors and the center of government. All the buildings are elaborately decorated.

Document 11.13: Wooden lattice work in one of the buildings of Yuyuan (豫园) in Shanghai (上海)

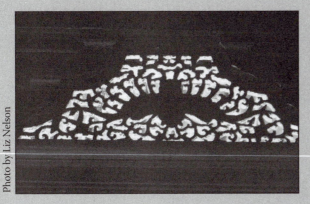

Photo by Liz Nelson

Yuyuan (Yu Garden) was created in the mid-16th century by a wealthy and influential public servant who had worked in Sichuan Province (四川). He had the garden built for his father to show filial affection. In one of several small buildings in the garden, the motif is part of the latticework running all the way around the room, just under the ceiling.

Document 11.14: Good fortune banner made of red paper

Courtesy of Ronald Knapp

Moving from right to left, the characters read *wu fu lin men*—meaning "five good fortunes have arrived at the door."

Document 11.15: Door hanging with traditional symbols of good fortune, Pangliu (庞留) village, Shaanxi (陕西) Province, 2004

Photo by Liz Nelson

Document 11.16: Front of a home with New Year's signs, Shanghai (上海), 2004

Photo by Liz Nelson

Document 11.17: Images of door gods hung to the left and right of a door, Pangliu (庞留) village, Shaanxi (陕西) Province, 2004

Photo by Liz Nelson

Door or gate gods (*menshen*, 门神) have decorated doorways of Chinese homes for centuries. They usually are put up in pairs, with each door god facing the other. *Menshen* vary from one region to another because they represent different historical or mythical men. The god on the left is Qin Qiong (秦琼) and the one on the right is Jingde (敬德). Qin Qiong is holding the character for sun in his left hand. Jingde is holding the character for moon.

» Activity 7: Discovering Chinese Home Ornamentation

Ask students what symbols appear in or around their homes that have special meaning. For example, are there any religious images/figures anywhere in their homes? Do they put up any symbols in conjunction with certain holidays? (hearts at Valentine's Day; cornucopias around Thanksgiving; candles or mistletoe around Christmas, menorahs around Hanukah?) Why do people hang permanent or temporary symbols in their homes?

More than a century ago, China scholar Edouard Chavannes wrote, "It seems to me that no other people in the world has so intense a feeling regarding the intrinsic value of life" (quoted by Ronald Knapp, *China's Vernacular Architecture: House Form and Culture*, p. 148–9). Through the use of many symbols, the Chinese welcomed good fortune into their homes and defended themselves against the bad. Divide Documents 11.11–11.17 among pairs or small groups of students. Display the characters for good fortune (*fu*) and double happiness (*shuangxi*) in the classroom (Item 11.A). Using books and online sources, ask the students to analyze the image they have so they can explain its importance to their classmates. Students should identify the date on their image and describe what it shows. In addition, their explanations should include information that answers questions specific to their image (Item 11.B). Both questions and the answer key (Item 11.C) are available on the CD-ROM.

Discuss as a class:

- Where does each symbol appear? Why might it be there?
- Several of the images include the color red. Why might that be?
- Several of the images are recent ones. What does that suggest about modern day use of traditional symbols?
- How is the use of symbols by Chinese people similar to or different from the use of symbols by other cultures?

As a follow-up activity, students can design an entryway to their homes, using whichever Chinese symbols they want.

» Activity 8: Extended Research

Using Web sites and books, explore

- the remarkable, cosmopolitan city of Chang'an during the Tang dynasty
- cave or earth-sheltered dwellings in north and northwest China
- regional differences among dwellings
- traditional building materials and practices
- fengshui as it applies to design of a home and placement of furniture within a home

Further Resources for Students and Teachers

Knapp, Ronald G. *China's Living Houses: Folk Beliefs, Symbols, and Household Ornamentation.* Honolulu: University of Hawai'i Press, 1999. (full of wonderful images; fascinating for anyone wishing for more information on the subject)

———. *China's Walled Cities.* New York: Oxford University Press, 2000.

———. *The Chinese House: Craft, Symbol, and the Folk Tradition.* New York: Oxford University Press, 1990. (81 pages; an excellent introduction)

———, and Kai-Yin Lo, eds. *House Home Family: Living and Being Chinese.* Honolulu: University of Hawaii Press, 2005.

Williams, C.A.S. *Outlines of Chinese Symbolism and Art Motives.* New York: Dover Publication, Inc., 1976.

Web Sites

http://www.wofs.com (online Fengshui magazine)

http://www.fastfengshui.com (includes a lot of basic information about fengshui practices)

http://depts.washington.edu/chinaciv/home/3homintr.htm (includes information on house architecture, regional variations, building materials, and decorative features)

http://afe.easia.columbia.edu/china/society/home.htm

http://www.newpaltz.edu/~knappr (site for Professor Ronald Knapp; multiple links to sites on Chinese architecture)

http://chinwu.com/fivedeadlyvenoms.html (five noxious creatures are referred to as "deadly venoms"; site includes a description of each one)

http://www.pem.org/yinyutang/ (an extensive Web site for *Yin Yu Tang:* A Chinese House at Peabody Essex Museum, includes photograph, videos, and text describing the Huizhou region of Anhui Province, history of the house, construction methods, use of rooms, and home ornamentation)

http://www.chinesepaintings.com/chinese-symbols.html (lists common Chinese symbols and their meanings)

For information on Zhong Kui:

http://www.pantheon.org/articles/z/zhong-kui.html

http://www.pureinsight.org/pi/

http://depts.washington.edu/chinaciv/painting/4courzho.htm

In the World Today

East-West Exchange of Architects

Chinese cities have seen an extraordinary burst in construction in the past fifteen years. Architects from overseas have played an increasingly active role in the building boom. The National Theatre in Beijing and the Shanghai Oriental Art Center in Shanghai were designed by Frenchman Paul Andreu. Rem Koolhaas of the Netherlands co-designed the China Central Television office building in Beijing. The spectacular 88-story Jin Mao Tower in Shanghai was the work of U. S. architects from Skidmore, Owings & Merrill. The company has more than two dozen projects in China at present. The design of the new terminal at Beijing airport was awarded to Britain's Lord Norman Foster, and Swiss architects Jacques Herzog and Pierre de Neuron designed the 2008 Olympic Stadium.

Chinese architects, on the other hand, have designed stunning buildings around the world. Ieoh Ming (I.M.) Pei, born in Guangzhou (formerly Canton) and raised in Shanghai, came to the United States in 1935, where he studied architecture at the Massachusetts Institute of Technology and Harvard University. Among his remarkable achievements are the Hancock Tower in Boston, the Javits Convention Center in New York City, the East Wing of the National Gallery in Washington, D.C., and the Pyramide du Louvre in Paris. In 1990, the 70-story Bank of China, designed by I.M. Pei, opened in Hong Kong. Pei's sons—Li Chung and Chien Chung—are architects in their own right. They designed the Bank of China headquarters in Beijing, which opened in 2001. Additional projects in China by Li Chung Pei and Chien Chung Pei include the 15,000-square meter Macao Science Center, restoration of the Peace Hotel in Shanghai, and a 43-story office building across the river from the Peace Hotel. The Bank of China headquarters in Beijing is of special interest because of the Chinese courtyard concepts the Pei brothers incorporated into their design. As a class, discuss what the advantages and disadvantages might be of Western architects working in China. Will the major cities of the world all begin to look alike?

Yin Yu Tang *(荫馀堂): A Chinese Home*

As a result of some remarkable coincidences and impressive collaboration, a traditional Chinese courtyard home now stands on the grounds of the Peabody Essex Museum in Salem, Massachusetts. For more than 200 years, the house was home to the Huang family of Huang Village in Anhui Province. Then, experts dismantled, crated, and shipped the house to Salem. In 1998, with the help of carpenters and stonemasons from China, the work of reassembling the home began. *Yin Yu Tang*, once the sixteen-bedroom home of prosperous merchants, opened to the public in 2003. Museum officials see it as an "ongoing effort to foster global awareness and understanding of Chinese culture." Discuss in class how bringing *Yin Yu Tang* over from China might do this. Ask students to identify at *Yin Yu Tang* features of Chinese homes and ornamentation they've learned about. Which building from their hometown would students send to China to help Chinese people understand how people in another nation live?

Lesson 12 CD-ROM Contents

Primary Sources

- Document 12.1: A chart showing different styles of script
- Document 12.2: A stone engraving of running script by Wang Xizhi (王曦之), 4th century
- Document 12.3: A scroll with a poem by Yuan Yi, a noted calligrapher, 1301
- Document 12.4: A photograph of the Treasures of a Study
- Document 12.5: A photograph of an ink stone with an engraved poem
- Document 12.6: A photograph of Chinese children practicing calligraphy, 2004
- Document 12.7: A photograph of a man writing calligraphy with a water brush, 2004

Supplementary Materials

- Item 12.A: Translation of characters on ink stone
- Item 12.B: Chinese basic character strokes
- Item 12.C 1–5: Writing practice sheets

Lesson 12 Calligraphy

Lesson Contents

- Calligraphy as "heart print"
- Treasures of the study
- Three Perfections
- Four Accomplishments

With the development of paper suitable for writing (around 100 C.E.), the opportunities for writing increased enormously. Government officials kept records on paper, people wrote letters to each other on paper, and they compiled books on paper. Writing with brush and ink soon became an art form, similar to painting. People prized works of fine calligraphy (*shufa*, 书法), framed them, and hung them on walls.

The word in Chinese for "writing" or "language," *wen* (文), also means "accomplished" and "refined." The Chinese considered calligraphy to be the mark of an educated and cultivated individual. As such, it was one of the subjects tested in civil service examinations. They believed an individual's calligraphy was his or her "heart print," *xinyin* (心印). It gave insight into that person's moral integrity, character, emotional state, and esthetic sensibilities. All this could be seen by the way the individual handled the brush as he or she worked and the manner in which the person presented the characters. Individuals learned calligraphy by first copying the great masters and then developing a style of their own.

The value placed on calligraphy was reflected in the "four treasures" (*si bao*, 四宝). Any scholar's study had to include an inkstick (*mo*, 墨), an inkstone (*yan*, 砚), writing brush (*bi*, 笔), and paper (*zhi*, 纸). A calligrapher prepared himself by grinding the hard inkstick on his inkstone and adding drops of water to get the right consistency. This process was a critical step in the calligrapher mentally preparing him or herself for the exacting and spiritual work ahead.

The Chinese believed calligraphy to be one of the Three Perfections (*sanjue*, 三绝), together with painting and poetry (see Lessons 13 and 14). Later music was added, and scholars aspired to excel in the Four Accomplishments (*siquan*, 四全). (see Lesson 15)

Note: This lesson is best taught in conjunction with Lesson 5 on Chinese Language.

Organizing Idea

Calligraphy—one the Four Accomplishments—has been valued among the Chinese for centuries not only as a means of communication, but also as an art form.

Student Objectives

Students will:

- understand that calligraphy has been and continues to be both a way to communicate words and ideas and an art form greatly admired in China
- know how calligraphy is practiced
- learn how to write several Chinese characters using the traditional tools of Chinese writing

Key Questions

- What is calligraphy and why is it practiced by people of all ages and positions in China?
- How has calligraphy changed over time?
- How is calligraphy similar to and different from western handwriting?
- What were the four Treasures of a Study and what was their significance to a calligrapher?

Supplementary Materials

Item 12.A: Translation of characters on ink stone
Item 12.B: Chinese basic character strokes
Item 12.C 1–5: Writing practice sheets

PRIMARY SOURCES *related to Activity 1*

 Document 12.1: A chart showing different styles of script

	horse	cart	fish	dust	see
Small Seal Script (*xiaozhuan*, 小篆) (246–207 B.C.E)	馬	車	魚	塵	見
Official Script (*lishu*, 隸書) (200 B.C.E—588 C.E)	馬	車	魚	塵	見
Standard Script (*kaishu*, 楷書) (after 588 C.E)	馬	車	魚	塵	見
Simplified Script (*jiantizi*, 簡體字) (after 1949 C.E)	马	车	鱼	尘	见

Characters from Ager, Simon, www.omniglot.com

SEAL SCRIPT was first developed during the Zhou (周) dynasty (ca. 1050–256 B.C.E.) and standardized again under Qin Shi Huangdi (秦始皇帝) into what is known as small seal script (*xiaozhuan*, 小篆).

CLERICAL or OFFICIAL SCRIPT (*lishu*, 隶书) became standardized in the 1st century B.C.E.

REGULAR STYLE (*kaishu*, 楷书) became the accepted formal script after 200 C.E., and was taught in all schools.

SIMPLIFIED SCRIPT (*jiantizi*, 简体字) has been in use in the People's Republic of China since 1949.

 Document 12.2: A stone engraving of running script by Wang Xizhi (王羲之), 4th century

Collection of the Shanghai Commercial Press

RUNNING SCRIPT (*xingshu*, 行书) is a simpler version of *lishu* (official script). It is the most likely style to show a calligrapher's artistic talent. Wang Xizhi is one of the most famous Chinese calligraphers.

›› Activity 1: Examining Styles of Calligraphy

Distribute copies of the four calligraphy styles (Document 12.1) and the example of running script by one of China's most famous calligraphers (Document 12.2).

- How are the styles similar and different?
- How do they change over time?
- Which appear to be the most "readable," the most beautiful, the most efficient?
- Why did *kaishu*, regular style, become the standard for so many centuries?
- Which style would most likely be used when artists write poems on paintings? (See Lesson 14 for more information on how the arts were combined.)

Hand out or project on a screen the image of the scroll on which Yuan Yi wrote his poem about the Qiantang River (Document 12.3). Which script did he use? Why might he have chosen this one for this poem? Students might want to create one of the characters using a pen.

Additional Primary Source

Document 12.3: A scroll with a poem by Yuan Yi, a noted calligrapher, 1301

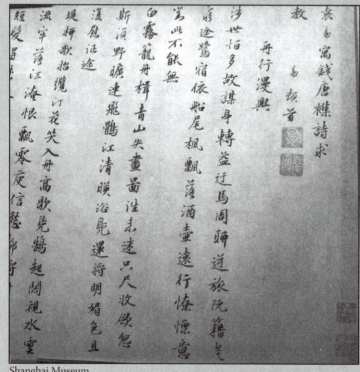

Shanghai Museum

Yuan Yi (1262–1306) was living in Hangzhou (杭州), renowned for its artistic community, at the time he created this scroll. He was thirty-nine.

PRIMARY SOURCES related to Activity 2

Document 12.4: A photograph of the Treasures of a Study

Collection of Steven Ratiner

Document 12.5: A photograph of an ink stone with an engraved poem

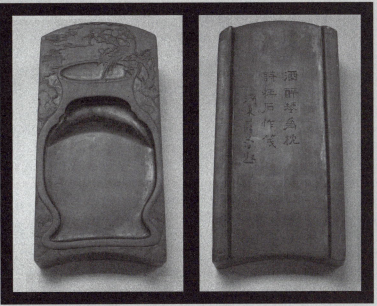

Collection of Steven Ratiner

» Activity 2: Treasures of a Study—Understanding Their Significance

Students may be familiar with routines baseball players, for example, have before a game, before they pitch, or before they bat. Students who dance, play a sport, play in a band, sing, or write may be surprised to recognize that they, too, have a routine they go through when their performance is important to them. Ask them to describe (orally or in writing) something they take pride in doing and how they prepare to start that activity. If several students report having a set routine, ask them why. How does it help them physically and mentally? What has happened on occasions when they have not gone through it?

Now distribute copies of Documents 12.4 and 12.5, showing the Treasures of a Study and a close-up of the inkstone, including the underside into which the writer etched a poem. (The translation of each character is available on Item 12.A on the CD-ROM.) Discuss:

- Why did scholars consider these items essential to their studies?
- What do students have at their places of work that they consider essential?
- What can they conclude about scholars' attitudes toward their "treasures" by examining the inkstone? Why did they call them "treasures"?
- What feeling does the etching on the frontside evoke?
- Why would the poet have etched a poem on the back?

PRIMARY SOURCES related to Activity 3

Document 12.6: A photograph of Chinese children practicing calligraphy, 2004

Photo by Joshua Silveira

These children living in Xi'an (西安) attend the private school once a week, beginning in July and ending in December each year. They practice for fifty minutes, take a recess break for ten minutes, then return to write again. That's the schedule for the four hours they are there. Their parents pay tuition. Calligraphy competitions are held regularly in China and prizes are awarded for both students and adults.

Document 12.7: A photograph of a man writing calligraphy with a water brush, 2004

This man was writing outside at the Summer Palace (颐和园) in Beijing (北京).

Photo by Liz Nelson

≫ Activity 3: Drawing Conclusions from Photographs of Individuals Writing Calligraphy

Distribute Documents 12.6 and 12.7, photographs taken in Beijing and Xi'an in 2004. Ask the students the ages of the key individuals in the photographs.

- What kind of script is the older man writing?
- What does each student have at his or her work station?
- How are they holding their brushes?

Children in China are on vacation in the summer just like students in the United States. What does it tell you about the attitude toward the art of calligraphy that parents pay for lessons at private schools and children go?

➤➤ Activity 4: A Workshop in Calligraphy

Materials

- Chinese basic character strokes and writing practice sheets (Item 12.B and 12.C)
- Heavy paper that isn't too absorbent
- Medium-sized calligraphy brush pens
- Black ink
- Small paper cups for ink and water
- Small paper plates for resting brushes
- Paper towels, newspapers to cover desks and old shirts to protect clothes

If at all possible, invite to the classroom a Chinese person adept at calligraphy to help with the activity. The individual may even be able to show how ink was made by grinding an ink stick on an inkstone with a little bit of water. When students are ready to begin, they should sit up straight with both feet flat on the floor. They should hold the brush straight up in relationship to the paper, not slanted in the way students are used to writing. Students will use their wrists and arms far more than they do in western writing. Demonstrate how to hold the brush correctly, dip it into the ink and wipe off excess ink. Wipe off the brush again before trying to write. Chinese writing is done in strokes. These should get slightly broader from beginning to end. Putting more pressure on the brush will make the strokes broader. Students cannot go backwards to fill in or finish a stroke. Calligraphy is difficult, and students will quickly understand why it takes at least a year of daily practice before someone has basic mastery of written Chinese.

After this activity is complete, ask students to look at the examples of calligraphy again (12.2 and 12.3). Ask students in a written response to give their impressions of the ancient calligraphy samples and why they believe the art of calligraphy continues to be valued so highly in China.

Further Student and Teacher Resources

Cherrett, Pauline. *An Introduction to Chinese Brush Painting*. New York: Barnes and Noble Books, 2004.

Fazzioli, Edoardo. *Chinese Calligraphy*. New York: Abbeville, 1986.

Fun With Chinese Characters, volumes 1, 2, & 3. The Straits Times Collection. Singapore: Federal Publications, 1980-1983.

McNaughton, William and Li Ying. *Reading and Writing Chinese*. Tuttle, 1999. (Gives stroke order for 2000 basic characters)

Qu Lei Lei. *The Simple Art of Chinese Calligraphy*. New York: Watson-Guptill Publications, 2002.

Rae, Nan. *The Chi of the Brush: Capturing the Spirit of Nature with Chinese Brush Painting Techniques*. New York: Watson-Guptill Publications, 2003.

Sullivan, Michael. *The Three Perfections: Chinese Painting, Poetry, and Calligraphy*. New York: G. Braziller, 1980.

Wei, Zhang. *The Four Treasures: Inside the Scholar's Studio*. San Francisco: Long River Press, 2004.

Web Sites

http://depts.washington.edu/chinaciv/callig/7calsixd.htm (for information on script types)

http://www.chinapage.com/wang1.html (for examples of Wang Xizhi's calligraphy; he was one of the most famous calligraphers)

http://www.chinavoc.com/arts/calligraphy.htm and http://www.asia-art.net/chinese_tech_brush.html (for links to sites describing techniques, resources, basic brush strokes, and more)

http://www.chinapage.com/callig1.html

In the World Today

The Debate Over Simplified Characters

For much of China's history, written language was confined to the most educated citizens. In 1956, the People's Republic of China adopted simplified characters with fewer strokes in order to raise the literacy level. Nevertheless, many parents, especially in mainland China's cities, want their children to learn Regular Script (traditional character) calligraphy. There are indications that people wishing to appear cultured use traditional characters, for example on business cards. Scholars in Taiwan, the Republic of China, (and some in PRC) offer a number of arguments against the use of simplified characters. They point out that traditional characters are very systematic, and when they're changed the origins are lost, too. They note that people will no longer be able to read older historical and literary texts, and that those who can, will become a scholarly elite. Taiwan has not adopted simplified characters; students there learn the traditional Regular Script. Chinese Language Schools around the world are divided; some teach children the simplified PRC script while others teach the traditional one. Ask the class to debate whether simplified characters seem to be a good idea or not? What is lost and what is gained? What is the result of Chinese people and people of Chinese descent using different scripts?

Lesson 13 CD-ROM Contents

Primary Sources

- Document 13.1: A selection of *jinti shi* (《近体诗》) poems from the Tang dynasty period (618–907)
- Document 13.2: Multiple translations of a single line of poetry by Wang Wei (ca. 699–761)
- Document 13.3: "Deer Enclosure" (《鹿柴》) by Wang Wei (王维) in Chinese characters, a translation of each character, and a translation of the poem by Wai-lim Yip
- Document 13.4: "Deer Enclosure" by Wang Wei, translated by James J. Y. Liu
- Document 13.5: "Zazen on the Mountain" (《独坐敬亭山》) by Li Bai (李白) (701–762) in Chinese characters with a translation of each character
- Document 13.6: "Zazen on the Mountain" by Li Bai, translated by Sam Hamill
- Document 13.7: Poems from the Song (宋) dynasty (960–1279)
- Document 13.8: "On the Border, First Series" (《前出塞》) by Tu Fu (杜甫) (712–770)

Lesson 13
Poetry Highlights
By Steven Ratiner

Lesson Contents
- *Shijing* and *Chuci*
- Critical qualities of the Chinese language
- Tang poetry
- Song poetry

In no other civilization has poetry played so important a role in the development and continuation of the culture, the function of the state, and the spiritual life of its people. The roots of Chinese poetry extend far deeper than its recorded literature. China possessed a rich oral tradition that continues even today and, in ancient times, incorporated folk songs; poems to accompany religious rites, agricultural labor, and communal celebrations; lyric poems, which detailed their understanding of the natural world; and narrative verse, which preserved historical events.

Shijing and *Chuci*

The origins of Chinese written poetry stem from dual sources, each with a unique character and derivation. The *Shijing* (《诗经》, *The Classic of Poetry*), the oldest anthology of Chinese verse, contains 305 poems consolidated around 600 B.C.E. from a body of some 3,000 poems. The anthology includes *Feng* (风, Airs), anonymous folk lyrics dealing with love, family, nature; *Ya* (雅, the Odes), describing the life of the court and state concerns; and *Song* (颂, Hymns), used at state and religious rituals.

As one of the Five Confucian Classics, the *Shijing* was considered a source book for understanding the life of the nation and the virtuous way to conduct one's affairs. For that reason the poems were memorized by any person aspiring to become a literate gentleman or lady, and such an education extended right up through the aristocracy to the emperor himself.

Daoism (see Lesson 8) lies at the heart of the *Chuci* (《楚辞》, *Lyrics of Chu*). This second anthology arose from the region south of the Yangtze River. Unlike the largely anonymous poems of the *Shijing*, many of these poems are attributed to the Chu aristocrat Qu Yuan (屈原) (340–278 B.C.E.), who fell from political favor at court and was exiled (see Lesson 8). The poems in this collection tended to be longer and looser in structure than those of *The Classic of Poetry*, more mystical in tone, and written with great imaginative flourish.

From these two main sources, the course of Chinese poetry was established. All through the ages, Chinese writers borrowed from these collections—for philosophical ideas, poetic models, and for figures of speech that would echo within a common understanding (the way Western writers might use allusions to Shakespeare or the Bible.)

The Centrality of Poetry

As one of the Four Accomplishments (*siquan*, 四全), poetry stood at the pinnacle of the cultural hierarchy. It was important because it demanded the deepest response from a disciplined mind in order to receive its meanings. It contained a record of what was valued by the culture, illustrating the proper ways to live and to conduct one's personal, professional, and political affairs. As hard as it would be to imagine Western prime ministers or presidents reciting poems as a normal part of their political discourse, it would be just as unusual to imagine the Chinese court *without* it. During three millennia of Chinese history, whether writers harked back to the past or developed new styles, poetry always maintained its central place in the culture.

Notes:

- This lesson lends itself to an interdisciplinary approach. Teachers may also wish to refer to "On Teaching Poetry," found in the Teacher Resources, for suggestions.
- Poets' names and titles of poems are written in Wade-Giles spelling rather than *pinyin* used throughout the book because almost all books of Chinese poetry use that spelling. We do, too, to avoid confusion. In Activity 7, poets' names written in *pinyin* appear in parentheses. (Please refer to the introduction for an explanation of Wade-Giles and *pinyin*.)

Organizing Idea

Chinese poetry has a central place in the matrix of art forms that comprised traditional culture. It contains vibrant imagery and compelling voices, which are still evocative after great stretches of time, and provide a first-hand perspective into specific eras of Chinese civilization.

Student Objectives

Students will:

- understand that two ancient anthologies are considered the wellspring of Chinese poetry
- understand the central place of poetry in Chinese culture and contrast it with that of other cultures
- learn to appreciate these ancient poems both for their literary qualities and the insight they provide into Chinese civilization

- explore some of the literary techniques borrowed by Western poets at the start of the 20th century that played an important role in the development of our modern poetry
- use the Chinese texts, and the ideas they embody, as the stimulus for their own creative writing, searching for an intimate connection between cultures

Key Questions

- If a Tang dynasty (618–907) and a contemporary Western poet somehow changed places, what conditions would each find most surprising about their role in the culture of the time? Which features would each appreciate and dislike the most?
- How did the structure of the classical Chinese language affect the writing of their poets?
- What are some of the similarities in style and technique between ancient Chinese poetry and Western contemporary free verse?
- How can the ideas and experiences of these ancient poets affect the way someone views her or her own experiences?

Student Activities

Note: These exercises have been used successfully with students from elementary school through graduate school (with small adjustments in how the exercise is presented and which model poems are read). Teachers are encouraged to use additional examples of Tang and Song dynasty poems, which can be found online and in poetry books listed at the end of the lesson.

›› Activity 1: Discussion of Language and Culture

Before the first writing exercise, two important discussions should take place.

The first: unique properties of the classical Chinese language dramatically affect the writing of the poets who work within its boundaries.

- sentences are more streamlined than in English, foregoing much of the connective tissue we use to bind our grammar together
- nouns do not necessarily specify their number
- verbs do not reveal their tense

- word order is more flexible, and reversing the order of two characters does not necessarily alter their meaning (where, in English, "the boy hitting the ball" means something quite different than "the ball hitting the boy")
- the commitment to a single perspective—central in the concept of English composition—is nowhere near as crucial to the thinking of a Chinese poet. As a result, any one line of Chinese poetry can be interpreted in a variety of ways.

Second: Introduce the students to the "four treasures"—brush, inkstone, inkstick, and paper—the traditional Chinese writing implements, and discuss the special approach to the written word that they created (see Lesson 12).

PRIMARY SOURCE related to Activity 2
Document 13.1: A selection of *jinti shi* (《近体诗》) poems from the Tang dynasty period (618–907)

"News of Home" by Wang Wei (王维) (ca. 699–761),
translated by Steven Ratiner

> Coming from my village,
> you must have news of home.
> The day you left, that winter plum tree outside my
>   window—
> was it blooming yet?

• Full text available on CD-ROM •

» Activity 2: Tang Poetry—Writing a *Jinti shi*

Begin by reading a selection of the short-form *jinti shi* poems of the Tang era (Document 13.1). In each case remind the students of the techniques that are crucial here: carefully focused subject, concise but expressive language, vivid images, streamlined syntax and, most important, *showing* a moment's experience rather than explaining it. Help them to tease out the broader scenes and deeper implications hovering just beneath the simple surface. In each piece, search for the "eye of the poem" (*shi yan*), that crucial word or image upon which the whole poem depends and through which the layers of meaning are revealed. For Wang Wei's "News of Home," explain to the students that emperors frequently assigned officials to provinces other than the one where they lived so they would not develop a loyal following. Ask them:

- If they were living far away, what would be the first three things they'd ask a traveler who had come from their hometown?
- Why does the poet focus on the plum tree? How might the fate of the plum tree inform him about his hometown and his life there?

In Tu Fu's "Traveling Northward,"

- Would an assignment to China's northern border likely have been something officials welcomed? Why yes or no?

- What mood does each line evoke? (consider: "yellowing leaves," "moaning owl," "scurrying mouse")
- How does the mood shift with the final image of the "white bones"? Whose bones might they be? Why have they been left on the field? What thought appears to have jumped into the poet's mind?

The writing exercise will help us attain that marvelous sense of observation these poems display *and* the intuited depths they lead us toward. Take the students outside to stand or sit in any open area around the school (playing field, garden, courtyard); each should find a little private space from which to observe the world. Since they cannot prepare their minds by grinding ink (see Lesson 12), students will do a simple breathing exercise to try to arrive at a state of mind akin to that of the Chinese masters. Have students close their eyes and hold their minds still on a single thought: a breath. Guide them with a quiet voice, urging them "to imagine the breath as it slowly fills you, then empties, gently rises, then falls." If any distracting thought intrudes, ask them to let it slip from attention and return to the slow breaths. After about a minute of this meditation, ask them to slowly open their eyes. Having relaxed their sight in darkness, and eased into a new state of mind, the world will instantly appear more vivid and alive when they open their eyes. The class can imagine what years of such practice might produce in the mind of a poet.

Once teachers say, "eyes open," there is to be *no talking whatsoever.* All will remain still, allowing only eyes and ears to travel, seeking that one image that will suddenly snare their attention and begin to open a moment of the world (a bird flying past, the treetops moving in the wind, or perhaps a mundane image such as the rusted points of a fence, a sheet of newsprint blowing across the street). Whatever pleases them, focuses perception, or stirs the imagination can become the central image of their poem. (It's not unusual to have students come up with poems about watching another student-poet at work.)

Ask them to capture, in a short poem, the crucial image as well as the thought and emotion around it. Explain that some students will immediately hit upon a concise four-line structure while others may have to write eight or ten lines on the subject. They can pare it down during the revision sessions. In a fifteen-minute period, students will usually compose between two and five little poems.

Back inside the classroom, share some of the rough drafts. (The teacher might want to be the first to share.) In subsequent lessons, have them choose one or two poems that most please them. For these, ask them to begin a thorough revision, slowly perfecting these brief luminous lines so that they will possess both visual clarity and the power to draw a reader into their deepest realms. It is consistently astonishing to read which moments, overlooked in our normally hurried days, will suddenly capture a student's mind and carry him or her to a moment of awakening. Often the students themselves will express surprise, as if the poem was "written for them" by a deeper voice or "just landed in their notebook like a gift."

Follow up with a homework assignment: Have students choose one favorite spot around their homes or neighborhoods (back yard, local park, bedroom window), and sit there with notebook in hand. They need to create that same inner quiet and concentration and then slowly view this familiar place with fresh eyes. Not only will this allow the young poets to bring us into their individual worlds, it will reinforce in them the understanding that they can tap into this powerful mode of being at any time.

PRIMARY SOURCE *related to Activity 3*

Document 13.2: Multiple translations of a single line of poetry by Wang Wei (ca. 699–761)

"So lone the hills; there is no one in sight there." (W.J.B. Fletcher, 1919)

"There seems to be no one on the empty mountain" (Witter Bynner and Kiang Kang-hu, 1929)

"No glimpse of man on this lonely mountain" (Chang Yin-nan and Lewis C. Walmsley, 1958)

• *Full text available on CD-ROM* •

›› Activity 3: The Art of Translation

Part 1: Exploring Multiple Interpretations of a Line of Poetry

Wang Wei's poem, "Deer Enclosure," opens with five characters: 空山不见人. They mean: "empty mountain not see man." Have students read Document 13.2 to see how scholars throughout the past century have chosen to translate those characters into a line of poetry in English. These translators have been compelled to give us not just Wang Wei's word-meanings but an interpretation of the event portrayed, something approaching what a reader of Chinese would receive. Hill or hills or mountains; man or men; see, seeing, saw, sight? Each choice alters the meaning of the poem and its effect on a reader. But in the hands of a master, these more ambiguous qualities of classical Chinese are the source of great evocative power and mystery.

Now provide the class with a character-by-character rendering and translation of the poem (Document 13.3) and a different translation (Document 13.4). Ask the students to discuss which of the translations comes closest to the original text and which *feels* most like the spirit they sense in the poem? If Buddhism has been introduced (see Lesson 8), ask them how that philosophy is reflected in Wang Wei's poem. The students might vote for the version that most pleases them or excites the imagination. Ask them why they think this seemingly simple poem is considered a masterpiece.

Additional Primary Sources for Activity 3

Document 13.3: "Deer Enclosure" (《鹿柴》) by Wang Wei (王维) in Chinese characters, a translation of each character, and a translation of the poem by Wai-lim Yip

空	山	不	见	人
但	闻	人	语	响
返	景	入	深	林
复	照	青	苔	上

Literal translation of each character:

empty	mountain	not	see	man
but	hear	man's	voice	sound
reflecting (i.e. sun's reflection)	shadow	enter	deep	forest
again/and	shine	green	moss	upon

The poem:

> Empty mountain: no man
> But voices of men are heard.
> Sun's reflection reaches into the woods
> And shines upon the green moss.

Document 13.4: "Deer Enclosure" by Wang Wei, translated by James J. Y. Liu

> On the empty mountains no one can be seen,
> But human voices are heard to resound.
> The reflected sunlight pierces the deep forest
> And falls again upon the mossy ground.

Primary Sources for Part 2

 Document 13.5: "Zazen on the Mountain" (《独坐敬亭山》) by Li Bai (李白) (701–762) in Chinese characters with a translation of each character

众	鸟	高	飞	尽
Numerous	birds	high	fly	finish/complete/exhaust

孤	云	独	去	闲
Lone	cloud	solitary	leave	idle/serene/empty

相	看	两	不	厌
Mutual	look	two	not	satisfied/bored

只	有	敬	亭	山
Only	exists	Jingting		peak/mountain

 Document 13.6: "Zazen on the Mountain" by Li Bai, translated by Sam Hamill

The birds have vanished down the sky.
Now the last cloud drains away.

We sit together, the mountain and me,
until only the mountain remains.

Part 2: Translating a Poem

Now hand out a new Tang dynasty poem in Chinese, accompanied only by a character-by-character English form (Document 13.5). First have the students consider what the poem is saying and what deeper ideas are hinted at in the text. Then ask the students to translate the poem. The goal is an English version they think does justice to the original. (If there is a Chinese speaker in your class, who is willing to read the poem, students will hear the true beauty of the rhythm and tonal qualities.) These sessions have often resulted in spirited debates among students about the hundreds of choices involved; they will also have the added benefit of appreciating the levels of complexity involved in poetry written in any language.

Once the class has had a chance to go over the variety of their translations, pass around a translation by a scholar (Document 13.6), so they can compare and contrast the versions.

PRIMARY SOURCE *related to Activity 4*
Document 13.7: Poems from the Song (宋) dynasty (960–1279)

Tune: "Pure Serene Music" (《清平乐》) by Li Ch'ing-chao (李清照) (ca. 1084–ca. 1151)

Year after year in the snow
we'd pick plum blossoms while we drank,
Pulling at all the petals to no good purpose,
drenching our clothes with pure white tears.

This year I'm at the end of the world,
strand by strand my hair turns gray.
Judging by the force of the evening wind
Plum blossoms will be hard to come by.

» Activity 4: Analyzing Song Dynasty Poems and Writing *Ci*

Distribute examples of Song dynasty poems (Document 13.7) and explain the origins and characteristics of the new *ci* form. Then read the *ci* aloud with the class. Discuss:

- What themes appear to recur? (for example, memory, seasons, passage of time, relationships, loss)
- What political and military developments were taking place during the period these poets were writing? How does this era compare with the Tang dynasty (618–907)?
- How might this have affected the themes that recur in the poems?
- How have these same themes occurred in the students' personal experiences?
- What national and international events have taken place in recent times that have created shared memories?

Ask the students to reflect on their own memories. Which ones came to mind when reading the *ci* poems or during the class discussion? Did students find themselves recalling "golden moments" or did other memories come to mind?

- Are "golden moments" perhaps better in hindsight than they were when they first took place?
- How are memories magnified or intensified when someone reflects on the past?
- Which memories stand out as important markers in their own lives, or, conversely, which simple little memories surprise them with their lasting power?

Using the Song poems as models, ask the students to close their eyes, to allow their minds to drift back until a single memory takes center stage. Ask them to envision the place this memory occurred and all the specific details that come to mind. Remind them that in the imagistic approach, they won't explain the importance of the memory, but will take the reader there. Their purpose is to open a poetic window so that, line by line and image by image, the reader will feel *present*, witnessing that moment.

The poems that arise from this exercise are often deeply-felt and yet surprising, even for the authors. This activity demonstrates how writing a poem is a double gift: first, for the poet who has re-experienced a vital piece of his or her life, and rendered it in an unforgettable manner. But second, and perhaps more surprising, is the way others in the class will discover pieces of their own lives in poetry written by their peers. Ask students to consider the commonality of experience, even over the span of millennia. Reading Su Shih's poem of longing for his dead wife, or Li Ch'ing-chao's lament about how quickly youth rushes by, one cannot help but feel more sharply what is most precious in life. As students write, they too are being instructed by and contributing to this long unfolding of the human story.

» Activity 5: Writing New Lyrics to Old Tunes

Ask each student to select a song, one that will be instantly recognized by the majority of the class. Giving students several days to work on this (perhaps as homework), ask them to create new lyrics to the old song. This exercise will raise many of the technical and stylistic issues any lyric poet must confront:

- how to work within a restricted form while maintaining a feeling of spontaneity and flow
- how to sketch out the pattern within the poem to keep on track, following the rhythm of the music
- what sort of tone and diction will be most appropriate for the mood of the new lyric
- whether to write in keeping with the mood of the original piece (a new love lyric that reflects or updates the old one), or to intentionally run counter to the original composition for the purposes of irony or satire. (Remind them how Li Ch'ing-chao used the tune "Pure Serene Music" for her poem about carefree youth slipping almost overnight into the loneliness of old age.)

There are many challenges to overcome in such a creation, but one of the new sensations that will spur them on is the interplay of expectation versus surprise. Because their readers are already familiar with the song at the heart of this piece, they will anticipate certain emotions and even rhymes; this gives the writer the opportunity to either satisfy those urges or lead them in surprising new directions. By the time these poems are ready to be shared (either read or, for the daring student, sung), there is usually a high-spirited mood in the class. Consider imitating the social atmosphere implied by the *ci* by setting up the classroom like a coffeehouse with shared tables and refreshments. The desire to impress, startle, or just plain move one's listeners frequently spurs the students' great creative ingenuity. This sense of poetry as a social bond between writer and audience, as a reflection of their shared cultural background, is a perfect reflection of one aspect of the literary milieu created during the Song dynasty. It's not hard to see its link to the performances by rap artists and poetry slammers today.

PRIMARY SOURCE related to Activity 6

**Document 13.8: "On the Border, First Series" (《前出塞》)
by Tu Fu (杜甫) (712–770)**

I.

We recruits have our commanders to send us off,
but, bound for distant duty, we're people too!
From here we go out to face life or death—
no cause for the officers to scowl at us so!
Along the route we come on someone we know,
give him a letter to hand to close kin.
Sad as it is, we and they are parted now,
no longer to share the same troubles and pain.

II.

If you draw a bow, draw a strong one;
if you use an arrow, use one that's long.
If you want to shoot a man, shoot his horse first;
if you want to seize the enemy, seize their leader first.
But killing people has limits too,
and when you guard a state, there are boundaries to be
    observed.
Just so you manage to keep invaders out—
Seeing how many you can slaughter—that's not the point!

›› Activity 6: Persona Poem—Writing From Behind a Mask

A persona poem is a form in which the author writes from somebody else's perspective, or with an alternate "voice." (The term traces its lineage through the Latin and Greek words for "mask," and students can think of it as similar to an actor putting on a mask and becoming a different character.) In a society where women were not encouraged to take up the literary arts, many male poets, for example, wrote lyrics in which they spoke in the voice of the loyal wife longing for a distant husband away in the emperor's service. In other cases, the mask might have acted as a shield, allowing a poet to express the true sentiments of the people, even those they would never normally proclaim in so public a manner.

In the body of Tu Fu's work there are a number of powerful poems that employ this device to great effect. Together read "On the Border, First Series" (Document 13.8) and discuss:

• From whose perspective or in whose voice is Tu Fu writing in the first stanza?
• What are the poet's feelings toward the soldiers?
• Is the voice in the first stanza the same as the one in the second stanza? If these are two different speakers, how are they different? If only one, what aspects of his personality do the stanzas express?
• Why might Tu Fu have chosen to write from this perspective?

One of the most powerful results when writing a persona poem is not what we disguise through this device but what the mask allows us to reveal from deep within ourselves, often feelings and ideas we had barely recognized before that we'd not likely give expression to in our normal voices.

After reading the Chinese persona poem, ask students to select one historical figure from their studies as the subject for a mask poem. Alternatively the students can choose an anonymous character (a soldier off to defend the borders, the wife left behind to care for the family, or a Buddhist monk watching from a hilltop as the battle rages below). In either case, discuss some of the stylistic considerations that might precede their writing:

- What sort of voice and personality would that individual possess?
- Which images from the character's daily life would be foremost in his or her mind and which would have to be rendered with a tangible presence if the poem is to work?
- What might this character reveal (or *not*) in the intensity of the moment?
- What similar emotions from the students' own lives might help them to understand what is happening in this person's life?

Once the poems are ready to be shared, the students might be coaxed to respond to each other's poems from two different points of view: as writers (examining each piece's effectiveness as imaginative writing); and as social scientists (considering how a distant historical era is brought to life through this technique.)

» Activity 7: Related Research—The Lives of the Poets

This activity can be done at any point while the students learn about Chinese poetry. Ask students to select a poet from the list below and then to research his or her life, using resources provided later in the lesson. Instruct students to look for the people, places, and events that influenced the poet.

The students will present their findings orally to the class, not in the form of a report but by taking on the role of the poet. They can introduce themselves to their audience and give pertinent details from their lives, or they might simply state their names and then take questions from the audience, which they must answer in character.

Note: The poets' names in *pinyin* are in parentheses. When students look for information, they should try looking under both spellings.

Qu Yuan, in whose memory the Dragon Boat Festival is celebrated, threw himself into a river after his state was conquered by the Qin state.

Ts'ao Chih (*Cao Zhi*) was the son of the great warlord Cao Cao, who, as the Han empire was breaking up, took over the north of China and founded the Wei dynasty. Ts'ao Chih was the leading poet of his time.

T'ao Ch'ien (*Tao Qian*) is thought of as the "revered grandfather" of Chinese verse and a model for the poet-as-recluse

Hsieh Ling-Yün (*Xie Lingyun*) is considered China's first great nature poet.

Empress Wu (*Wu Tse-T'ien* or *Wu Zetian* in *pinyin*) was not only an accomplished poet, but, by seizing power from her husband and sons, she was the only empress in Chinese history to rule in her own right.

Li Bai (*Li Bo*) was one of the three great Tang poets. He is still the most popular poet in all Chinese literature.

Tu Fu (*Du Fu*), although unappreciated during his lifetime, is not only one of the great Tang poets, but is generally considered the best Chinese poet of all time.

Wang Wei is the third of the Tang great talents. Before he retired to his mountain home, one of his poems helped him escape certain imprisonment and execution for treason.

Po Chu-I (*Bai Juyi*): Popular among the common people, he took pride in finding his poems copied onto the walls of inns and monasteries.

Kuan P'an-P'an (*Guan Panpan*): A great courtesan during the Tang period, she became the concubine of the statesman Zhang Qian. She was celebrated in the work of many other poets because of her loyalty to her lord.

Han Shan took the name "Cold Mountain" from the misty T'ien T'ai (*Tian Tai*) mountains, where he became a recluse.

Li Yü (*Li Yu*) was the last emperor of the Southern Tang dynasty. The new Song emperor placed him under house arrest.

Su Tung-P'o (*Su Dongpo*) was also known as Su Shih (*Su Shi*). Those who live near West Lake in Hangzhou even today benefit from something this poet-official created for the people.

Lu Yu (*Lu You*): In his nearly ten thousand poems, he frequently focused on taking pleasure in everyday life. This explains his pen name: "The old man who does as he pleases."

Li Ch'ing-chao (*Li Qingzhao*) is generally considered China's foremost female poet. Of the twelve collections of poetry and prose listed in her biography, less than one hundred poems survive today.

Ou-Yang Hsiu (*Ouyang Xiu*): Largely self-educated, he rose to the heights of government only to be toppled by political enemies.

Further Student and Teacher Resources

Landau, Julie, trans. *Beyond Spring: Tz'u poems of the Sung Dynasty*. New York: Columbia University Press, 1994. (includes brief biographies of all the Song dynasty poets)

Owen, Stephen, trans. *An Anthology of Chinese Literature*. New York: W.W. Norton & Co., 1996.

Watson, Burton, trans. *The Columbia Book of Chinese Poetry.* New York: Columbia University Press, 1984.

Weinberger, Eliot and Octavio Paz. *Nineteen Ways of Looking at Wang Wei.* Mt. Kisco, N.Y.: Moyer Bell Limited, 1987. (examines one poem and its nineteen translations)

Yip, Wai-lim, trans. *Chinese Poetry.* Durham, N.C.: Duke University Press, 1997. (includes character-by-character translations)

Web Sites

Tang poems:

http://etext.lib.virginia.edu/chinese/frame.htm

http://www.chinapage.org/poem2e.html

http://afe.easia.columbia.edu/ (Columbia University's Asia for Educators site. Go to "Literature," then "Classical Literature.")

Tang and Song poems:

www.chinese-poems.com (with a sampling of material from other eras; presents poems in Chinese characters, *pinyin*, and English)

http://en.wikipedia.org/wiki/Chinese_poetry (free online encyclopedia featuring extensive selections of Chinese poems plus a variety of essays on poetry styles and historical context)

In the World Today

A Bridge Between Cultures

Early in the twentieth century, the American poet Ezra Pound popularized the idea that the pictorial nature of the Chinese language represented an ideal means of expressing poetry, of showing rather than explaining what a moment or an experience was like. His concept grew into *imagism* and became the dominant poetic style of the twentieth century. Pound borrowed the concise, clear-eyed imagery he found in Tang dynasty poems as well as some of the other unique qualities of classical Chinese writing to present his reader with the feeling of a spontaneous experience. The large number of translations that began to appear in the twentieth century introduced Western poets to a Chinese sensibility and writing style that gradually became integrated with their own. This established a bridge between the cultures that still has great influence today. Have students compare poems by William Carlos Williams, Gary Snyder, Mary Oliver, Robert Frost, James Wright, and Sylvia Plath to the Chinese poems they have been reading. Which poets from the West are most like the poets of the Tang and Song dynasties? How are they similar and different?

苦々緑深草風の吾が目に

Lesson 14 CD-ROM Contents

Primary Sources

- Document 14.1: A segment from the handscroll "Admonitions of Court Ladies" (《女史箴图》) attributed to Gu Kaizhi (顾恺之), 4th century

- Document 14.2: "Travelers by Stream and Mountains" (《溪山行旅图》) by Fan Kuan (范宽), 1070

- Document 14.3: A close-up of a section of "Travelers by Stream and Mountains" by Fan Kuan, 1070

- Document 14.4: "Walking on a Mountain Path in Spring" (《春晓》) by Ma Yüan (马远) (ca. 1190–1230)

- Document 14.5: "Magpies and Hare" (《双喜图》) by Cui Bai (崔白), 1061

- Document 14.6: "The Fisherman" (《渔父图》) by Wu Zhen (吴镇) (1280–1345)

Lesson 14
Traditional Painting

By Dr. Huajing Maske, Renee Covalucci, and Christine Vaillancourt

Lesson Contents

- Figure painting
- Birds, plants, and flowers
- Landscaping painting
- Literati-artists

Chinese art history is an extraordinarily rich and complex subject that includes many genre and spans millennia. The earliest known brush paintings on silk were found in tombs that date back to the fifth through the third centuries before the Common Era. During the Han (汉) dynasty (202 B.C.E.–220 C.E.), art focused on portraits of ancestors and served to illustrate Confucian values. In the centuries that followed, as Daoism and Buddhism became the prevalent beliefs, art increasingly reflected the Chinese quest for harmony, and nature became the subject. Landscape painting, in particular, has dominated Chinese art since the tenth century.

The Six Principles

In the sixth century, Chinese art critic Xie He established six principles by which great art should be judged. They have had a profound effect on Chinese art. Five of the principles addressed brush technique, fidelity to the subject, composition, use of color, and respect for tradition. The first one, perhaps more than anything else, speaks to the heart of Chinese art: A painting must have *qi* (气), defined as "cosmic spirit that vitalizes all things" (Sullivan, p. 88). Many think of *qi* as the breath of life.

Calligraphy

Chinese painting has much in common with the art of calligraphy since both come from the same creative source and artists use many of the same materials and techniques as calligraphers. The artist works with the same types of brushes, ink, and paper.

Brush work for both requires mastery of precise, swift, and delicate strokes. Painters, like calligraphers, developed their art by copying ancient masters and through disciplined training. Writers or poets, calligraphers, and artists in that order were, and still are, highly respected.

Poetry

For hundreds of years, the relationship between calligraphy and poetry was very close. During the Tang (唐) dynasty (618–907 C.E.), visual art began to be linked with them as well. In the centuries that followed, proficiency in the Three Perfections (*sanjue*, 三绝) would be seen as the hallmarks of a refined and educated person. In the late eleventh and early twelfth century, poems were spoken of as "formless paintings, while paintings were poetry with form." Artists incorporated poems into their compositions, both supplementing and complementing the painting's effect. Sometimes, others would respond to a piece of art by adding a poem.

Seals

In the seventh century, a Tang dynasty emperor was the first to start stamping the paintings in the imperial household. The art of seal engraving added another dimension to painting, beginning in the Song (宋) dynasty (960–1279 C.E.) and continuing until the early twentieth century. Seals stamped in red ink added an aesthetic appeal to the monochromatic paintings. Many paintings were the joint product of a painter, a poet, a calligrapher, and a seal maker. This unique combination of poetry, calligraphy, seals, and painting—all important aspects of Chinese culture—makes Chinese landscape painting mesmerizing and formidable.

Notes:

• This lesson lends itself to an interdisciplinary approach.
• Since traditional Chinese painting closely reflects culture and beliefs, this lesson is best introduced after students are familiar with Lesson 7 on Confucianism and Lesson 8 on Chinese Belief Systems.

Organizing Idea

Traditional painting served as a mirror of prevalent beliefs in China at the time. In subject matter, style, and approach, it has a unique place in world art.

Student Objectives

Students will:

  • understand the major genre of traditional Chinese painting
  • recognize how art reflected Chinese beliefs
  • recognize landscape painters' approach to perspective
  • recognize common symbols in Chinese art

Key Questions

  • What purpose did paintings such as "Admonitions of Court Ladies" serve?
  • What goals did landscape painters have in mind as they worked?
  • How did academy-trained artists and literati-artists differ?

Vocabulary

admonition
brush stroke
concubine
cun
literati-artists
perspective
scroll
Three Perfections

Student Activities

≫ Activity 1: Recognizing Confucian Beliefs in "Admonitions of Court Ladies"

Distribute copies of the section of the painting (Document 14.1) or project it on a screen. Introduce or review Document 10.3 in the lesson on Family Life. It describes the ideal of women's behavior during the Han dynasty. Read the text for "The Rejection Scene." Discuss its meaning.

- What are women meant to accept?
- What is their role?
- Should they expect any personal satisfaction?

Now examine the painting:

- How is the emperor responding to the concubine?
- What is the message here for women?
- Why would this image be part of the "Admonitions" scroll?
- Gu Kaizhi's scroll was copied and studied for centuries. Why?

Look at the lines and paint strokes. Ask students to compare the emperor's body stance to that of the woman. What is the artist communicating by depicting them this way? (The emperor has a solid stance while the concubine is full of movement, almost dancing.) Additional sections of the scroll can be seen on the British Museum Web site, http://www.thebritishmuseum.ac.uk/compass/ixbin/goto?id=OBJ2100.

PRIMARY SOURCE *related to Activity 1*

Document 14.1: A segment from the handscroll "Admonitions of Court Ladies" (《女史箴图》) attributed to Gu Kaizhi (顾恺之), 4th century

In figure paintings, such as this one by Gu Kaizhi, forms were outlined and painted with rich colors. Confucian ideals were illustrated in the work. Typical subjects were virtuous women, dutiful children, Confucian gentleman, loyal subjects, and just and wise emperors. In this painting, Gu Kaizhi was illustrating a text on correct behavior, written for women living at court. He was a master of figure painting and was also a writer on Chinese painting. His work, including this masterpiece, was often copied by artists as part of their training.

The text for "The Rejection Scene" reads: "When love has reached its highest pitch, it changes its form. For whatever has reached fullness must require decline. This law is absolute."

PRIMARY SOURCE *related to Activity 2*

Document 14.2: "Travelers by Stream and Mountains" (《溪山行旅图》) by Fan Kuan (范宽), 1070

National Palace Museum, Taiwan, Republic of China

Chinese landscape paintings tried to capture the spirit of a scene rather than to give a literal representation of it taken from one viewpoint. Often painted on hanging scrolls, the paintings invite the viewer to take a spiritual and physical journey.

The arts went through a renaissance as a result of the patronage of Song dynasty emperors. Fan Kuan worked as one of the professional court artists. He learned from the paintings of a famous artist of the late 10th century. As his skill developed, he decided he should study nature itself rather than "learning from a man" and then that "better than either of these methods is the way of learning from my own heart." This piece of art is a hanging scroll, painted with ink on silk. It is approximately a foot wide and two feet long (103 cm by 206 cm).

» Activity 2: Understanding Shifting Perspective in Landscape Painting

The video *A Day on the Grand Canal* (see Lesson 16), in which a scholar shows sections of a 72-foot scroll and explains issues of perspective, is an excellent way to introduce the concept.

Display "Travelers by Stream and Mountains" (Document 14.2) on a screen or have students look at their own copies. Ask the students where the artist was "standing" when he painted this? The answer is that it was not in any one place. The mountain is enormous if one stands at its base. The figures are tiny if one stands on top of the mountain. Chinese landscape paintings make the viewer an active participant. They invite the viewer to wander with the painter through the scenes he depicts. Imagine traveling in this region in the 11th century; it could take days or even weeks. Ask the students to let themselves travel through the picture and write spontaneously as they do. Why might the artist have left part of the painting in mist? Ask them to use all of their senses. What do they see, hear, feel, smell? What allows them to respond with all their senses?

Now have students look at the close-up of the lower section of the painting (Document 14.3 available on the CD-ROM).

- How far are the tops of the pine trees from the trail in the foreground?
- From what angle are the rocks shown?
- How high is the waterfall?
- Just as the perspective shifts, the distances are ambiguous. What feeling does that evoke?

Daoists accepted that they could never fully comprehend Dao; rather their goal was to be in harmony with Dao.

- What elements in this painting reflect Daoist thinking?
- How does this painting capture a sense of harmony?
- Does it have *qi*, breath of life? Where? How?

» Activity 3: Comparing and Contrasting Earlier and Later Song Dynasty Art

Ask students to look at "Walking on a Mountain Path in Spring" (Document 14.4) and to jot down words that come to mind, especially what feelings the painting evokes. Identify:

- Who is in the painting? (Notice the servant on the lower left carrying a *qin*.)
- What is happening and what may happen in the near future?
- What in the painting identifies the time of year?
- What sounds does this painting capture?

Have students write a four-line poem in response to the painting. Then ask them to consider the poem that appears in the top right corner of the painting. It was written not by Ma Yüan but by his concubine. Ask students to compare her poem to their own. Ask them whether it seems to fit the feel of the painting? If they perceive the poem as being different, ask them to speculate on why that might be? At the time Ma Yüan created the piece of art, the Song dynasty was being threatened by invaders from the north. What appears to be his response to this pervading threat? How does the poem reflect this threat? How does an individual's state of mind affect how he or she responds to a piece of art?

PRIMARY SOURCE *related to Activity 3*

Document 14.4: "Walking on a Mountain Path in Spring" (《春晓》) by Ma Yüan (马远) (ca. 1190–1230)

National Palace Museum, Taiwan, Republic of China

Ma Yüan's father, grandfather, and great-grandfather all painted at the Royal Academy of Painting (翰林书画院). His son became a painter, too. This painting is done on silk in ink and light colors and is ten by seventeen inches in size. The poem on the right reads: "Brushed by his sleeves, mountain flowers dance in the wind. Fleeing from him, the hidden birds cut short their songs."

Next, compare this painting to "Travelers by Stream and Mountains" (Document 14.2). Explore among other points:

- How is nature portrayed in each?
- How big a piece of nature is Ma Yüan rendering as compared to Fan Kuan? How does this choice of subject affect the painting?
- How are people represented?
- Compare the composition of the two works of art.
- Compare the brush strokes.
- How did each artist appear to view nature? How did each see man's relationship to nature?

PRIMARY SOURCE *related to Activity 4*

Document 14.5: "Magpies and Hare" (《双喜图》) by Cui Bai (崔白), 1061

National Palace Museum, Taiwan, Republic of China

After the 8th century, birds and flowers and plant life became popular subjects. Things in nature symbolized moral and ethical values for instructional purposes. For example, pine trees, bamboo, plum blossoms, and chrysanthemums symbolized endurance and strength to withstand harsh conditions and survive; gulls, egrets, peonies, and peacocks were symbols of wealth and rank. Willow trees and ancient cypresses represented constancy and wisdom.

Cui Bai painted at the Royal Academy of Painting (翰林书画院). As the favorite painter of one of the emperors of the Song dynasty, his only responsibility was to paint for him. The Chinese title of this painting is *Shuang Xi Tu* (《双喜图》). *Xi* (喜) means happiness. The painting is done in ink and color on a silk hanging scroll, approximately two feet long and a foot wide (194 cm by 103 cm).

≫ Activity 4: "Magpies and Hare," Identifying the Symbolism

Show the students the painting by Cui Bai (Document 14.5).

- Note the Chinese name for this painting and ask them what the symbol for happiness might be in the scroll (magpie). It is a Chinese belief that if a magpie sings in a tree in front of your home, the family will have good luck and happiness. Since there are two in the painting, what might that suggest?
- Consider what sounds are present in this painting as well.
- Notice the details in the painting. What is the season? What are the weather conditions?
- How does the viewer's eye travel as he or she looks at the painting? Why?
- Describe the interaction between the hare and the magpies. Are the birds cautioning the hare? Mocking it? Or singing to it?
- Why might Cui Bai have chosen to leave it ambiguous? How does this, too, reflect Daoist beliefs?
- How does this painting evoke *qi*?
- Show the students some examples of Western art depicting animals and birds, such as "After the Hunt" by William Michael Harnett (see http://www.thinker. org/fam/education/publications/guide-american/24.html).
- How is the result different?
- Though Western artists also painted live creatures, a Chinese artist would never have painted a dead one. What do the paintings suggest about the cultural attitude toward nature?

≫ Activity 5: Exploring the Art of Literati-Artists

Distribute copies of Document 14.6, "Fisherman" by Wu Zhen. Students have become familiar with certain key qualities of Chinese art. Have them work in small groups and write three critical questions about "Fisherman." If they need guidance, suggest they consider composition, use of space, man's relationship to nature, and use of calligraphy and seals. Have each group pose at least one of its questions to the class to stimulate discussion. Then ask students to compare and contrast the three landscape paintings. What unique qualities does the one by the literati-artist have? The artists believed that a painting should express the painter's emotions. Does "Fisherman"? What feelings does it express? Ask students to write a poem in response to the painting.

PRIMARY SOURCE *related to Activity 5*

Document 14.6: "The Fisherman" (《渔父图》) by Wu Zhen (吴镇) (1280–1345)

Photo by Malcolm Varon. Photo © 1991 The Metropolitan Museum of Art.

In the 12th century, a new style of painting evolved created by literati-artists. Their approach was very different from that of artists trained at the Royal Academy. The art of literati-artists was more expressive—a visual poem. They believed art should be an outlet for the painter's emotions just like poetry and calligraphy. After the Mongols invaded China in 1279, numbers of scholar-officials turned away from government service and devoted themselves to furthering the literati-artist genre. Efforts at realism vanished completely. Instead their goal was to capture man's response to nature.

Wu Zhen was one of the four great artists of the Yuan (元) dynasty (1279–1368). He withdrew from society and became known as a hermit-artist. Besides his landscapes, he is also celebrated for his renderings of bamboo done in ink.

≫ Activity 6: Painting a Landscape Experimenting with Chinese Techniques and Approaches

Materials

- white heavy-weight paper
- watercolors brushes, a variety of sizes
- water in small cups
- black watercolor

Students may choose to create either a horizontal or vertical format. The final paintings can be painted as hand or hanging scrolls. (A hand scroll can be comfortably held between two hands.) Either precut the paper or have students cut their own.

Students will want to practice using some of the painting techniques ahead of time. (See the resources list for suggestions.) Encourage them to look at many more Chinese paintings in art books and online.

Each student will create his or her own composition beginning with the foreground, creating visual depth, adding fading mountains in the distance, or clouds and mist for mood. The teacher should remind the students to pay attention to the composition. Ask the students what viewpoint(s) they have. Are they sitting on top of a mountain looking down on a river or small village? Or are they on a riverbank looking up at tall mountains with a temple on top? Or will they be in several places? Remind them that not every space has to be filled.

Ask them to add their own poetry to the painting. They may want to try writing their poetry in Chinese characters. They can complete the piece of art by adding a seal, or by making their own seals (see Lesson 5) and then stamping their work. Multiple seals could be painted on as though this were a painting that had passed through many hands. When the painting is finished, mount it on light brown or gray paper to represent silk.

≫ Activity 7: Extended Research

Traditional scholar-official and scholar-literati painting are but two of many types of art of ancient China. Teachers can encourage students to use books and Internet sources to explore other art forms in China, among them:

- Neolithic pottery with its extraordinary human-facial, animal, and geometric design
- laquerware, which dates back more than 6000 years, and was used on plates, coffins, musical instruments and furniture
- bronzes (see Lesson 3)
- Buddhist art, especially in statuary
- porcelain from the Jingdezhen region
- paper arts, especially pattern-cut paper used to make fans and lanterns, and to decorate doors and windows. It dates back to the 6th century
- Wood block printing used to illustrate books beginning in the Song dynasty (960–1279)

Students can work in small groups to create an exhibit on the art form they have researched. Each exhibit should include information about the origin of the art form, a description of the level of craftsmanship needed, a description and examples of the art form, and an explanation of the purposes the art served.

Further Student and Teacher Resources

Cahill, James. *Chinese Painting*. New York: Rizzoli International Publications, Inc. 1985.

Sullivan, Michael. *The Arts of China*. Berkeley: University of California Press, 1984.

Xin, Yang and Nie Chongzheng, James Cahill, Lang Shaojun, and Wu Hung. *Three Thousand Years of Chinese Painting*. New Haven: Yale University Press, 2002.

Yangmu, Wu. *The Techniques of Chinese Painting*. Beijing, China: Morning Glory Press, 1996.

Web Sites
For Chinese paintings:

http://www.chinapage.com/paint1.html

http://www.npm.gov.tw/ (National Palace Museum, Taipei)

http://depts.washington.edu/chinaciv/painting/4schyuan.htm (focuses on Song and Yuan painting from the point of view of painting as social record and as fine art)

http://www.asia.si.edu/collections/chineseHome.htm (Freer and Sackler galleries)

http://www.indiana.edu/~ealc100/Art1.html (Indiana University site on literati painters)

http://losangeles.china-consulate.org/eng/Topics/chinabrief/t83970.htm (on Gu Kuazi)

http://www.asia-art.net/chinese_tech_brush.html (for brush painting techniques)

http://www.metmuseum.org/explore/Chinese/html_pages/glossary.htm (excellent glossary)

http://www.chinesepaintings.com/chinese-symbols.html (common Chinese symbols and their meanings)

http://www.thinker.org/fam/education/publications/guide-american/24.html (for an image of and information about "After the Hunt")

In the World Today

A Revival of Traditional Chinese Brush Painting

Dr. Julia Andrews, co-curator of the Guggenheim Museum's major exhibition, "China 5000 Years," writes that "two decades of steady contact with the outside world have yielded an intense reconsideration of China's native artistic traditions." Official communist party patronage and proscribed subjects and styles have eased. Contemporary artists seek to rediscover and renew the traditional medium of ink on paper, delving into the forms and aesthetics that make their art Chinese.

The audience for today's artists, however, is very different: The museum-going public view their work rather than fellow artists in private settings. Paintings are no longer limited to albums and hand scrolls; some are more than six feet. Artists such as Li Keran, Andrews points out, use traditional brushwork to "go beyond representation to achieve the timeless quality sought by artists of the classical past." To see some superb examples of recent Chinese art, visit http://kaladarshan.arts.ohio state. edu/exhib/gug/indxs/tran/tranchinptg.html. Ask students what similarities and differences they see between the art in the lesson and the twentieth-century paintings.

Lesson 15 CD-ROM Contents

Primary Sources

- Document 15.1: Excerpts on music from the *Analects of Confucius* (《论语》)
- Document 15.2: Image of sixty-five bells from the tomb of Marquis Yi of Zeng (曾侯乙), ca. 433 B.C.E.
- Document 15.3: Image of thirty-two chime stones from the tomb of Marquis Yi of Zeng (曾侯乙), ca. 433 B.C.E.
- Document 15.4: Lyrics for "Gentle Girl" in *Shijing* (《诗经》, *The Classic of Poetry*)
- Document 15.5: Mural of dancers and musicians in the Yulin Grottoes (榆林石窟), Tang (唐) dynasty (618–907)
- Document 15.6: Statues of musical ensemble from a Tang (唐) dynasty tomb
- Document 15.7: Ceramic model of a group of musicians on a camel, Tang (唐) dynasty
- Document 15.8: Marble relief of musicians from a 10th-century tomb, Hebei (河北) Province
- Document 15.9: Close-up of musician playing a *sheng* (笙), from marble relief of musicians in a 10th-century tomb, Hebei (河北) Province
- Document 15.10: Painting of Emperor Huizong (宋徽宗) playing a *qin* (琴), Song (宋) dynasty (960–1279)

Supplementary Materials

- Item 15.A Additional vocabulary for primary source
- Item 15.B Questions related to Documents 15.5, 15.6, 15.7, and 15.8
- Item 15.C Descriptions of several ancient Chinese instruments

Selections of Music

- *Jiangnan sizhu*
- Guangdong music: *Gaohu* solo
- Music for wind and percussion: *Guanzi* solo
- *Sheng* solo
- *Qin* solo

Lesson 15
Music

Lesson Contents
- Role of music
- Instruments of ancient China
- Influence of the silk routes trade

China's ancient historic texts, such as *Liji* (《礼记》, *The Book of Rites*) and *Shijing* (《诗经》, *The Classic of Poetry*) make clear that the Chinese have long considered music as central to everyday life. Confucians saw it as essential to a meaningful, moral life; knowledge of and appreciation for music was something a person had to cultivate in order to be considered educated. Together with calligraphy, poetry, and painting, it was one of the Four Accomplishments (*siquan*, 四全). China's early philosophers believed that music was something that man discovered rather than invented. According to tradition, "wise men heard the singing of phoenixes and imitated the sounds they made" (Major, p. 29).

Ancient Chinese believed that "music comes from within" and that it created serenity (Major, p. 23). The written character for music (乐, *yue*) can also be read as *le* (乐), meaning joy. Music was enjoyed widely as entertainment and had an important role in courtship. The Chinese also recognized that music could be a very powerful political instrument since it can unite the feelings of large groups of people through song, dance, or military drill. They saw music as a key component of good government.

Confucius referred to the important role of music several times in the *Analects*. During the Han (汉) dynasty (202 B.C.E.—220 C.E.), the emperor created an Imperial Bureau of Music (*Yuefu*, 乐府). It was responsible for collecting music, training choirs and orchestras, and performing music at official ceremonies and private court events. During both the Han dynasty (206 B.C.E.–220 C.E.) and, later, the Tang (唐) dynasty (618–907), extensive trade via the silk routes (see Lesson 18) brought into the country musicians from other cultures, playing instruments and types of music previously unknown, further enriching China's music.

Instruments of Ancient China

While much has been known for centuries about the importance of music in ancient China, historians had less information about which instruments might have been used and what was actually performed. Archaeological discoveries of the past half-century have begun to change this. Archaeologists have unearthed models of musicians (made of pottery, bronze, or wood) in tombs. This confirms that the Chinese saw music as so important that they should have it with them in the afterlife, too. Images on wall paintings or inscribed in brick and stone provide information about musical performances. Finally, the discovery of actual instruments, some inscribed with detailed information, have contributed enormously to what is now known.

The most extraordinary archaeological find for our knowledge of ancient music was the discovery in 1977 of the perfectly preserved tomb of Marquis Yi of Zeng (曾侯乙), the ruler of a small state in the Yangtze (长江) valley. He died about 433 B.C.E. Two of the four burial chambers were filled with 124 instruments, including bells, stone chimes, drums, zithers, mouth organs, and flutes. The collection represents "the oldest musical ensemble surviving from any culture" (Major, p.7).

Organizing Idea

Both ceremonial and folk music were central to life in ancient China. Archaeological discoveries in the twentieth century have significantly enriched our understanding of this central role.

Student Objectives

Students will:

- recognize the centrality of music in ancient China
- be introduced to the sounds of ancient instruments
- recognize how trade via the silk routes brought new instruments into China

Key Questions

- Why did Confucians hold music in such high esteem in ancient China?
- How have historians learned about different types of music in China?
- How are the roles of music in ancient China similar and different to the roles of music in the United States and other cultures today?

Vocabulary

bamboo
ceremonial
ensemble
grotto
mural
tomb

Supplementary Materials

Item 15.A: Additional vocabulary for primary source
Item 15.B Questions related to Documents 15.5, 15.6, 15.7, and 15.8
Item 15.C Descriptions of several ancient Chinese instruments
Selections of music

Student Activities

≫ Activity 1: Understanding the Role of Music for Confucius

Students should work with a partner to read what Confucius believed about music (Document 15.1). Then answer the following questions:

- If Confucius were alive today, what kind of music would he like and what types would he not like? Why?
- How were music and songs important in people's lives, according to Confucius?
- What purpose did they serve?
- If music is not "merely bells and drums," what is it?

If students are familiar with the role of Confucius in Chinese culture (Lesson 7), ask them to consider why his thoughts about music may have been influential and when they might have been most influential.

PRIMARY SOURCE related to Activity 1

Document 15.1: Excerpts on music from the *Analects of Confucius* (《论语》)

8.9 Confucius said, "Find inspiration in *The Classic of Poetry*, steady your course with the ritual; find your fulfillment in music."

17.9 The Master said: "Little ones, why don't you study *The Classic of Poetry*? *The Classic of Poetry* can provide you with stimulation and with observation, with a capacity for communion, and with a vehicle for grief…"

• **Full text available on CD-ROM** •

PRIMARY SOURCES *related to Activity 2*

Document 15.2: Image of sixty-five bells from the tomb of Marquis Yi of Zeng (曾侯乙), ca. 433 B.C.E.

The Marquis Yi's tomb was discovered in 1977. It included four burial chambers. Two of these were filled with musical instruments. The collection in the largest central room included these bells. Each had been cast in bronze in an elliptical shape that gives it two tones, depending where it is struck. Each also has descriptive text cast into the bronze with information explaining the bell's pitch and that the set was a gift from the king of Chu.

Document 15.3: Image of thirty-two chime stones from the tomb of Marquis Yi of Zeng (曾侯乙), ca. 433 B.C.E.

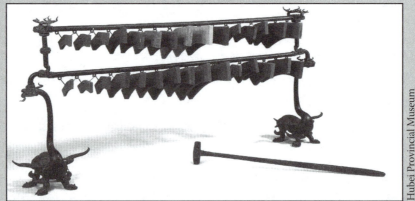

The collection in the largest central room included this set of chimes.

≫ Activity 2: Examining Ceremonial Music in Ancient China

Have students examine documents 15.2 and 15.3 and read additional information about Marquis Yi's tomb online.

Discuss:

- Why do historians believe the instruments were used for ceremonial occasions?
- What kind of technology would be necessary to create the bells? (see Lesson 3 on China's Bronze Age)
- How do the inscriptions on the bells add to our knowledge of that time period and the bells themselves?
- How many musicians do they think played the bells or played the chimes?
- Can they compare the sound of either instrument to any they are familiar with?
- What kinds of ceremonial music do we have? If students are familiar with ceremonial music of other cultures, ask them to share what they know.
- Are there particular instruments we play primarily or exclusively in our ceremonial music?
- What role does ceremonial music play in any culture?
- What do students find most remarkable about these ancient Chinese instruments?

PRIMARY SOURCE related to Activity 3

Document 15.4: Lyrics for "Gentle Girl" in *Shijing* (《诗经》, *The Classic of Poetry*)

A gentle girl and fair
awaits by the crook of the wall;
in shadows I don't see her;
I pace and scratch my hair.

A gentle girl and comely
gave me a scarlet pipe;
scarlet pipe that gleams—
in your beauty I find delight.

Then she brought me a reed from the pastures,
it was truly beautiful and rare.
Reed—the beauty is not yours—
you are but beauty's gift

>> Activity 3: The Role of Folk Music

Explain to students that this folk poem, which also served as the lyrics for songs, dates back to about 600 B.C.E. Read it aloud, and then ask students to read it to themselves. Discuss:

- Who is speaking?
- What is the relationship between the two individuals? What lines suggest this relationship?
- How old might the two individuals be?
- What emotions are present in the lyrics?
- Who or what does the speaker consider beautiful?
- Do these lyrics fall into a particular category of songs? (Love songs, perhaps?)
- Did anything about these lyrics surprise students?
- Ask students if they know of love songs in other cultures. They can explore online to find examples.
- What do all the lyrics appear to have in common? Why do they share certain features?
- Do songwriters today write love songs? Why?

Explain to the class that this is but one of many courtship songs and songs about relationships between men and women in this ancient book of poetry and song lyrics. What can they conclude about the role of songs (and music) in the everyday lives of common people?

PRIMARY SOURCES related to Activity 4

Document 15.5: Mural of dancers and musicians in the Yulin Grottoes (榆林石窟), Tang (唐) dynasty (618–907)

Courtesy of Dunhuang Academy

The Yulin Grottoes are one of five groups of caves in the Dunhuang (敦煌) region of Gansu (甘肃) Province. There are hundreds of caves filled with statues, carvings, and murals. The work of digging out the caves and creating the art, which celebrates Buddhism, began in the 4th century.

Document 15.6: Statues of musical ensemble from a Tang (唐) dynasty tomb

Shaanxi Provincial Museum

This group of figures, each about 3½ inches tall, was discovered in Shaanxi (陕西) Province in 1983.

Document 15.8: Marble relief of musicians from a 10th-century tomb, Hebei (河北) Province

Hebei Provincial Cultural Relics

This painted relief was set into one side of a coffin chamber for a member of the royal family. A complete orchestra is shown, as well as a conductor and two small dancers dressed in Central Asian clothing.

Document 15.7: Ceramic model of a group of musicians on a camel, Tang (唐) dynasty

Shaanxi Provincial Museum

» Activity 4: Musical Ensembles and Influences from Abroad

Divide the students into small groups and have each group examine Document 15.5, 15.6., 15.7, or 15.8. Students should respond to the questions specific to their image (Item 15.B), using Item 15.C for reference (both available on the CD-ROM). Then regroup the students so that each new group has a representative from one of the original groups. Students should share information about their image with the rest of the new group.

Note: If students are not familiar with burial practices of ancient China, explain that people believed that in the afterlife they would need to have with them all that was important in their earthly lives. They buried models of these things with themselves or carved them into the walls of tombs. The more important an individual was, the more things archaeologists have uncovered in the tomb.

Ask students to jot down notes for themselves on all the facts they've learned from these four images about music during the period from about 600 to just after 900. After organizing their notes, they should write a description of music in that time period. Alternatively they can create a poster or a simple picture book for younger students.

PRIMARY SOURCE related to Activity 5

Document 15.9: Close-up of musician playing a *sheng* (笙), from marble relief of musicians in a 10th-century tomb, Hebei (河北) Province

Hebei Provincial Cultural Relics

This painted relief was set into one side of a coffin chamber for a member of the royal family. A complete orchestra (Document 15.8) includes twelve musicians. The *sheng* is one of the oldest instruments in China. It dates back more than 3,000 years. The original *sheng* were made out of gourds; now they're made of wood. According to tradition, the *sheng* was created to imitate the call of a phoenix, itself a legendary bird.

Students can get a sense of traditional Chinese ensemble music by listening to three selections played by twenty-first century musicians. The first is a piece of music from Jiangnan, south of the Yangtze River. Its title is "*Xing jie*" ("Walking on the Street"), and it is most commonly played at events such as festivals or weddings, when people are parading. The second selection, "*Yu Da Ba Jiao*" ("Raindrops falling on banana leaves"), features a solo by a stringed instrument (*gaohu*). It comes from the province of Guangdong. The third piece of music includes a flute (*guanzi*) solo. Its title is "*Fang Lu*" ("Herding donkeys"). Have students listen with their eyes closed. What images or words come to mind as they listen? Ask them to give a title to each selection, and to be ready to explain why they chose it. Compare their titles to the ones provided. Ask students to compare the selections to music with which they are familiar.

» Activity 5: Creative Extension to the Sound of a *Sheng*

Have students examine Document 15.9 and listen to the selection of music (available on the CD-ROM) from Shanxi Province played on a *sheng*, a Chinese mouth organ. As a class discuss the questions that follow:

- Do you know of other instruments that take their shape from a part of a plant?
- How do you think a *sheng* is played? (Answer: The neck serves as a mouthpiece, and the player blows air in and sucks it out while fingering the holes.)
- Do you know of other instruments that are played somewhat like this?
- What images and feelings come to mind when you listen to the *sheng*?

Play the selection of music at least once more. Ask students to listen with their eyes closed and then to write words that come to mind as a result of the music. Ask them to write a poem in response to the music. They can incorporate words they've listed or use them as a launching pad. When students have shared some of their poems with the class, ask them if there are common themes in the poems. Why?

Alternatively, students can create an instrument out of a part of a plant, for example a gourd, reed, bamboo, dried seeds and so on.

PRIMARY SOURCE *related to Activity 6*

Document 15.10: Painting of Emperor Huizong (宋徽宗) playing a qin (琴), Song (宋) dynasty (960–1279)

聽琴圖

Palace Museum, Beijing

Emperor Huizong (1082–1135) is remembered for his love of painting, calligraphy, and music. Here he has painted himself playing a *qin*. This string instrument dates back more than 2,000 years. The oldest ones had up to twenty strings. Confucius was very fond of the *qin*, which probably explains why it was so popular among scholars.

» Activity 6: Examining the Role and Setting of Solo Instruments

Ask students to examine the painting by Emperor Huizong (15.10) and to describe exactly what they see in this picture that is almost 1,000 years old. (Consider each person and what he is doing, the objects and their function, and the natural elements.)

- What words come to mind when students examine the painting as a whole?
- What words come to mind after they listen to a selection of music ("Flowing Water" or "*Liu shui*" is available on the CD-ROM) played on a *qin*? Are they the same types of words? Why yes or no?
- The *qin* was played as a solo instrument. What instruments can students name that are usually played that way?
- Do they know of any instrument in the United States that is only played by the most "educated" people? In other cultures?
- What effect might it have on the way an individual governs a country if he or she is an accomplished artist, be it musician, author, or painter?

Ask students to create a piece of art that represents an individual playing an instrument alone in a setting they feel fits best. Display the art and ask students to share with their classmates their reasoning behind selecting the setting. Discuss what roles solo instruments play in people's lives.

Further Resources for Students and Teachers

Debaine-Francfort, Corinne. *The Search for Ancient China.* Discoveries Harry N. Abrams Publishers, 1998.

Grotenhuis, Elizabeth Ten, ed. *Along the Silk Road.* Washington, D.C: Smithsonian Institute, 2002.

Kah Joon, Liow. *A Musical Journey: From the Great Wall of China to the Water Towns of Jiangnan.* Quebec: SilkRoads Networks, Inc., 2004. (The book includes a CD with 12 lively musical selections representing each of the highlighted regions; some of which are based on folk melodies. Each song is introduced on an appended spread, but the information about each one is brief, and a list of individual instruments played on the track is not included. No textual sources are listed.)

Major, John S. and Jenny F. So. "Music in Late Bronze Age China," in *Music in the Age of Confucius*. Jenny F. So, ed. Freer Gallery of Art and Arthur M. Sackler Gallery, Washington, D.C: Smithsonian Institution, 2000.

McLean, Jacqueline. "Confucius's Influence on Chinese Music," *Calliope*, Cobblestone Publishing, Inc., Oct. 1998.

Web Sites

http://teachers.silkroadproject.org (extensive lessons on aspects of the Silk Road, including one on music)

http://www.china.org.cn/english/travel/42101.htm (information on the Dunhuang Grottoes)

For descriptions of Chinese instruments:

http://www.paulnoll.com/China/Music/China-musical-instruments.html

http://depts.washington.edu/chinaciv/archae/2marmusi.htm

For information about the Tomb of Marquis Yi:

http://depts.washington.edu/chinaciv/archae/2marmain.htm,

http://www.nga.gov/education/chinatp_s111.htm, and

http://www.archaeology.org/0005/etc/museum1.html

In the World Today

The Silk Road Project

In 1998, world-renowned cellist Yo-Yo Ma founded the Silk Road Project. His goal was to "study the ebb and flow of ideas among different cultures" along the historic trade route between Asia and Europe, to "plant the seeds of new artistic and cultural growth, and to celebrate living traditions and musical voices throughout the world." The Project acts as an umbrella organization for a number of artistic, cultural, and educational programs. In recent years, Silk Road Ensembles have performed all over the world, including Carnegie Hall in New York, and other localities in the United States, Singapore, and the United Kingdom. In 2002, in partnership with the Smithsonian Institution, the Project recorded a two-CD set "The Silk Road: A Musical Caravan." Encourage students to explore the myriad ways that music travels among cultures. Ask them to bring in music selections and discover their roots. For further information on the Silk Road Project see http://www.silkroadproject.org.

Lesson 16 CD-ROM Contents

Primary Sources

- Document 16.1a–f: Photographs of the Great Wall (长城)

- Document 16.2: Excerpt from *Records of the Historian* (*Shiji*, 《史记》) by Sima Qian (司马迁), written between 105 and 90 B.C.E., describing the Qin (秦) emperor's projects

- Document 16.3: "Song: I Watered My Horse at the Long Wall Caves" (《饮马长城窟行》), a poem by Chen Lin (陈琳) from 207 C.E.

- Document 16.4: Images of *hangtu* (夯土) (tamped earth) construction from the 4th and 20th centuries

- Document 16.5a and b: Images from a scroll painting "Kangxi Emperor's Southern Inspection Tour" (《康熙南巡图》), Scroll 7, by Wang Hui (王翬), 1698

Supplementary Materials

- Item 16.A: Additional vocabulary for primary sources
- Item 16.B: Table of measurement
- Item 16.C: Foreign currency exchange tables
- Item 16.D: Maps of the Great Wall during four dynasties

Lesson 16
Public Works and Centralization Projects

By Peter Lowber

Lesson Contents

- Dujiangyan irrigation project
- Qin Shi Huangdi
- The Great Wall
- Standardization decrees
- The Grand Canal

Chinese history is marked by periods of unification under strong empires and fragmentation. During the periods of unification, the dynastic emperors created huge central bureaucracies, which often executed expansive public works projects, like the Great Wall (长城) and the Grand Canal (大运河). Yet, curiously, one of the most successful projects—the Dujiangyan (都江堰) irrigation project—took place during a period when various Chinese kingdoms were at war with each other. It has continued to function well for more than 2,000 years.

The Dujiangyan Irrigation Project

Li Bing (李冰), governor of a region near Chengdu (成都) (in present day Sichuan Province, 四川) began an extensive flood prevention and irrigation project in 256 B.C.E., and his son, Er Lang (二郎), completed it. Li Bing's goal was to manage the Minjiang River (岷江), the longest tributary of the Yangtze (长江). The Chengdu plain was an area often affected by the extremes of flood or drought. Li Bing had men divide the river by building a long bank in the middle. The inner river was directed into a canal dug through Mount Yulei. It served to irrigate thousands of acres of land. In the outer river, Li Bing ordered weirs built (out of bamboo cages filled with stones) to harness the river when it flowed high. He also put in place an annual maintenance plan to remove silt buildup. The plain has stayed almost completely free of floods and drought since the project was completed. Farmers can grow up to four crops a year on the same land, earning Sichuan Province the name "land of abundance" (天府之国). The Dujiangyan project continues to be maintained and enlarged.

The Great Wall

Most of the original Great Wall was constructed in a brief period during the Qin (秦) dynasty (221–206 B.C.E.). King Zheng named himself Shi Huangdi (始皇帝)—first august emperor—after he led the Qin to military victories over the states of Han, Zhao, Wi, Chu, Yan, and Qi—thus ending the Warring States Period. Shi Huangdi united the country by abolishing the aristocracy and creating a vast central bureaucracy. To further demonstrate his power and control, and to keep out the Xiongnu (匈奴) invaders to the northwest, he initiated the Great Wall construction project, which, incredibly, was completed in eleven years. The Great Wall stretched for about 2,600 miles. It incorporated about 500 miles of walls that had been constructed by individual states during the Warring States Period (战国时期), but the remaining 2,100 miles or so represented new construction.

Though it was a remarkable engineering feat, Qin Shi Huangdi's Great Wall was built at great human cost. Meng Tian (蒙恬), an adviser and military commander who organized over a million men to build the wall, wrote an account of its construction. Peasants and others too poor to pay taxes were forcibly conscripted to build the wall. Convicts worked on it while wearing chains. Historians estimate that between four hundred thousand and one million men died building the wall. Those with power and wealth may have benefited, but those with neither suffered. Indeed the great abuses during Qin Shi Huangdi's reign undermined the strength of the Qin dynasty, leading to its rapid decline and fall after his sudden death in 206 B.C.E.

For the next 1,500 years, some repairs were made on the wall, but generally its condition deteriorated. Much of the Great Wall that exists today was built in the Ming (明) dynasty over a 276-year period from 1368 to 1644. Its purpose was to keep out the Mongols and to establish control. The Ming wall was about 3,000 miles long. Though much of it was new, it followed the course of the Great Wall it replaced.

Standardization Decrees

Though his greatest triumph, the Great Wall was not the only measure of achievement during Qin Shi Huangdi's reign. Like Napoleon in Europe 2,000 years later, he extended his power and influence by standardizing weights and measures, and building roads. Also like Napoleon, he accomplished his goals through absolute power. Qin Shi Huangdi was a dictator who tolerated no dissent. Recognizing the power of the written word, he decreed that all non-legalist philosophical books be burned, saving only technical books on subjects such as agriculture and medicine.

By imperial decree, Qin Shi Huangdi standardized writing, into one seal script (see Lesson 5) weights; measures; money, and the axle width of carriages. Besides the Great Wall, he also ordered the construction of an elaborate network of roads. (For additional information about Qin Shi Huangdi, see Lesson 4.)

The Grand Canal

Built in the Sui (隋) dynasty (581–618), the Grand Canal, which now extends over 1,100 miles in eastern China from Hangzhou (杭州) north to Beijing (北京) is still the largest man-made waterway in the world—far surpassing the Erie, Suez and Panama canals. Like the Qin dynasty, the Sui dynasty was a period of unification after centuries of disintegration. The Sui also strengthened and standardized institutions of political control, including a strong central bureaucracy and military.

In 604–610, Emperor Yangdi (隋炀帝), had the canal sections that had already been built integrated and ordered construction of new sections to greatly expand the canal. The Grand Canal interconnected the great rivers that run from western to eastern China—the Yangzi, Yellow, Huai, Hai, and Qiantang rivers. Eventually the canal connected the cities of Beijing, Tianjin, Hebei, Shandong, Jiangsu, and Hangzhou at its southernmost end. More than 2,000 years old, some parts of the Grand Canal are still in use today.

The Grand Canal enabled the imperial power to extract levies of grain and cloth from the fertile east central region of China. First it connected this region with Chang'an (present day Xi'an), which was the capital during the Sui dynasty. Later, during the Ming dynasty it connected the fertile region with the new capital, Beijing. The canal also created a thriving economy, allowing for the transportation and trade of up to 200,000 tons of rice per year, as well as all kinds of other goods (clothing, fruits, fish, meat, cooking oil, sugar, porcelain, bamboo, timber, mineral ores, etc.). Like the Great Wall, however, its construction resulted in enormous human suffering. Of the 600,000 peasants who were conscripted to build it, almost half died during construction.

Note: This lesson will be more meaningful to students if they are familiar with the geography of China (see Lesson 2).

Organizing Idea

Great public works projects like the Great Wall and the Grand Canal over time become mythical and symbolic representations of empire. Although these projects were incredible accomplishments, they came at great human cost. The Dujiangyan project, on the other hand, the oldest of the three, has benefited people for more than 2,000 years.

Student Objectives

Students will:

- understand the value of standardized measurements
- explain the historical, geographic, cultural, political, and social significance of the Dujiangyan irrigation project, the Great Wall, and the Grand Canal
- understand the human cost and benefits of massive public works projects
- understand ways in which rulers consolidate power

Key Questions

- Why was the Dujiangyan irrigation project begun?
- What is its significance?
- Why and how was the Great Wall built?
- Who built the wall, and what was the impact on the people who built it?
- During which dynasties were the Great Wall and Grand Canal built?
- Why was the Grand Canal built?
- What was life like along the Grand Canal?
- What is the significance of the Great Wall today?
- What were the moral choices posed by the Great Wall?

Vocabulary

aristocracy
empire
hangtu
Huangdi
irrigation
li (measure of distance)
Xiongnu

Supplementary Materials

Item 16.A: Additional vocabulary for primary sources
Item 16.B: Table of measurement
Item 16.C: Foreign currency exchange tables
Item 16.D: Maps of the Great Wall during four dynasties

Student Activities

» Activity 1: Exploring the Impact of Standardization

Explain that during the period of the Warring States (475 B.C.E.–221 B.C.E.), there were different standards for writing, measurements, and money. When Qin Shi Huangdi conquered these states in 221 B.C.E., he changed this.

Ask the class whether different units of measurement exist today. They may only be familiar with the U.S. units of inches, miles, ounces, and pounds. Point out that most of the world uses the metric system (centimeters, kilometers, grams, kilograms, and liters). Have them look at Item 16.B (available on the CD-ROM), Tables of Measurement. Ask the students:

- Which system of measurement would they choose for a single standard? Why?
- What are the advantages of having standard weights and measures?
- How might standardization of measurements have made the building of the Great Wall more efficient in 200 B.C.E.?

Divide the class into pairs, and assign each pair a country from the list on Foreign Currency Exchange Tables (Item 16.C). Distribute copies of the tables.

Tell the students they are traveling in China by car. The task of each student pair is to calculate how much money in their own country's currency it will cost them to fill up their car with gas. It costs 250 Chinese yuan to fill up the car. The currency table is standardized according to the Chinese *yuan*.

Create a table on the board of the cost to fill up a tank of gas as expressed in each currency. The teacher lists the cost in *yuan* first. Then have each pair write the amount in their country's currency on the board. What difficulties are created by having these different currencies? Now ask students to imagine they are living in China during the Warring States Period. Each state has its own currency.

- What kinds of problems might that create?
- How might these different currencies affect trade and economics?
- Why do they think Qin Shi Huangdi standardized currency in China once he conquered all the states?

Tell students that regarding currency, Europe today is like China under Qin Shi Huangdi. Europeans are accustomed to traveling in different European countries and, until recently, each time they crossed a border, they were faced with a different currency. France had the franc, England the pound, Germany the mark, Italy the lira, and so on. In 2000, Europe adopted the euro as a standard currency. If you go to Europe today in most countries you will pay in euros. Ask the class if they think something has been lost. Has abolishing individual countries' currencies diminished local culture?

PRIMARY SOURCES related to Activity 2
Document 16.1a–f: Photographs of the Great Wall (长城)

Photo by Pamela Tuffley

This section of the Great Wall is in Mutianyu, northeast of Beijing.

• *Additional photographs of the Great Wall are available on the CD-ROM* •

>> Activity 2: Learning about Walls Around the World

Write the following question on the board: "What are some uses of walls throughout history?" Have students write their responses in their notebooks. Elicit their responses and write them on the board. Have students take notes on these responses.

Then show students pictures of walls in history (see resource list). Consider including the Great Wall of China, the Berlin Wall, the Vietnam War Memorial, Hadrian's Wall, a city wall (for example, of Carcassone, Xi'an, or Pingyao), and the Wailing Wall in Jerusalem, among others.

Assign each student a number from 1-6. For homework, students will research the wall they have been assigned. (For example, all "1's" learn about the Berlin Wall; all "2's" about the Vietnam War Memorial, and so on. Do not include the Great Wall in this exercise.) They are to write a brief report on when the wall was built, why it was built, and the significance of the wall today, if any. (www.wikipedia.org is an excellent resource for this assignment.)

During the following class period, have students form groups according to the wall they researched. Each group discusses their findings and a note taker records them. Another group member presents the findings to the class, and a third person writes the findings on the board.

When all the groups have finished their presentations, the teacher should facilitate a class discussion on the similarities and differences of these historic walls.

Now introduce the Great Wall of China (and the other major Chinese public works projects) by having the students read the introduction to the lesson or by sharing the information with them. Show photographs of the Great Wall taken in the past decade (Document 1a–f). Tell the students many more photographs are online (see Web sites in the resource list). Encourage them to take notes and to ask questions.

» Activity 3: Mapping Exercise

In order to successfully do this activity, students should be familiar with China's geography (see Lesson 2), in particular the country's topography. Each student should have colored pencils, copies of a blank map of China (available in Teacher Resources on the CD-ROM), and maps showing the Walls of the Warring States (475 B.C.E.–221 B.C.E.), the Great Wall of Qin Shi Huangdi (221 B.C.E.–210 B.C.E.), the Ming Wall, and the Grand Canal of the Ming dynasty (Item 16.D).

Encarta's desktop mapping tool is a good resource if it is possible to display it. Review China's major rivers, mountain ranges, desert, and bordering countries. Place Beijing, Hangzhou, and Chengdu on the outline map. Have students work in small groups so they can help each other, or independently if they prefer, but each student should have his or her own map. They will create maps that show the Minjiang River and Chengdu Plain, the Great Wall(s), and the completed Grand Canal. Student will need to:

- add the Minjiang River to their maps and identify where the Dujiangyan project began
- create a legend key identifying the walls of the Warring States, the Great Wall of Qin Shi Huangdi, and the Ming Wall. A different color for each helps.
- include the time periods for each wall in their legend keys. (Emphasize the huge amount of time that elapsed between the Warring States Period, the Qin, and the Ming dynasties.)
- plot the walls on the blank map
- add the Grand Canal

The teacher may wish to make his or her own map and show a transparency of it on an overhead projector. Alternatively students can create a Big Map for the classroom. (See Teacher Resources on the CD-ROM for instructions on how to make Big Maps.)

In the following class period, conduct a class discussion about the maps and the photographs students have seen, what they know about the three projects, and their observations. Have students write their observations, and those of the class, in their notebooks. To stimulate their thinking, you might ask:

- In what terrain was the Dujiangyan project done?
- What was its purpose?
- How successful was it then and has it been since?
- What kind of terrain does the Great Wall cover?
- Given that some of the terrain is extremely harsh, why was the wall built there?
- What purposes might the Great Wall have served? (Note that one of the silk routes ran along the Great Wall for a fair distance. Why?)
- What purposes did the Grand Canal serve?
- Why might it have been built where it was?
- What questions do students have and where can they find the answers?

PRIMARY SOURCES related to Activity 4

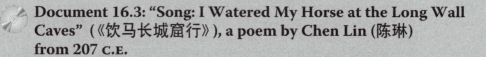

Document 16.2: Excerpt from *Records of the Historian* (*Shiji*, 《史记》) by Sima Qian (司马迁), written between 105 and 90 B.C.E., describing the Qin (秦) emperor's projects

[T]he First Emperor of Qin dispatched Meng Tian, to lead a force of a hundred thousand men north to attack the barbarians. He seized control of all the lands south of the Yellow River and established border defenses along the river, constructing forty-four walled district cities overlooking the river and manning them with convict laborers transported to the border for garrison duty. He also built the Direct Road from Chiuyuan to Yunyang. Thus he utilized the natural mountain barriers to establish the border defenses, scooping out the valleys and constructing ramparts and building installations at other points where they were needed. The whole line of defenses stretched over ten thousand *li* from Lintao to Liaodong and even extended across the Yellow River and through Yangshan and Beijia…

• Full text available on CD-ROM •

Document 16.3: "Song: I Watered My Horse at the Long Wall Caves" (《饮马长城窟行》), a poem by Chen Lin (陈琳) from 207 C.E.

I watered my horse at the Long Wall caves,
water so cold it hurt his bones;
I went and spoke to the Long Wall boss:
"We're soldiers from Taiyuan—Will you keep us here
   forever?"
"Public works go according to schedule—
swing your hammer, pitch your voice in with the rest!"
A man would be better off to die in battle
than eat his heart out building the Long Wall!
The Long Wall—how it winds and winds,
winds and winds three thousand *li*;
here on the border, so many strong boys;
in the houses back home, so many widows and wives.

• Full text available on CD-ROM •

>> Activity 4: Reliving the Period When the Great Wall Was First Built

Distribute copies of Documents 16.2 and 16.3. Divide the class into groups of four and assign each group one paragraph of Sima Qian's history or sections from the poem to read. Ask each group to paraphrase their reading and then explain its meaning to the class. Ask them whether it matters that these documents were written hundreds of years after the wall was built? What does it suggest about people's experience that so many generations later, others were still writing about it?

To get a full understanding of the poem, students should consider the following questions:

- The poem is written in the first person. Who is this person? How do you know?
- How do we know that the poem is about the building of the wall? Be specific.

There are several places in the poem where the soldier expresses his emotions about building the wall. Write down in your own words what emotions he expresses, and quote some lines in the poem to demonstrate this.

- Why does the soldier tell his wife to remarry?
- Why does he tell his wife to bear only daughters?

As a final exercise, each student will read the primary sources in their entirety. Using what they have learned from these documents, have the students write a summary of the Great Wall under Qin Shi Huangdi. Students are to explain the historic change that happened under Qin Shi Huangdi (paragraph one), the purpose and breadth of the Great Wall (paragraph two), the difficulties faced by the people (paragraph three), and the problem of supplying provisions (paragraph four).

Document 16.1e: Great Wall (长城) at its western end in Jiayuguan, Gansu Province

Photo by Renee Covalucci

• Additional photographs of the Great Wall are available on the CD-ROM •

PRIMARY SOURCE *related to Activity 5*

Document 16.4: Images of *hangtu* (夯土) (tamped earth) construction from the 4th and 20th centuries

Courtesy of Ronald Knapp

Photo by Robert E. Murowchick

This method of wall construction was used from at least 300 B.C.E. through the Ming (明) dynasty (1368–1644). The name comes from two Chinese words: *hang* (夯), meaning pounded or beaten, and *tu* (土), which means earth.

» Activity 5: Learning How the Great Wall was Built

Distribute copies showing *hangtu* construction (Document 16.4) and either show photographs of the Great Wall on the screen or have students look at their own copies. Students will need large sheets of drawing paper. Explain to the class that the essential construction method that Chinese workers used to build walls from at least 3000 B.C.E. during the Neolithic period through the Ming dynasty was called *hangtu*. The *hangtu* method is still used today to build homes in some regions of China. Ask students to look at the images of *hangtu* construction. (While these show a house being built, the same method was used to build the Great Wall.)

• How does the *hangtu* method appear to be done?

(Answer: Workers would construct a frame of bamboo or wood. The frame would include a mould a few inches thick. Workers would pour a few inches of earth into the mould and pound the earth with thick wooden sticks until it was almost solid. They would thus build the wall one layer at a time.)

- How did the workers get the earth to the point of construction? What equipment existed more than 2,000 years ago?

(Answer: During Qin Shi Huangdi's reign it is likely that thousands of workers would form a line and hand baskets of earth, stones, and pieces of bamboo or wood along the line to the point where the wall was being built. By the time of the Ming dynasty, the wheelbarrow had been invented, so that made transporting the earth easier.)

- How were building materials moved in the mountains?

(Answer: Workers used ropes and baskets to pull up earth and stones.)

- Can they tell on the photographs how tall and wide the walls were?

(Answer: The wall built during the Ming dynasty was typically thirty feet [nine meters] high and twenty to thirty feet [six to nine meters] wide on top.)

- How might the construction materials have varied, considering the changing geography—from desert (in the west), to the plains (central region), to the mountains (in the northeast)?

(Answer: On high mountains, stones were used with earth; on the plains, earth was used; in the desert, walls were built using reeds and tamarisk twigs layered with sand.)

- How were workers able to survive attacks from invaders, like the Xiongnu?

(Answer: Under Qin Shi Huangdi, at least 300,000 soldiers protected the workers while they were building the Great Wall. The Great Wall also included gates that were guarded by the soldiers, watch towers to spot invaders, and signal towers to send smoke signals to warn others of invaders.)

- What were the differences between the Great Wall built during Qin Shi Huangdi's reign, and the Great Wall built during the Ming dynasty between 1368 C.E. and 1644 C.E.?

(Answer: The hangtu *was the basic construction method for building the walls, but the Ming period had the advantage of some technology breakthroughs like the wheelbarrow and the pulley system, making it easier to lift heavy baskets of earth and stones up mountains, and to the top of the wall as the wall grew higher during construction. In addition, the Ming dynasty also had the kiln. The Ming Great Wall was covered with bricks, making it much stronger than the original wall. The bricks were made of earth that was baked in kilns that were erected at the point of construction.*

Another innovation of the Ming Wall was the inclusion of drains. This was very important—the drains kept water in the winter from gathering and freezing within the walls, which would have caused rapid deterioration (see Document 16.1f).

By the 1500s quarrying techniques had been developed, making it easier to cut and transport stone. So the workers building the Ming Wall also had the ability to use these cut stones to build more effective walls and towers in the mountain regions. The signal stations allowed soldiers on guard to send a smoke signal to warn soldiers at other stations or towers that invaders were coming.)

Finally divide the class into pairs. Based on the preceding discussion and the images, each pair is to make drawings on a large sheet of paper. The drawings will include: the *hangtu* method, a section of the wall itself (showing the wall and a tower or signal station), and at least three innovations from the Ming dynasty. All drawings should be labeled, and should include a title for the project. Excellent projects will include details like the drains that the Ming used. Have students share their drawings, explaining them to the class.

PRIMARY SOURCE *related to Activity 6*

Document 16.5a and b: Images from a scroll painting "Kangxi Emperor's Southern Inspection Tour" (《康熙南巡图》), Scroll 7, by Wang Hui (王翚), 1698

This section shows the Chang Gate of Suzhou (苏州).

Suzhou (苏州), Jiangsu (江苏) Province.

» Activity 6: A Day on the Grand Canal

Show the class the video *A Day on the Grand Canal*, created by David Hockney and Philip Haas (see Resource list for information). This video is about a seventy-foot-long scroll that was painted in 1698. It was commissioned by the emperor to show his journey on the Grand Canal. The video is forty-four minutes long. David Hockney explains the scroll "frame by frame." He shows about three feet (a meter) of the scroll at a time. As he shows the scroll, have students jot down in their notebook what they observe. (You will want to pause the video at different points.) For example, they might write down: fish merchant, cattle, ducks, rice merchant, vegetable garden, horses, canal boats, building homes, tiling roofs, three non-Chinese merchants, and so on. This scroll is an incredibly rich representation of the social and economic life of the Chinese people in 1698. In addition, distribute copies of two sections of the scroll (Document 16.5a and b). This allows students to spend lots of time studying the details. (Additional images can be found at http://worldart.sjsu.edu.)

In the class period following the showing of the video, have the students share their observations. The teacher should summarize these observations, and also emphasize that every Chinese person in the scroll (and there are hundreds, maybe thousands of them) is portrayed as an individual. People of all ages, occupations, men and women, and some religions (Buddhist monks) are portrayed. And the emperor is portrayed like any other person. He is the same size as his subjects and is modest in his dress.

Ask students to imagine they are traveling down the Grand Canal. Have them write a diary of one day's experiences and observations. Or they can be an individual living in a town along the Grand Canal. They should write about what they did on that day, and what they observed around them and on the canal. Ask them to illustrate their writing. Their final product should demonstrate what they have learned about the social and economic lives of Chinese people living by the Grand Canal in the 17th century.

» Activity 7: A Debate: Were the Projects Worth the Human Cost?

This activity is best done in conjunction with Lesson 19 about how the Chinese interacted with their nomadic neighbors. Throughout history, political leaders of great empires have reduced their enemies to negative stereotypes. In doing so, there is no need to foster understanding or to seek reconciliation, and it makes it easy to justify war and killing. The United States is no exception. American Indians were called "savages," and it was easier to justify their near extermination. Chinese history had a similar experience. The Great Wall was built to keep out the "barbarians."

- Who were the barbarians?
- Do walls like the Great Wall create "national security," or do they create ethnic divisions and hostility?
- What if the Great Wall had never been built or if it had been torn down?

Given all they have learned about three monumental public works projects in China, ask the students to take a stand: Was either the Great Wall or the Grand Canal worth the human cost? We don't have information about the human cost of the Dujiangyan project, but does it appear to have been worth doing? Students will need to select which of the building projects they wish to address. Then they will prepare their arguments for a debate in class. Alternatively, students can be assigned a paper, where they present an argument for or against the Dujiangyan irrigation project, the Great Wall, or the Grand Canal. It might be interesting to note that between 1991 and 2006 when the Big Dig construction project took place in Boston—the largest public works project in U.S. history—two individuals died on the job.

Further Resources for Students and Teachers

DuTemple, Lesley. *The Great Wall of China*. Minneapolis: Lerner Public Co., 2003.

Jan, Michael (text), Michaud, Roland and Sabrina (photography). *The Great Wall of China*. New York: Abeville Press, 2001.

Luo, Zhewen and Zhao Luo. *The Great Wall of China in History and Legend*. Beijing: Foreign Language Press, 1986.

McNeese, Tim. *The Great Wall of China*. San Diego: Lucent Books, 1997.

Pin, Liao, ed. *The Grand Canal—An Odyssey*. Beijing: Foreign Language Press, 1987.

Video

A Day on the Grand Canal. A Milestone Video release. A film by David Hockney and Philip Haas, 1988. (available at Milestonefilms.com and Amazon.com)

Web Sites

For the Dujiangyan irrigation project:

http://www.regenttour.com/chinaplanner/ctu/ctu-sights-dujiangyan.htm

http://www.travelchinaguide.com/attraction/sichuan/chengdu/dujiangyan.htm

For the Great Wall:

http://www.chinahighlights.com/beijing/greatwall1.htm (designed for tourists with some good pictures of the Great Wall as it looks today)

http://www.travelchinaguide.com/china_great_wall/ (brief, historical overview of the Great Wall, and an excellent source for details and pictures about the construction of the Wall in the Qin, Han and Ming dynasties)

http://library.thinkquest.org/20443/greatwall.html (concise overview of the Great Wall of China, with photos)

http://www.thebeijingguide.com/great_wall_of_china/ (interactive panoramic view of the wall; gives you the feeling of walking on the wall and is accompanied by Chinese flute music.)

http://en.wikipedia.org/wiki/Great_Wall_of_China (Wikipedia's history of the Great Wall is an excellent summary; it also includes pictures.)

http://encarta.msn.com/encyclopedia_761569621/Great_Wall_(China).html (article describing the myth of the Great Wall)

http://www.travelchinaguide.com/picture/china_great_wall/ (map of the Great Wall, with pictures of the wall from each geographic area)

For the Grand Canal:

http://www.asianartmall.com/grandcanalarticle.htm (excellent high-level overview)

http://en.wikipedia.org/wiki/Grand_Canal_of_China

http://encarta.msn.com/map_701512661/Grand_Canal_(China).html (an interactive map)

http://artworld.uea.ac.uk/teaching_modules/china/spatial/inland/welcome.html (detailed analysis of the Grand Canal's design, engineering, and commercial purposes)

http://www.asiasociety.org/arts/chinaphotos/ketchum.html (Robert Glenn Ketchum's photos of Suzhou [the "Venice" of China] on the Grand Canal)

Elsewhere in the World

Around the time that Li Bing was directing the Dujiangyan project and forty years later when Qin Shi Huangdi was building the Great Wall:

• **In the Second Punic War, Rome fought against Carthage (218 B.C.E.–202 B.C.E.).**

• **Paracas culture was thriving in Peru (700 B.C.E.–200 B.C.E.).**

• **Latin drama emerged with Plautus (225 B.C.E.–184 B.C.E.).**

• **Eratosthenes, Greek scientist and mathematician, was alive (276 B.C.E.–194 B.C.E.).**

When the Grand Canal was built (604–610 C.E.) during the Sui dynasty:

• **The Mayan civilization in Central America was in its classical period (250–850 C.E.).**

• **Prophet Mohammed, founder of Islam was alive (570–632 C.E.).**

During the Ming dynasty (1368–1644 C.E.):

• **Gutenberg invented the printing press in Germany in 1455.**

• **Columbus sailed to America in 1492.**

• **The Spanish Inquisition took place in 1492.**

• **The Sultan Mohammed II's mosque was constructed in 1496.**

• **The Spanish conquered the Aztecs in Mexico and the Incas in Peru in the 1500s.**

• **The Russians conquered Siberia (1581–1598).**

• **The English established colonies in North America in the early 1600s.**

In the World Today

Building the Transcontinental Railway

The first Transcontinental Railway, completed in 1869, could not have been accomplished without the Chinese. The Central Pacific Railroad Co. was established in 1863 to build the railroad east from Sacramento over the Sierra Nevada Mountains to Utah, but there was no labor force available in California to build it. There was no practical way of shipping thousands of European immigrants to California, so the labor supply had to come from elsewhere. Railroad magnates turned their attention across the Pacific and recruited thousands of Chinese men. Racist attitudes abounded. One supervisor was furious when ordered to hire them: "I will not boss Chinese. I will not be responsible for work done on the road by Chinese labor. From what I've seen of them, they're not fit laborers anyway. I don't think they can build a railroad."

The Chinese brought with them skills passed from generation to generation since the time of building the initial Great Wall over 2,000 years ago. There was no heavy machinery to traverse the Sierra Nevada, but the Chinese could navigate their way around transporting rocks and materials using ropes and baskets.

More than 13,000 Chinese men built the Transcontinental Railway from Sacramento to Utah. Over 3,000 died. Many Chinese froze during the harsh winter in the Sierras because they did not have winter clothing, and the railroad owners did not supply them with the clothing they needed.

Despite the recognition the Chinese workers won from some of the white railroad men, racism pervaded the country. In a famous photograph showing railroad officials and workers commemorating the completion of the Transcontinental Railway in Promontory, Utah, in 1869, not a single Chinese worker is visible.

Refer to the http://cprr.org/Museum/Fusang.html for further information. Discuss as a class how the Chinese contributed to the Transcontinental Railway and the significance of their experience with huge public works projects.

Note: Refer back to "In the World Today" in Lesson 2, which introduces the Three Gorges Dam project. Students can also compare and contrast that with the three projects discussed in this lesson.

Lesson 17 CD-ROM Contents

Primary Sources

- Document 17.1: Image of rider on a horse, Tang (唐) dynasty (618–907 c.e.)
- Document 17.2: Image of brick relief found in a Han (汉) dynasty tomb (202 b.c.e.–220 c.e.)
- Document 17.3: Model of the earliest known compass

Supplementary Materials

- Item 17.A: Instructions for making paper
- Item 17.B: Instructions for making a compass
- Item 17.C: A list of Chinese inventions and innovations

Lesson 17
Inventions and Innovations

"One of the greatest untold secrets of history is that the 'modern world' in which we live is a unique synthesis of Chinese and Western ingredients. Possibly more than half of the basic inventions and discoveries upon which the modern world rests come from China" (Temple, p. 9). For centuries the Chinese knew more about technology, astronomy, and health than any other civilization on earth. Of the many Chinese contributions, arguably the single most important one is their invention of paper.

The earliest surviving bit of paper-like material was found in a tomb and dates back to the reign of the Han emperor Wu (汉武帝) (140–87 B.C.E.). At first, paper was not used for writing. Instead, people made clothes out of thick paper—jackets, hats, and shoes. They also used it for blankets and even as protective armor.

Paper used for writing was produced in 105 C.E., during the later Han (汉) dynasty under the direction of an inspector of public works called Cai Lun (蔡伦). For centuries the Chinese had been writing on silk, bamboo, or wooden strips (see Lesson 5). Like many others, Cai Lun recognized that writing on silk was expensive and that documents written on bamboo strips tied together were very heavy. He set out to create a more practical material.

The material that he and his staff invented was made by boiling and pounding bits of tree bark, hemp, old rags, and fishnets to make a rather sticky, pulpy paste, mixing it in a vat of water, and then lifting out a thin layer onto a screen. The water drained away, leaving a layer suitable to write on once it had dried. The most important use for this paper was to record government business and to send letters.

After the Han dynasty ended (220 C.E.), this method of papermaking spread first throughout China and then beyond. It soon reached Korea and Vietnam. In the seventh century, Japan and India were making paper. In the following three centuries, papermaking made its way through the Muslim world in Central Asia and West Asia into Europe. Spain set up a paper factory in 1150. More than 1,000 years after the Chinese had first invented paper, it spread through Western Europe.

The creation of paper is but one of many technological advances originating in China. In his book, *The Genius of China*, Robert Temple argues: "The technological world of today is a product of both East and West to an extent which until recently no one had ever imagined. It is now time for the Chinese contribution to be recognized and acknowledged, by East and West alike" (p. 12).

Note: This lesson lends itself to an interdisciplinary approach with a science teacher.

Organizing Idea

China was a technologically advanced country between 2,500 and 400 years ago. Much of mankind's progress is based on Chinese inventions.

Student Objectives

Students will:

- gain insight into the invention of what we now see as very simple things
- understand how and why early paper was made
- learn how to make paper
- construct a simple water compass
- each be responsible for researching and presenting one Chinese invention
- learn about dozens of Chinese inventions and their significance to human progress

Key Questions

- Why was the invention of paper important to civilization?
- What is the significance of the invention of the compass?
- How have inventions originating in ancient China influenced events in world history?

Supplementary Materials

Item 17.A: Instructions for making paper
Item 17.B: Instructions for making a compass
Item 17.C: A list of Chinese inventions and innovations

Student Activities

PRIMARY SOURCES related to Activity 1

Document 17.1: Image of rider on a horse, Tang (唐) dynasty (618–907 C.E.)

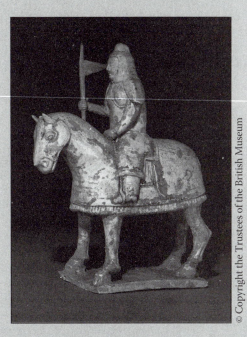

Document 17.2: Image of brick relief found in a Han (汉) dynasty tomb (202 B.C.E.–220 C.E.)

>> Activity 1: Brainstorming Inventions

Throughout this activity, it is helpful to record student responses on the board. Ask students to define "invention." Distribute copies of Documents 17.1 and 17.2. Ask students what in each image might be a significant invention. (Answer: the stirrup and the wheelbarrow.) Do these fit their definitions of an invention? Suggest that they modify their definitions if need be. How have these things—stirrups and the wheelbarrow—helped people for centuries? (If students have learned about the Great Wall in Lesson 16, they might remember that wheelbarrows were used to build it.) Evidence exists that the Chinese used wheelbarrows in the 1st century B.C.E., while in Europe they did not exist until the 11th or 12th century C.E. A pottery figure from 302 C.E. shows that stirrups existed in China by that date. The earliest mention in Europe is in a text from 580 C.E.

As a class, brainstorm a list of everyday inventions and then ask students to speculate where each invention originated. Why do they think the object was invented in that place? Ask students if they know of any Chinese inventions? Invite them to use books and/or the Internet to verify their ideas about the origin of certain inventions.

Ask students when and by whom paper was invented. Then brainstorm a list of things in the classroom and in their homes that are made out of paper. What important documents are made of paper? Where does paper come from? Share the information in the lesson introduction with the class.

>> Activity 2: Paper Making

Have students work in pairs or groups of three to create their own paper. Detailed instructions are available on the CD-ROM (Item 17.A).

PRIMARY SOURCE related to Activity 3
Document 17.3: Model of the earliest known compass

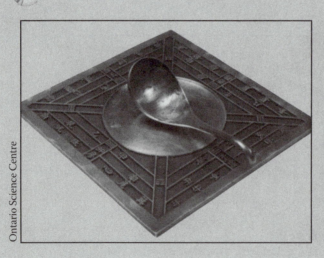

Ontario Science Centre

A section of a stone relief dating back to 114 C.E. shows a figure looking at a compass such as is shown in this model. The ancient compass had a spoon made of magnetic lodestone resting on a bronze plate. The circle in the center represents heaven and the square is symbolic of earth. The eight directions—north, south, east, west, northeast, northwest, southeast, and southwest—are written in Chinese characters. The handle of the spoon points south.

>> Activity 3: Making a Compass

Note: See Item 17.B for list of materials necessary to complete this activity.

Distribute copies of Document 17.3 or show it on a screen. Ask students to speculate what this might be. If no one guesses, tell the class it's a compass. The spoon is a magnetic lodestone and it rests in a smooth bronze plate. Explain that though the origin of the compass is not clear, there is mention of one in a Chinese text, *Book of the Devil Valley Master*, from the 4th century B.C.E. It says, "When the people of Cheng go out to collect jade, they carry a south-pointer with them so as not to lose their way."

The magnetic piece of lodestone and later the needle on all compasses is aligned north-south. In Western cultures, the needle is marked so that north is what is considered of interest. Chinese compasses emphasize the end of the needle that points south. That is primarily because compasses were used in siting buildings and graves, and south was the direction that the Chinese believed they should face. (See Lesson 11 for information about *fengshui.*)

A description in a 6th-century book suggests that the first compass that had a needle was made by 570 C.E. An 11th-century essay exists describing a compass: "Magicians rub the point of a needle with the lodestone; then it is able to point to the south...It may be balanced on the fingernail, or on the rim of a cup, where it can be made to turn more easily, but these supports being hard and smooth, it is liable to fall off. It is best to suspend it by a single cocoon fiber of new silk attached to the center of the needle by a piece of wax the size of a mustard seed, then, hanging in a windless place, it will always point to the south" (*Dream Pool Essays* by Shen Kua, p. 1086). Four years later, another text describes how Chinese sailors used compasses to navigate. The first mention of a magnetic compass in Europe comes a century later.

Have each student work with a partner and distribute copies of Item 17.B, instructions for making a compass. After the students have completed the list of instructions, as a class discuss:

- What are the similarities and differences between the compasses they made and modern compasses?
- What materials are they made from?
- What are the benefits of using a modern compass?
- How might life have been different in China than in Europe for the approximately 1,500 years that the Chinese knew how to make compasses and Europeans didn't?

≫ Activity 4: The Invention Convention

Have students work independently or with a partner. They will conduct research on one Chinese invention. (This list is also available on Item 17.C.)

abacus	kite	rocket and multi-staged rocket
cast iron	lacquer ware	
crossbow	locks on canals	rudder
decimal system	matches	seismograph
fishing reel	paddle-wheel boat	sericulture (silk production)
gunpowder	paper money	suspension bridge
horse collar or trace	porcelain	watertight compartments on ships
iron plow	printing	

Their project will include written and visual materials. An extensive list of Web resources is provided at the end of the lesson.

- Written information must include the date of the invention, the item's various uses, its significance for China, and when it became available (or was invented) in Europe.
- For the visual component, students can represent their invention by choosing to make a model, provide samples (if appropriate), have pictures, create a poster, and so on.
- The class will hold a Chinese Invention Convention, to which the school community and parents will be invited. Each project will be displayed, and the students should be prepared to answer questions from the public.

Further Student and Teacher Resources

Beshore, George. *Science in Ancient China.* New York: Franklin Watts, 1988.

Ross, Frank Jr. *Oracle Bones, Stars, and Wheelbarrows.* Boston: Houghton Mifflin Co., 1982.

Temple, Robert. *The Genius of China 3,000 Years of Science, Discovery and Invention.* New York: Simon and Schuster, 1986. (An excellent and thorough survey of the scientific and technological achievements of ancient China. Temple's book is based on the work of Professor Joseph Needham, the world's foremost scholar of the history of Chinese science. The book has many examples of primary sources, including photographs and drawings. A must-read book for educators who will be teaching about ancient Chinese inventions.)

Williams, Suzanne. *Made in China: Ideas and Inventions from Ancient China.* Berkeley, CA: Pacific View Press, 1996. (visually attractive survey book highlighting twenty inventions or discoveries of ancient China)

Web Sites

General information on Chinese inventions:

http://sln.fi.edu/tfi/info/current/inventions.html (Franklin Institute: Images and information about Chinese Inventions)

http://www.smith.edu/hsc/museum/ancient_inventions/home.htm (the Museum of Ancient Inventions)

http://afe.easia.columbia.edu/song/readings/inventions_ques.htm

http://www.inventions.org/culture/asian/chinese.html

http://www.computersmiths.com/chineseinvention/

http://www.usc.edu/isd/archives/arc/libraries/eastasian/china/toqing.html

http://www.engr.sjsu.edu/pabacker/history/china.htm

http://inventors.about.com/od/chineseinventors/

http://www.sdcoe.k12.ca.us/score/chinin/chinintg.htm (a California Online Resource for Education Resource)

http://www.uh.edu/engines/epi377.htm (for information about the wheelbarrow)

In the World Today

Scientific Contributions, Ancient and Modern

How is it that given all of China's contributions, few people in the world, including the Chinese themselves, knew about them? During the nineteenth century, while the West was in the midst of the Industrial Revolution, China struggled with major rebellions and social upheaval. Chinese leaders focused on preserving the imperial state and the Confucian order; the West looked toward the future. Dr. Joseph Needham, who is responsible for bringing to light China's remarkable early inventions, added his insight in a 1946 lecture:

"I personally believe that all Westerners, all people belonging to the Euro-American civilization, are subconsciously inclined to congratulate themselves, feeling with some self-satisfaction that, after all, it was Europe and its extension into the Americas which developed modern science and technology. In the same way I think that all my Asian friends are subconsciously inclined to a certain anxiety about this matter, because their civilization did not, in fact, develop modern science and technology."

When Needham made this observation, he had just begun his exploration into Chinese scientific achievements, a vast publication project, which has spanned almost fifty years and is continued by others to this day. This project has demonstrated that Chinese civilization did not lack a scientific and technological base. Historians of science are still debating what were the particular circumstances that enabled industrialization to occur in Europe and North American long before it spread to China. For more information on Needham's extraordinary work, visit www.nri.org.uk. Ask the students why most people remain ignorant of China's contributions.

Lesson 18 CD-ROM Contents

Primary Sources

- Document 18.1: Excerpts describing the "barbarians" who lived outside the Chinese empire from *Records of the Grand Historian* (《史记》) by Sima Qian (司马迁), written between 105 and 90 B.C.E.

- Document 18.2: Excerpt describing the diplomatic efforts of Zhang Qian (张骞) on behalf of Han emperor Wudi (汉武帝) from *Records of the Grand Historian* (《史记》) by Sima Qian (司马迁), written between 105 and 90 B.C.E.

- Document 18.3: Photograph of a Buddhist mural in the Mogao Grottoes (莫高窟), Dunhuang (敦煌), 705–780 C.E.

- Document 18.4a–c: Photograph of a five-stone pagoda, late 5th, early 6th century; two close-up views of carved stones on the pagoda

- Document 18.5a and b: Images of silk processing, 1696

- Document 18.6: Excerpts from *The Travels of Marco Polo*, describing his travels from Italy to China for trade, ca. 1299

- Document 18.7: Photograph of a painted terracotta figurine of a merchant on a two-humped Bactrian camel, Tang (唐) dynasty (618–907 C.E.)

- Document 18.8: Photograph of silver bowl, 5th–6th century, found in Xinjiang Uygur Autonomous Region (新疆维吾尔自治区)

Supplementary Materials

- Item 18.A: Additional vocabulary for primary documents
- Item 18.B: Brief description of history of silk in ancient China

Lesson 18
The Silk Routes

By Shirley Moore

Lesson Contents

- Silk routes
- Political goals
- Infusion of new ideas and culture
- Silk in China
- Commerce

The Silk Road (丝绸之路) is the name given to various land routes, first developed during the Han (汉) dynasty (202 B.C.E.–220 C.E.), over which China traded its goods to empires in what are now India, Pakistan, Afghanistan, Iran, and as far west as Rome.

These trade routes were first called the Silk Route by a nineteenth-century European explorer, but the name is a misnomer. Silk (丝绸) *was* traded along the routes, but so were many other commodities. And traders were not the only people traveling the routes; government officials, monks, soldiers, missionaries, and itinerant musicians and dancers also traveled along the silk routes.

Purpose of the Silk Routes

From a Chinese perspective, the silk routes provided, first of all, a strategic corridor for defense and expansion of the empire. Second, they were trade routes for high priority goods, such as horses and alfalfa (for the Chinese) and silk (for Europeans). Third, the silk routes were a route for the transmission of ideas, including Buddhism, Nestorian Christianity, and Islam, and the arts. The last was especially true during the Tang (唐) (618–907 C.E.) and Yuan (元) (1279–1368 C.E.) dynasties. However, few people traveled from one end to the other; rather, goods were traded along the route, passing from one merchant to the next.

Commerce and Travel

Commercial trade along these routes was primarily carried out by Central Asian merchants—for example, Bactrians, Parthians, and Kushans. Caravans, numbering between sixty and a hundred people, most on two-humped camels, traversed challenging terrain from one trading center to another.

Travel along the silk routes could be exceptionally hazardous. Travelers setting out from Chang'an (present day Xi'an) would first have to negotiate the Gobi and Taklamakan deserts. The latter was particularly dangerous because of its great heat and famously shifting sands. When the winds blew up, they caused violent noises that could terrorize travelers. If a merchant caravan got to Kashgar, it would then have to negotiate the steep and lengthy ascent into the Pamirs, where bandits were often waiting in ambush. Travelers proceeding on to South Asia had also to negotiate the Hindu Kish mountains and a precipitous and terrifying descent into the Indus valley. Only the most determined travelers passed along this route.

Changes Over Time

In order for trade along the silk routes to flourish, there had to be stability in China and in Persia. Strong governments on both "ends" protected the caravan routes. When the Han dynasty was in its decline, the government withdrew from garrisons along the route, and trade diminished significantly. The routes continued to be used for travel, however. When China was strong again during the Tang dynasty, trade flourished. Since the Tang was among the most cosmopolitan of the dynasties, not only was commerce successful, but the silk routes had a significant cultural impact. The Chinese were exposed to music and dance from Central Asia, for example, which they incorporated into their own. (See Lesson 15 for examples of instruments from other areas that became part of traditional Chinese music.)

In the centuries following the Tang dynasty, use of the silk routes slowed. When Genghis Khan united the nomad tribes of Mongolia and proceeded to conquer China, Central Asia, and Eastern Europe, the region was once again stable. As a result, in the thirteenth century, the routes were busy. One of the most famous travelers of that era was Marco Polo. Another was the Chinese Christian monk Rabban Sauma, who traveled west as far as Paris.

For centuries at a time the silk routes brought China into contact with the empires and people of Central and Western Asia. The exchange of commercial goods, culture, and ideology changed all the peoples involved.

Organizing Idea

The Silk Road is a misnomer in that it was not a single road, but rather a network of trade routes linking China with South, Central, and West Asia, and the Mediterranean. Not only were these routes used for trade of myriad goods, including silk, but also for military expansion and cultural exchange.

Student Objectives

Students will:

- be familiar with the geography of the area traversed by the silk routes
- understand the various uses of the silk routes, including military, trade, and cultural exchange
- learn about specific historic figures who played a role in founding or using the silk routes

Key Questions

- Where were the silk routes?
- What were conditions like along the silk routes?
- Why did people use the silk routes?
- What were the effects on China of trade along the silk routes with Central Asia and Mediterranean countries?

Vocabulary

Buddhism
diplomat
grottoes
merchant
monk
pagoda
pilgrim
sutra
Xiongnu

Supplementary Materials

Item 18.A: Additional vocabulary for primary documents
Item 18.B: Brief description of history of silk in ancient China

Student Activities

PRIMARY SOURCES related to Activity 1

Document 18.1: Excerpts describing the "barbarians" who lived outside the Chinese empire from *Records of the Grand Historian* (《史记》) by Sima Qian (司马迁), written between 105 and 90 B.C.E.

The Xiongnu are descended from the rulers of the Xia dynasty [ca. 21st century–16th century B.C.E.]. …They live among the northern barbarians, moving to follow their flocks. They primarily raise horses, oxen and sheep, but also keep unusual animals like camels, asses, mules, and wild horses. They move about in search of water and grass, having no cities, permanent dwellings, or agriculture. Still, they divide their territory into regions. They have no written language, so make oral agreements. Little boys are able to ride sheep and shoot birds and mice with bows and arrows. When they are somewhat older they shoot foxes and rabbits for food. Thus all the men can shoot and serve as cavalry…

• *Full text available on CD-ROM* •

Document 18.2: Excerpt describing the diplomatic efforts of Zhang Qian (张骞) on behalf of Han emperor Wudi (汉武帝) from *Records of the Grand Historian* (《史记》) by Sima Qian (司马迁), written between 105 and 90 B.C.E.

[Zhang Qian] set out…accompanied by Kanfu, a Xiongnu slave…They traveled west through the territory of Xiongnu and were captured by the Xiongnu and taken before the shanyu [king]. The shanyu detained them and refused to let them proceed. "The Yuezhi people live north of me," he said. "What does the Han mean by trying to send an envoy to them! Do you suppose…the Han would let my men pass through China?"

The Xiongnu detained Zhang Qian for over ten years and gave him a wife from their own people, by whom he had a son. Zhang Qian never once relinquished the imperial credentials that marked him as an envoy of the Han, and after he had lived in Xiongnu territory for some time and was less closely watched than at first, he and his party finally managed to escape and resume their journey toward the Yuezhi.

After hastening west for twenty or thirty days, they reached the kingdom of Dayuan. The king of Dayuan had heard of the wealth of the Han empire and wished to establish communication with it, though as yet he had been unable to do so. When he met Zhang Qian, he was overjoyed and asked where Zhang Qian wished to go…

• *Full text available on CD-ROM* •

» Activity 1: The Chinese and Their Neighbors: Writing a Letter of Advice to the Emperor

Have students read Document 18.1, which describes the Xiongnu from a Chinese historian's point of view, and discuss the differences between the Han Chinese and the nomadic life of the Xiongnu. (For additional information on how China interacted with her neighbors to the north, see Lesson 19.)

Distribute copies of Document 18.2 about Zhang Qian's diplomatic attempts in northwestern China. Remind the students that the first travelers known to history went for political reasons. Have students discuss answers to the following questions:

- Why did Zhang Qian set out to travel west?
- What was the purpose of Zhang Qian's mission? Include specific groups and people in the answer.
- Was Zhang Qian successful? How?

Ask students to imagine they are the emperor's adviser traveling along with Zhang Qian. They have concluded their travels and will now write a letter of advice to the emperor on how to deal with the "barbarians" who live just outside the borders of the empire.

» Activity 2: Creating Big Maps

Show the students a topographical map that includes China, Central Asia, and Turkey. Identify Xi'an, China, (formerly Chang'an, the Han and Tang capital), and Antioch, Turkey, on the Mediterranean Sea. Ask them to identify the best land route between the two cities that served as end points to the silk routes. Note their ideas, and later in the lesson compare the routes traders took with the ones students suggested. How are they similar and different? What might be the reasons for the differences?

Using the instructions for making Big Maps (in Teacher Resources on the CD-ROM) and the additional resources provided at the end of this chapter, create large maps of the area of the silk routes. Additional details can be added as students complete activities. For easy reference students should also create their own desk maps of the key aspects from the class Big Maps.

Possible Big Map topics include the following:

- Geographic: Include key cities/landscape involved in the silk routes, such as Kashgar, Yarkand, Khotan, Turfan, Dunhuang, Lanzhou, Xi'an, and Beijing, as well as Pamir Mountains, Taklamakan Desert, Gobi Desert and Yellow River. Include pictures from the Internet or drawings to illustrate the different kinds of terrain in each place. Add the routes used as the silk routes.
- Economic: Research the regional goods produced and traded in China; glue to the maps stickers, drawings, dried foods, cotton balls, etc., to illustrate the different kinds of products exchanged.
- Political: Using different colors to outline, or plastic overlays, show the area controlled by the Han, Tang, and Yuan dynasties.
- Cultural: Research and indicate regions in which particular imported religions flourished.

PRIMARY SOURCES *related to Activity 3*

Document 18.3: Photograph of a Buddhist mural in the Mogao Grottoes (莫高窟), Dunhuang (敦煌), 705–780 C.E.

Courtesy of Dunhuang Academy

This illustration of the Pure Land of the West shows Buddha in the center and attendant bodhisattvas on his left and right. Pure Land was a popular form of Buddhism in China. The bottom panel illustrates whirling dancers from Central Asia accompanied by musicians.

Document 18.4a–c: Photograph of a five-stone pagoda, late 5th, early 6th century; two close-up views of carved stones on the pagoda

Courtesy of Gansu Provincial Museum

Early pagodas, *ta* (塔), were multistoried towers built as monuments, where a relic of Buddha was said to be buried. In time, they were constructed to commemorate sacred places, to house objects used in worship, or to achieve a balance of life forces. Thousands were built all over China. This one was created as a model. Each side of the five levels shows a story or legend related to Buddha or his life.

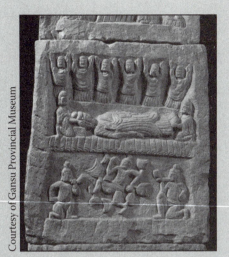

This carving shows the famous conversation, recorded in a sacred text, that took place between the Bodhisattva of Wisdom and a man called Vimalakirti, a wealthy aristocrat who lived the life of an exemplary Buddhist. Additional bodhisattvas stand on both sides and below. Three monks are among the figures below, too.

One of the carvings on the fourth level, this one shows Buddha dying. His youngest and favorite disciple (Ananda) is holding his head. His oldest disciple (Kasyapa) kneels at Buddha's feet. Mourners stand above. The three figures below, however, appear in complete contrast: They are active, moving, and blowing horns.

» Activity 3: Recognizing the Spread of Buddhism in China

Teachers may wish to review (or introduce) information about Buddhism and its spread into China as a result of the silk routes. (Refer to Item 8.F in Lesson 8.) Distribute copies of Documents 18.3 and 18.4 or project them on a screen. Discuss the images together or divide the students into small groups and have them examine the images (especially the close-ups) carefully. (For more information about Pure Land Buddhism, see Document 8.7 in Lesson 8.) If the students work in groups, one student should record everyone's observations.
Discuss:

- What does the pagoda (of which there were thousands in China) suggest about the spread of Buddhism?
- What is being depicted on the panels of the pagoda? In the close-up photographs?
- What do the meticulous stone carving and the paintings in the grottoes indicate?
- What feelings does the art evoke?
- What surprised students about the images?
- What questions do the students have and how can they find answers to the questions?

» Activity 4: Extended Research on the Spread of Buddhism

Students can use online resources and books to discover more about the spread of Buddhism in China. In small groups, they can research

- Faxian, a monk who traveled to India
- Xuanzang, a monk who also traveled to India
- The Big Goose Pagoda in Xi'an
- The White Horse Temple in Luoyang
- The extent of the discoveries in the grottoes at Dunhuang
- Buddhist temples
- Cliff carvings at Longmen and Yungang grottoes

Students can share their findings with classmates through oral or PowerPoint presentations or posters.

PRIMARY SOURCES *related to Activity 5*
Document 18.5a and b: Images of silk processing, 1696

Library of Congress

These two images are from a set of forty-six scenes depicting silk production, painted in ink and color on silk.

>> **Activity 5: An Introduction to Silk in Ancient China**

While silk was not the only product traded on the silk routes, it was one of the major ones that the Chinese exported. To learn more about silk in China, distribute copies of the two images of silk production or display them on a screen (Documents 15.5a and b).

- Who is in the pictures?
- What does each person appear to be doing?

Now have the students read Item 18.B (available on the CD-ROM) about silk and information at http://www.sewing.org/enthusiast/enthusiast.html. How do the two images fit into what students have learned about the process? How labor intensive was the production of silk? How costly do students think silk would have been? Students may wish to explore further to learn how silk is made today and how its cost compares to other fabrics.

PRIMARY SOURCE *related to Activity 6*

Document 18.6: Excerpts from *The Travels of Marco Polo*, describing his travels from Italy to China for trade, ca. 1299

[Charchan]

I will tell you next of another province of Turkestan, lying east-north-east, which is called Charchan. It used to be a splendid and fruitful country, but it has been much devastated by the Tartars. The inhabitants worship Mahomet. There are villages and towns in plenty, and the chief city of the kingdom is Charchan. There are rivers producing jasper and chalcedony, which are exported for sale in Cathay and bring in a good profit; for they are plentiful and of good quality.

All this province is a tract of sand; and so is the country from Khotan to Pem and from Pem to here. There are many springs of bad and bitter water, though in some places the water is good and sweet. When it happens that an army passes through the country, if it is a hostile one, the people take flight with their wives and children and their beasts two or three days journey into the sandy wastes to places where they know that there is water and they can live with their beasts. And I assure you that no one can tell which way they have gone, because the wind covers their tracks with sand, so that there is nothing to show where they have been, but the country looks as if it had never been traversed by man or beast...

• **Full text available on CD-ROM** •

≫ Activity 6: Travel and Trade-Discussion of Conditions

An early 15th-century traveler from Spain, sent to Samarkand on an official mission, described how

> "The best of all merchandise coming to Samarkand was from China: especially silk, satins, musk, rubies, diamonds, pearls and rhubarb. The Chinese were said to be the most skilful workmen in the world....Cambalu, the chief city of Cathay [in Mongol-era China], was six months from Samarkand, two of which were over steppes. In the year of [one official mission], eight hundred laden camels came from Cambalu to Samarkand" (quoted in *The Silk Road: Two Thousand Years in the Heart of Asia,* p. 13-14).

This activity can be conducted as a "Read, Pair, Share" discussion. Reading can be done in class or as homework. Explain that the writing of Marco Polo comes hundreds of years after men first started to travel the silk routes. Have students read Documents 18.6 to get a sense of the life of a traveler during the Yuan dynasty. Locate places described in the reading on maps from Activity 2. Check http://en.wikipedia.org/wiki/Genghis_Khan to see the areas of control by various Mongolian leaders during the Yuan dynasty when Marco Polo was traveling. Students can answer the following questions alone or in pairs then be prepared to share their answers with the class.

- According to Marco Polo, what kinds of conditions did a traveler on the silk routes encounter?
- What provisions needed to be taken in order to survive the travel? Where should travelers have stopped and restocked? Why?
- Few Europeans traveled all the way to China along the silk routes. Most international trade was handled by a series of Central Asian middlemen between the Black Sea and Chinese cities like Kashgar. How might the travel conditions along the silk routes explain why trade was conducted this way?
- Which would most likely have been the products the Polos would take back to Venice with them? Why?
- What was life like for inhabitants under the control of the Yuan dynasty (Great Khan)?

PRIMARY SOURCES *related to Activity 7*

Document 18.7: Photograph of a painted terracotta figurine of a merchant on a two-humped Bactrian camel, Tang (唐) dynasty (618–907 C.E.)

Photo: Thierry Ollivier. Réunion des Musées Nationaux/Art Resource, NY.

Because of its splayed feet, a camel can carry more weight across desert regions than any other pack animal. The two-humped Bactrian camel had been the main beast of burden in Turkestan (now Xinjiang Province, 新疆) for thousands of years, and was used extensively in trade along the Silk Routes. This is one example of the many terracotta and porcelain figurines made.

Document 18.8: Photograph of silver bowl, 5th–6th century, found in Xinjiang Uygur Autonomous Region (新疆维吾儿自治区)

Bayingolin Mongolian Autonomous Prefecture Museum

Persian artisans excelled at silversmithing, and the skill was first brought to China during the Tang (唐) dynasty, via the silk routes.

»» Activity 7: Creative Extension—Cultural Influences

The influence of Persian art motifs on Chinese work and vice versa has been well documented. However, recognizing these patterns requires extensive knowledge of both cultures. The last two primary sources in the lesson serve as examples of a fascinating and complex subject. Have students examine the photographs of the terracotta camel and the silver bowl (Documents 18.7 and 18.8).

- In what region do camels live and work?
- Who is riding the camel? What else is on its back?
- Why would someone make a figurine of this? Many figurines of camels have been found. Why would so many be made?
- What creature decorates the silver bowl?
- In what region does it live?
- How did this bowl come to be found in Xinjiang? What connection does it suggest?

Have each student decide what piece of art he or she will create (painting, sketch, sculpture). Ask them to find a pattern or subject matter that is typical of another culture and to use it to decorate the piece they make. Alternatively, a student can create on a piece of paper a design for fabric. When the students display their finished work, have others try to identify where the design ideas come from.

»» Activity 8: Extended Research

Using additional resources, students can conduct research and present projects on:

- other religions introduced along the silk routes—e.g. Nestorian Christianity, Islam, Judaism
- art (especially images of the Buddha)—and the merging of Western and Eastern elements
- Ferghana horses and other specific regional goods
- music introduced via the silk routes (see Lesson 15)

»» Activity 9: Essay Writing on Aspects of the Silk Routes

Students choose one the following topics and write essays that demonstrate their understanding of the lesson. They will likely need to do some more research.

- Various commodities were traded and ideas and knowledge exchanged as a result of the silk routes. What happens when languages, religions, and cultures are exchanged? Give one or more examples of similar situations today.
- Countries in East and Central Asia were often at war with each other. What might they have been fighting about? What conflicts are taking place there now? Why?

- Describe how people traveled across Central Asia, the obstacles and dangers they faced. What did they need to prepare for their journey?
- What faiths could be found along the silk routes? Which made their way to China? What evidence remains of their presence in China?

Further Teacher and Student Resources

Boulnois, Luce. *Silk Road: Monks, Warriors & Merchants on the Silk Road.* Translated by Helen Loveday. Airphoto International Ltd., 2004.

Gilchrist, Cherry. *Stories from the Silk Road.* New York: Barefoot Books, 1999. (Stories from the journey along the ancient trade route between East and West. Includes tales of dragons, demons, goddesses and spirits. Background statements introduce each region.)

Guishan, Li, trans. *Frescoes and Fables: Mural Stories from the Mogao Grottoes in Dunhuang.* New World Press, 1998. (Tales as told by residents of Dunhuang to the translator, which are illustrated by or explain the origins of some of the murals at the Mogao Grottoes in Dunhuang. Color plates of murals included.)

Latham, Ronald, trans. *Marco Polo: The Travels.* London: Penguin Classics, 1958. (accessible translation of Marco Polo's retelling of his experience in China during the Yuan dynasty. Index and maps included.)

Rossabi, Morris. *Voyager from Xanadu: Rabban Sauma and the First Journey from China to the West.* Tokyo: Kodansha International, 1992.

Schafer, Edward H. *The Golden Peaches of Samarkand.* Berkeley, Calif.: University of California Press, 1963. (brilliant study of the silk routes trade by one of America's great Sinologists)

Watt, James C. Y., et al. *China: Dawn of a Golden Ages, 200–750 A.D.* New Haven: Yale University Press, 2004. (Metropolitan Museum of Art's catalog to accompany the exhibition. A scholarly and fascinating book. Note especially the introductory essay by James C. Y. Watt "Art and History in China from the 3rd through the 8th Century," highlighting the synthesis of Western with Eastern art styles in China as a result of migration and trade along the silk routes.)

Wood, Frances. *The Silk Road: Two Thousand Years in the Heart of Asia.* Berkeley: University of California Press, 2002. (A richly illustrated and thorough chronological account of the silk routes from the Mediterranean to China.)

Wriggins, Sally Hovey. *Xuanzang: A Buddhist Pilgrim on the Silk Road*. Boulder, Colo.: Westview, 1996.

Historical fiction:

Schneider, Mical. *Between the Dragon and the Eagle*. Boston: Houghton Mifflin, 1997. (Set in 100 C.E., the short chapter book, gives students an inside look at what a traveler might have experienced at major stops along the trade route. The 150-page book is written at about a sixth-grade level.)

Whitfield, Susan. *Life Along the Silk Road*. Berkeley: University of California Press, 1999. (Roughly modeled on Geoffrey Chaucer's *Canterbury Tales*, Whitfield has written short vignettes illuminating the lives of different kinds of people who lived along or traveled the silk routes. Note especially "The Monk's Tale" for the conditions and perils of travel during the Tang dynasty. Pre-read stories and consider editing out periodically racy elements in each tale.)

Web Sites

For information to use in Big Maps activity:

http://plasma.nationalgeographic.com/mapmachine/ (excellent topographic maps)

For maps of the silk routes:

http://www.ancientroute.com/hotmap2.htm

http://depts.washington.edu/uwch/silkroad/maps/maps.html

http://www.newton.mec.edu/Angier/DimSum/Silk%20Road%20Lesson.html (excellent summary of the way trade worked along the silk routes)

For general information on the silk routes:

http://Chinapage.com/silksite.html (good reference maps, silk route pictures and information about the Dunhuang project)

http://www.silk-road.com (Silk Road Foundation Web site has resources and information about the culture and art of Central Asia and the silk routes)

http://www.monkeytree.org/dunhuang/dunhuang.html

Maps of dynasties:

http://afe.easia.columbia.edu/china/geog/M_Hist.gif

For information about Chang'an (present day Xi'an):

http://depts.washington.edu/uwch/silkroad/cities/china/xian/xian.html

Video

Along the Silk Road: People, Interaction, and Cultural Exchange. Stanford, Calif.: Stanford University, 1993. (Using both hardcopy activities and video clips included on the accompanying video, this curriculum unit challenges students to "take" Xuanzang's journey that linked China to the West during the Tang dynasty.)

The Silk Road. New York: Central Park Media, 2000. 630 min. (three-disc DVD set containing twelve episodes, each running about fifty-five minutes, of historical background on the different locations and trades that comprised the Silk Road.)

CD-ROM

The Silk Road: A Digital Journey. Vancouver, Canada: DNA Media, Inc., 1998. (This CD-ROM includes photographs of landscapes, art, and people, along with examples of regional music, sample phrases in various languages, animated maps, and an interactive time line. There are a few errors to note, however. Marco Polo is incorrectly placed in the 12th century (rather than the 13th) and the Han Chinese are said to be a minority in Kashgar, which is no longer the case after recent migrations.)

In the World Today

China Joins the World Trade Organization in 2001

The World Trade Organization (WTO) is an international economic organization that makes agreements on the rules of trade between nations, including tariffs. The process to admit China took sixteen years, with the U.S. taking the role as one of the chief negotiators. China's entry into the WTO was an important development in the history of China's economic reform. It was also a controversial event in terms of the effects it has had on the global economy. As a member of the WTO, China has experienced faster development of its industries, increased foreign investment, higher rates of employment, and an improvement in the standard of living. However, many international human rights organizations believe that since other countries can no longer use economic sanctions, they cannot hold the Chinese government account-able for human rights violations. Economic relations between China and the West have become increasingly complex. For example, China's accession to the WTO has resulted in job loss in the United States, Canada, and countries in Europe and Latin America because it is cheaper for companies to move manufacturing jobs to China, where wages are much lower. In addition, because of the trade deficit, China is now financing much of the U.S. national debt. Ask students to describe the differences between trade along the silk routes and global trade in the twenty-first century. Why is there so much more international trade today than ever passed along the silk routes? What additional benefits are likely to result from China's membership in the WTO? How will other nations benefit?

Lesson 19 CD-ROM Contents

Primary Sources

- Document 19.1a–g: Photographs of Chinese farmers and steppe nomads
- Document 19.2: "The Xiongnu" (匈奴) in *Records of the Historian* (《史记》) by Sima Qian (司马迁), written between 105 and 90 B.C.E.
- Document 19.3: "To the tune, 'Song of the Six Prefectures,'" a poem by Zhang Xiaoxing (1132–1169)
- Document 19.4: "Final Essay on the Legitimate Succession of Dynasties" (《帝王基命录》), by Fang Xiaoru (方孝孺), written around 1380
- Document 19.5: An exchange of diplomatic letters between the Han (汉) emperor and the chief ruler of the Xiongnu (匈奴), 176 B.C.E.
- Document 19.6: A chart showing Han Chinese (汉族) gifts of silk to the Xiongnu (匈奴)
- Document 19.7: *The Han Koong Tsu* (*Autumn of the Palace of Han*), a short 13th century play

Supplementary Materials

- Item 19.A: Additional vocabulary for primary sources
- Item 19.B: Brief summaries of the interaction between four Chinese dynasties and nomadic neighbors
- Item 19.C: Answers for Activity 4 (Documents 19.2–19.4)
- Item 19.D: Answers for Activity 5 (Documents 19.5 and 19.6)

Lesson 19
Relations with Nomadic Neighbors

By Cara Abraham

"A Chinese dynasty is like an accordion," writes Albert Craig, "first expanding into territories of its barbarian neighbors and then contracting back to its original, densely populated core area" (*Heritage of World Civilization*, p. 229).

The nomadic tribes of the north and west have often been troubling neighbors to various Chinese dynasties and their people. Sometimes they were at peace and sometimes at war. The Chinese called them "barbarians," a term applied to anyone who did not read Chinese, believe in the Confucian rituals of kinship and, most strikingly, did not farm.

Farming

Farming was a fundamental way of life for many settled Chinese. Many ancient Chinese myths are centered around the beginnings of or advances in agricultural practices: Fuxi domesticated animals, Shennong invented the plow and hoe, and Yu dredged the rivers into manageable irrigation canals (see Lesson 6). From early times, the Chinese family was organized around labor-intensive agriculture. Big families meant more laborers to plant and harvest the crops. Even children's labor was necessary to the survival of the family. The staple foods were millet and later wheat in the north and rice in the south. Other common foods were barley, soybeans, and sometimes vegetables, fruit, and fish or meat.

All Chinese dynasties relied on agriculture to support the people and the government. In peacetime, farmers could produce enough food to feed millions of Chinese people. Improved technology, such as iron plows and wheelbarrows, resulted in greater yield. (See Lesson 17.) Grain harvests were the major source of income for the government. But when natural disasters or poor government policies worked against farmers, hundreds of thousands could starve in a single season. Poor farmers rarely owned their own land; rather they rented land or worked for wealthy families who controlled large estates.

A Nomadic Culture

The tribes in the north and west of China, on the other hand, were mostly pastoral. In the dry climate of the northern steppe, people relied on grazing animals, rather than on farming, for their livelihood. They maintained a nomadic life, moving seasonally with their herds of cattle, sheep, goats, and camels, and also organized themselves into kinship groups. Their animals were a source of food and provided skins or fur for clothing and shelter (including circular tents called *gers* in Mongolia). Camels carried the nomads' possessions, and the people used their horses to help shepherd the flocks. When brutal snowstorms (called *zud* by the Mongolians) or the droughts of summer killed off too many animals in their herds, nomadic warriors attacked settlements on the Chinese border. Warriors on horseback had a significant advantage over the infantry of the Chinese. The terrifying raids came swiftly and left death and destruction in their wake.

Relations with Nomadic Tribes

Every Chinese emperor was charged with the protection of China from these marauding bands. They tried building defensive walls, sending diplomatic missions, and even waging war. One example of a defensive strategy was the Great Wall (长城). Qin Shi Huangdi (秦始皇帝) used a conscripted labor force to connect and expand a vast network of walls that had been constructed by individual states to protect their borders. It was rebuilt centuries later during the Ming (明) dynasty. (See Lesson 16.)

China's success in maintaining dominance in relation to its neighbors depended heavily on its own economic strength and internal stability. Traditionally the center of Asian culture, China modeled imperial government and promoted science, writing, literature, and music. These features set China apart as a source of knowledge for her neighbors. When the imperial house was in order, China projected an image of strength, and her neighbors kowtowed to the emperor and laid expensive tributes at his feet. China could pick and choose what foreign goods and ideas it wished to import. (See Lesson 18.) To maintain peace, officials negotiated payments of tribute from the nomadic tribes in exchange for diplomatic recognition by the emperor. This arrangement continued even when the nomadic chiefdoms proved stronger than the Chinese imperial forces. When China was weakened by internal disputes however, the nomadic tribes took the upper hand and demanded the Chinese government exchange gifts that far exceeded the worth of the goods offered as tribute. Still, the "barbarians" were always expected to recognize China's supremacy as *Zhongguo* (中国)—the Middle Kingdom—center of all civilization.

The Mongol Invasion

International diplomacy was conducted in this way for hundreds of years, and relative peace and stability prevailed in East Asia during the Han, Tang, and Song dynasties. In the thirteenth century, however, after a period of steady dynastic decline, Genghis Khan launched the Mongol conquest of China, which his successors completed. The Mongol Yuan (元) dynasty ruled for a mere eighty-nine years before the Chinese reestablished dominance over the Mongolians under the Ming dynasty (1368–1644). This dynasty survived 270 years until peasant rebellions and invading Manchu forces from the northeast brought it down. The Manchus would rule China until 1911.

China's history has often been described as cyclical with the rise and fall of dynasties. It can also be described by its interaction with its nomadic neighbors. By investigating five key periods in Chinese history, students can gain a broader and more comparative overview of international relations and economic interdependence in East Asia.

Note: For an overview of the complex relationship between various Chinese dynasties and China's nomadic neighbors, please read Item 19.B on the CD-ROM.

Organizing Idea

Exchanges across China's northern borders involved trade and political negotiations as well as armed incursions, to ensure stability between China's agricultural society and the nomadic tribes.

Student Objectives

Students will:

- compare and contrast the lifestyles of sedentary farmers with nomadic herders
- identify and describe the interaction between the settled Chinese people and the nomadic tribal groups from five key periods in history (Han, Tang, Song, Yuan, and Ming dynasties)
- judge which type of interaction brought about the best foreign relations between China and its nomadic neighbors

Key Questions

- What happens when settled and nomadic cultures collide?
- What were the results of diplomacy between Chinese emperors and nomadic tribal chiefs?
- How did the tribute system maintain a balance of power in East Asia?
- Was there a pattern to the interaction between the Han Chinese and their neighbors to the north and west? If so, what was it?

Vocabulary

balance of power
barbarian
cavalry
diplomacy
envoy
ethnocentrism
infantry
kowtow
nomad
tribute and tribute system

Supplementary Materials

Item 19.A: Additional vocabulary for primary sources
Item 19.B: Brief summaries of the interaction between four Chinese dynasties and nomadic neighbors
Item 19.C: Answers for Activity 4 (Documents 19.2–19.4)
Item 19.D: Answers for Activity 5 (Documents 19.5 and 19.6)

Student Activities

» Activity 1: Comparing Farmers and Nomads

Display photographs of farmers and herders from East Asia (Documents 19a–g). Have students note the clothing, housing, diet, working hours/seasons, and conditions. Students will need to extrapolate from the sources to get an overall sense of how each group lived from day to day. Note taking can be in the form of a Venn diagram or a T-chart. Conduct a class discussion to check for understanding.

Ask students to identify the advantages/disadvantages and benefits/problems of each type of lifestyle. Explore the question of superiority and inferiority of lifestyles.

- Is one lifestyle better than the other?
- Is it possible for each lifestyle to be the best given a certain environment?
- Have students choose which lifestyle they would rather live and explain why.

Have students pair off and write a dialogue between a farmer and a herder in which they identify two or three common values and interests and two or three differences. Ask for volunteers to present in front of the whole class. Ask students if they know of similar cultural contacts in their nation's history or in other parts of the world. (One example would be the spread of Euro-American culture into Native American lands from the 1600s through the early 1900s.)

PRIMARY SOURCES *related to Activity 1*

Document 19.1a–g: Photographs of Chinese farmers and steppe nomads

Tea farm on terraced land, Yunnan (云南) Province.

Photograph of steppe nomads near Karakorum, Mongolia.

• *The remaining photos are available on the CD-ROM* •

Document 19.1a–g: Photographs of Chinese farmers and steppe nomads

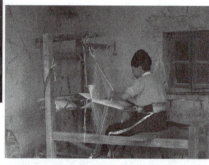

Photos by Michael Abraham

Women at work in Kashgar, Xinjiang Province

Photograph taken in Mongolia

• The remaining photos are available on the CD-ROM •

» Activity 2: Making Big Maps

Divide students into five dynasty groups named Han, Tang, Song, Yuan, and Ming. Distribute a map of East Asia that represents the political boundaries of the Chinese dynasty to the corresponding group. (Maps can be found in most world history transparency resource binders and online at http://www.mnsu.edu/emuseum/prehistory/china/map/map.html.) Following the directions for Big Maps (Teacher Resources on the CD-ROM), students should trace the political boundaries of the Chinese dynasty and label the nomadic tribes along the northern border, title their maps, and write the dates that the dynasty was in power.

» Activity 3: Constructing a Time Line of Chinese–Nomad Relations

Using the template for a time line (Teacher Resources on the CD-ROM), students should label each of the five dynasty names and dates (Han 202 B.C.E.–221 C.E.; Tang 618–907 C.E.; Song 960–1279 C.E.; Yuan 1279–1368 C.E.; Ming 1368–1644 C.E.). Then ask them to create two symbols: one representing the Chinese farming lifestyle and one representing the nomadic herding lifestyle. These symbols should be noted in a key or legend on the time line. Ask students to add their symbols above the time line to represent the dominant power in East Asia for each dynasty time period. For example, during the Han dynasty, students should draw in a Chinese farmer symbol above the time line to illustrate that the Han dynasty was strong during its contact with the Xiongnu. During the Yuan dynasty, students should draw in a nomadic herder symbol above the time line illustrating that the Mongols dominated China.

PRINCIPLE

PRIMARY SOURCES related to Activity 4

Document 19.2: "The Xiongnu" (匈奴) in *Records of the Historian* (《史记》) by Sima Qian (司马迁), written between 105 and 90 B.C.E.

The Xiongnu are descended from the rulers of the Xia dynasty (ca. 21st century–16th century B.C.E.)…They live among the northern barbarians, moving to follow their flocks. They primarily raise horses, oxen and sheep, but also keep unusual animals like camels, asses, mules, and wild horses. They move about in search of water and grass, having no cities, permanent dwellings, or agriculture. Still, they divide their territory into regions. They have no written language, so make oral agreements. Little boys are able to ride sheep and shoot birds and mice with bows and arrows. When they are somewhat older they shoot foxes and rabbits for food. Thus all the men can shoot and serve as cavalry…

• Full text available on CD-ROM •

Document 19.3: "To the tune, 'Song of the Six Prefectures,'" a poem by Zhang Xiaoxing (1132–1169)

I think of the arrows that hung at my waist and my sword in its scabbard,
    now moth-eaten or covered with dust.
What did they accomplish? How fast the time has gone.
My heart is still passionate but my years are numbered.
I see how our delightful capital plays music for the foreigners.
The beacon fires have been extinguished, the soldiers given rest.
Envoys, with their fine hats and carriages, hurry back and forth, unfeeling.
Yet I have heard that the old who were left behind in the central plains constantly look towards the south hoping to see the decorated imperial chariots.
Arriving at this place makes this traveler's feelings well up and his tears fall like rain.

• *Full text available on CD-ROM* •

Document 19.4: "Final Essay on the Legitimate Succession of Dynasties" (《帝王基命录》), by Fang Xiaoru (方孝孺), written around 1380

Common notions are formed when people become imbued with something and, over a long time, just accept it without realizing what they have done. For example, in the Song [dynasty] (960–1279), people thought it strange whenever they saw barbarian costumes or heard barbarian speech. They would have thought it shameful and repugnant to submit to a barbarian ruler, or to become barbarized themselves. However, during the century of Yuan rule (1279–1368), everyone became barbarized in their eating and living habits, in their speech, and in objects of daily use. People raised their sons and grandsons under these conditions. They were acclimated to these things for so long that it all seemed quite appropriate to them. In the Yuan era, everyone would have been shocked and amazed to hear them [Mongol rulers] repudiated on the grounds of barbarism. This is the skewed outlook that was prevalent in that era. It is not an outlook that is in accord with the Way and therefore destined to prevail forever…

• *Full text available on CD-ROM* •

≫ Activity 4: Researching Chinese Views of the Northern Barbarians

Introduce or review imperial government in China, Confucian values, and the roles of literature and music in Chinese culture. Students should be able to identify China's view of itself as *Zhongguo* (Middle Kingdom). Ask students if Americans have adopted a similar cultural attitude in the modern world. Introduce the term "ethnocentrism" and discuss its implications in viewing other cultures.

Distribute the documents describing Chinese views of the northern barbarians (19.2–19.4). Have students answer the following comprehension and interpretation questions (Answers are available on Item 19.C on the CD-ROM.):

Document 19.2
1. What battle tactics made the Xiongnu into formidable warriors?
2. According to the author, how did the Xiongnu lifestyle differ from that of the Chinese?

Document 19.3
1. How does Zhang Xiaoxing describe the loss of northern China to the Jurchen?

Document 19.4
1. How does the author use the teachings of Confucius and *The Spring and Autumn Annals* to justify his definition of "legitimate succession"?

Discuss as a class:
1. What bias is present in all three documents?
2. Why were the Chinese so fearful of the northern barbarians?

Going beyond the documents:

• What might have been the consequences of the Chinese bias against the northern tribes?
• What do students think would likely have happened when the Chinese were militarily and economically stronger than their northern neighbors?
• What do students think would have happened when the Chinese were militarily and economically weaker than their northern neighbors?

PRIMARY SOURCES related to Activity 5

Document 19.5: An exchange of diplomatic letters between the Han (汉) emperor and the chief ruler of the Xiongnu (匈奴), 176 B.C.E.

The Han has made a pact of brotherhood with the Xiongnu, and for this reason we have sent generous gifts to you. Any violations of the pact or ruptures of the bonds of brotherhood have been the work of the Xiongnu. However, as there has been an amnesty since the affair of the Wise King of the Right occurred, you need not punish him too severely. If your intentions are really those expressed in your letter, and if you will make them clearly known to your various officials so that they will henceforth act in good faith and commit no more violations of the pact, then we are prepared to honor the terms of your letter.

• Full text available on CD-ROM •

Document 19.6: A chart showing Han Chinese (汉族) gifts of silk to the Xiongnu (匈奴)

Year (B.C.E.)	Silk Floss (catties)	Silk Fabrics (pieces)
51	6,000	8,000
49	8,000	9,000
33	16,000	18,000
25	20,000	20,000
1	30,000	30,000

Note: One catty equals approximately half of a pound or 250 grams.

» Activity 5: Researching the Tribute System

Ask students to think of times when they needed to resolve a conflict between themselves and friends, especially if the conflict was caused by the actions of another person. How was it resolved? What are ways to resolve a conflict so that both sides gain something? Introduce the term "diplomacy," and discuss how leaders today and in the past have tried to use it to resolve international conflicts.

Distribute the documents describing the tribute system (19.5 and 19.6) and have students answer the following comprehension and interpretation questions. (Answers are available on Item 19.D on the CD-ROM.)

Document 19.5
1. What event prompted the exchange of these letters between the Xiongnu *shanyu* (ruler) and the Chinese emperor Wen?
2. What outcome is expected from this exchange of letters?
3. Why did the Chinese ministers advise the emperor to make peace with the Xiongnu?
4. What trade goods accompanied these letters? Which side received more valuable goods?
5. Why would both leaders send gifts with their letters?

Document 19.6
1. What does this chart tell you about the interaction between the Chinese and the Xiongnu?

Introduce the terms tribute and tribute system. Explain to students that all of China's neighbors were expected to pay tribute to the Chinese emperor on a regular basis by sending envoys with gifts to the Chinese capital. Once granted an audience with the emperor, the envoys were expected to kowtow, that is, prostrate themselves in front of the emperor and knock their heads against the floor in submission. In exchange, the envoys would carry back to their leaders documents with official seals recognizing them as allies of and under the protection of the Chinese emperor. Most times the envoys would return with very expensive gifts as well. Trading missions often followed these official diplomatic exchanges.

PRIMARY SOURCE *related to Activity 6*

Document 19.7: *The Han Koong Tsu* (*Autumn of the Palace of Han*), a short 13th century play

Minister. I am a minister of Han. In the western palace of the Emperor is a lady, named Chaoukeun, of rare and surpassing charms. When your envoy, great king, came to demand a princess, this lady would have answered the summons, but the Emperor of Han could not bring himself to part with her, and refused to yield her up. I repeatedly renewed my bitter reproaches, and asked how he could bear, for the sake of a woman's beauty, to implicate the welfare of two nations. For this the Emperor would have beheaded me; and I therefore escaped with the portrait of the lady, which I present, great king, to yourself. Should you send away an envoy with the picture to demand her, she must certainly be delivered up. Here is the portrait. [Hands it up.]

Khan. Whence could so beautiful a female have appeared in the world? If I can only obtain her, my wishes are complete. Immediately shall an envoy be dispatched, and my ministers prepare a letter to the Emperor of Han, demanding her in marriage as the condition of peace. Should he refuse, I will presently invade the South: his hills and rivers shall be exposed to ravage. Our warriors will commence by hunting, as they proceed on their way; and thus gradually entering the frontiers, I shall be ready to act as may best suit the occasion. [Exit.]

• *The full play is available on the CD-ROM or online at* *http://www.fordham.edu/halsall/eastasia/eastasiabooks.html* •

» Activity 6: Role Playing between the Chinese and Mongolians

Have students recall the ways in which the Chinese and the nomads interacted: warfare, diplomacy, and exchange of goods. Tell students that there was an additional, very personal way in which these two groups made peace: intermarriage. Since family was so important to both groups, by marrying a Chinese princess to a tribal chief, one could ensure peace.

Conduct a dramatic reading of the negotiations between the Chinese emperor and the Mongolian khan for the marriage of a Chinese princess. Distribute copies of *Han Koong Tsu*, and assign roles to students. Have them act it out in front of the room with props if possible. At the end, conduct a class discussion on the motivations of each of the four main characters: Hanchenyu, khan; Yuente, emperor; Mao Yen-Shou, minister; and Wang Chao-chun, princess. How was peace finally achieved? Is this method a good way to resolve conflict?

Optional extension activity: Have students produce their own skits that recreate one or several methods that were used to resolve conflicts between the Chinese and their northern neighbors. Encourage short multiple-scene skits with action, intrigue, and dialogue. Students can use their Big Map groups and can retell an episode from that dynasty's history.

» Activity 7: Choosing a Foreign Policy Option

Prompt students to list and describe the policy options faced by the Chinese in relating to their nomadic neighbors (isolation, war, diplomatic negotiation, and trade). Ask them to choose an option and defend it: Which foreign policy strategy best ensured peace and prosperity in East Asia?

Further Teacher and Student Resources

Cleaves, Francis Woodman. *Secret History of the Mongols.* Adapted by Paul Kahn. Boston: Cheng & Tsui Co., 1998. (adaptation of what is recognized today as the oldest Mongolian text tells the Mongols' version of the origin of their nation)

Craig, Albert, M. et al. *Heritage of World Civilizations.* Upper Saddle River, N.J.: Prentice Hall, 2000.

Grousset, René. *The Empire of the Steppes: A History of Central Asia.* Translated by Naomi Walford. New Brunswick: Rutgers University Press, 1999.

Morgan, David. *The Mongols.* Oxford, U.K.: Blackwell Publishers Inc., 1990.

Rossabi, Morris, ed. *China Among Equals: The Middle Kingdom and its Neighbors, 10th–14th Centuries.* Berkeley: University of California Press, 1983.

Rossabi, Morris. *Khubilai Khan: His Life and Times.* Berkeley, University of California Press, 1988.

Young adult historical fiction:

McCaughrean, Geraldine. *The Kite Rider.* New York: Harper Collins Publishers, 2001. (gives a strong sense of the way the Chinese viewed the Mongols as "other")

Wilson, Diane Lee. *I Rode a Horse of Milk White Jade.* New York: Harper Collins Publishers, 1998. (though elements in the plot are historically improbable, the book gives a lot of excellent and accurate detail about nomadic beliefs, customs, and superstitions)

Web Sites

http://www.mnsu.edu/emuseum/prehistory/china/ (time lines, maps, and short narratives, including pictures of artwork, about each dynasty in China. Includes a bibliography.)

http://www.fordham.edu/halsall/eastasia/eastasiasbook.html (site of direct links to primary source documents, including maps and images, about cultural origins, religious traditions, Chinese dynasties, modern history, and other East Asian countries)

Maps of dynasties:

http://sll.stanford.edu/projects/wworld/highlights/ww/Atlas.html

http://afe.easia.columbia.edu/china/geog/M_Hist.gif

Video

Mongols: Storm from the East. Films for the Humanities and Sciences. Princeton, New Jersey, 1994. (Four 50-minute episodes detailing the history of the Mongol Empire. Episode 1, Birth of an Empire, examines the rise of Genghis Khan. Episode 2, World Conquerors, illustrates the building of the capital, Karakorum, and has a good description of Mongol fighting tactics and comparison of Mongol warriors with their European counterparts. Episode 3, Tartar Crusaders, explores the relationship between Europe and the Mongol Empire and details the spread of Christianity into East Asia. Episode 4, The Last Khan of Khans, traces the life of Kublai Khan and the subjugation of China under the Yuan dynasty.)

Elsewhere in the World

During the Han dynasty:

- **The Roman Empire defeated Germanic tribes in Gaul and eventually added Britain.**

- **Christianity and Rabbinic Judaism arose in Palestine and Asia Minor.**

During the Tang dynasty:

- **Vikings invaded Britain and France.**

- **Umayyad and Abbasid dynasties consolidated Islamic rule in Middle East.**

- **Muslim armies defeated Tang forces at Battle of Talas River in 751.**

During the Song dynasty:

- **Europeans fought Crusades in the Middle East.**

- **Mayan Empire was at its height in the Yucatan.**

During the Yuan dynasty:

- **Under Genghis Khan and his successors, Mongols established the world's largest land empire.**

- **Dante (1265–1321) wrote *Divine Comedy*.**

During the Ming dynasty:

- **The Ottoman Empire captured Constantinople in 1453.**

- **The Italian Renaissance fostered a new humanism in Europe.**

In the World Today

A New Image for Genghis Khan

Genghis Khan claimed his armies killed 40 million people, and the peoples he defeated have been quite harsh in their descriptions of his savage character and actions. Yet his reputation has always remained heroic in Mongolia. "He is like a god to us," said Bat-Erdene Batbayar, a historian and adviser to Mongolia's Prime Minister Elbegdorj Tsahkia. "He is the founder of our state, the root of our history" (*Boston Globe*, July 3, 2005).

Nearly 800 years after his death, Genghis Khan is receiving overwhelming attention to better his image in Mongolia. Now one can see evidence of a renewed interest in Genghis Khan everywhere. "Children, streets, hotels, vodka, cigarettes, banks, candy bars, beer, products, and businesses of almost every type all carry his name; his face is on Mongolian money, stamps, and official buildings, and is spray-painted on street corners," writes Jehangir Pocha for the *Boston Globe*. Young people, even music bands, see Genghis as a hero.

Other nations are helping Mongolia find out more about Genghis. For example, in October 2004, a Japanese-financed research team searching for the ruler's tomb said it had found it at Avraga, about 155 miles east of Ulan Bator, the capital. China is spending about $20 million to renovate a mausoleum it built for Genghis Khan in 1954 at Ejin Horo Banner on the Ordos Highlands in its province of Inner Mongolia.

Ask students to define "hero." Is the "founder of [a] state, the root of [a country's] history" necessarily a hero? What happened to Mongolia in the twentieth century that might be spurring the move to establish Genghis Khan as an ancestor to be revered? How can historians learn more about an individual who ruled 800 years ago?

Lesson 20 CD-ROM Contents

Primary Sources

- Document 20.1: "Ships, Chinese and Western, on the World Map of Fra Mauro," 1459
- Document 20.2: A sailing chart from *Wu Bei Zhi* (《武备志》, *Treatise on Military Preparation*), 1621
- Document 20.3: Stone inscription on stele erected by Zheng He (郑和), 1431–1432
- Document 20.4: Fei Xin's description of the country of Champa (part of present-day Vietnam), 1436
- Document 20.5: Fei Xin's description of Calicut, India in 1436
- Document 20.6: Introduction to Fei Xin's "Overall Survey of the Star Raft," 1436
- Document 20.7: Description of Calicut, India, in *Yingyai shenglan* (*The Overall Survey of the Ocean's Shores*) by Ma Huan (马欢), published mid-15th century
- Document 20.8: "Tribute Giraffe with Attendant," 1414
- Document 20.9: Hymn of Praise to Emperor Chengzu (明成祖), 1414

Supplementary Materials

- Item 20.A: Additional vocabulary for primary sources
- Item 20.B: Zheng He's treasure ship and Columbus's *Santa Maria*
- Item 20.C: Outline map of the world
- Item 20.D: Suggested activities for Ma Huan's account

Lesson 20
China and the South Seas

By Philip Gambone

Lesson Contents

- Early maritime history
- The treasure fleets of Admiral Zheng He

A longstanding misconception holds that the Chinese were never a seafaring people. This is far from the truth. Chinese ships, which later the Portuguese came to call *juncos* (from which we get our word "junk"), probably reached Malaysia and Sri Lanka by the fourth century C.E. By the Tang (唐) dynasty (618–907 C.E.), the Chinese were trading via the sea with kingdoms in Southeast Asia, India, and the Persian Gulf. During the Southern Song (南宋) dynasty (1127–1279), when half of China's land was ruled by foreigners, Emperor Gaozong (宋高宗) promoted overseas trade in order to generate more income. He enlisted the help of merchants to build a fleet that would challenge the Persian and Arab traders who, since the eighth century, had dominated trade in the Indian Ocean. In 1132, he also established China's first permanent navy. By the thirteenth century, the Chinese had developed the most reliable ocean-going ships in the world, with watertight bulkheads and moveable rudders.

The Motive for the Treasure Fleets

The most impressive Chinese maritime achievements occurred during the early days of the Ming (明) dynasty (1368–1644). Between 1405 and 1424, Emperor Chengzu (明成祖), who had usurped the throne, launched six expeditions to foreign countries under the command of his close confidant, the Chinese Muslim eunuch warrior Zheng He (郑和). These expeditions were among the ways Chengzu strove to establish himself as the legitimate ruler of China. The aim was, as the Chinese put it, to "proceed to the end of the earth to collect tribute from barbarians beyond the sea" and to "attract all under heaven to be civilized in Confucian harmony." The new emperor intended to ensure his supremacy throughout the South Seas.

Zheng He's Treasure Fleet

The original fleet carried more than 27,800 people in over 300 vessels, a number that surpassed the combined fleets of all Europe at that time. The largest vessels were nine-masted "treasure ships," 444 feet long and 180 feet wide, which would have towered over Columbus' ships. (By comparison Vasco Da Gama traveled with 3 ships and 170 men.) These magnificent vessels combined the best features of several different kinds of reliable Chinese ships. Accompanied by a vast array of support vessels, the treasure fleet could remain at sea for months, covering great distances without stopping for food and water. Although they were also outfitted with cannon, they were not primarily warships. Rather than colonial exploitation, their mission was to exact promises of loyalty to the Ming state and to engage in commerce.

The Expeditions

The fleets visited an officially recorded thirty-seven countries in South and Southeast Asia, the Persian Gulf, and East Africa. There is some evidence that they may have rounded the tip of Africa and reached the Atlantic. To cross the Indian Ocean, Zheng He followed the monsoon winds: south in winter, north in summer. The mariners navigated principally by means of the compass, which the Chinese had invented several centuries before (see Lesson 17), and by burning graded incense sticks to mark the passage of time. They determined latitude by measuring the altitude of the North Star above the horizon. The captains also consulted sailing charts, providing instructions for traveling from port to port.

The commodities that the Chinese used in trade included gold, silver, silk and cotton cloth with printed designs, porcelain, rice and cereals, and brass and iron implements. Foreigners particularly admired the gorgeous and unique Ming porcelain called blue-and-white ware. In exchange for such goods, and as "tribute"—showing their recognition of Chinese superiority—foreign rulers presented Zheng He with cargoes of luxury items including dyes, spices, precious gems and pearls, medicinal herbs, rhinoceros horns, ivory and rare woods, and exotic animals, including a giraffe.

In their book *East Asia: The Great Tradition*, Edwin Reischauer and John Fairbank wrote: "The voyages [of Zheng He] must be regarded as a spectacular demonstration of the capacity of early Ming China for maritime expansion, made all the more dramatic by the fact that Chinese ideas of government and official policies were fundamentally indifferent, if not actually opposed, to such an expansion" (p. 323).

The End of the Treasure Fleet

The voyages led by Zheng He continued throughout Emperor Chengzu's reign. But officials distrusted such demonstrations of eunuch authority and lobbied against the voyages, on grounds of their expense. By the end of the sixth voyage, the emperor was preoccupied with moving his government from Nanjing to the new capital of Beijing, which he had been constructing for fourteen years. He died soon after in January 1425. His grandson, Xuanzong, followed in Chengzu's footsteps and sponsored one more voyage. Sometime during the return journey, in 1433, Admiral Zheng He died and is believed to have been buried at Nanjing. Not long afterwards, high officials, who had always opposed foreign trade, brought a halt to the construction of further treasure ships. Emphasis shifted away from foreign tribute relations to internal commerce along the recently reopened Grand Canal. As a final expression of distaste for foreign commerce, the official records of Zheng He's voyages were apparently burned in 1477 by Liu Daxia, a director in the Transportation Bureau. He damned the records as "deceitful exaggerations of bizarre things far removed from the testimony of people's eyes and ears."

In 1525, an imperial edict authorized destruction of all oceangoing ships and the arrest of merchants who sailed them. China as a state began to close itself off from the seagoing world. Less than fifty years later, Spanish galleons found their way across the Pacific to and from Manila, bringing shiploads of silver and returning to the New World with Chinese goods. This transpacific silver trade, which flourished for 200 years, would transform the Chinese and world economies.

Organizing Idea

The voyages of Zheng He are one of the most extraordinary accomplishments of the Chinese, "a spectacular demonstration of the capacity of early Ming China for maritime expansion." They also raise one of the great "what if's" of history: What if the Chinese had maintained this maritime tradition, instead of conceding the initiative to the Portuguese and Spanish explorers?

Student Objectives

Students will:

- understand the pre-Ming naval accomplishments of the Chinese
- appreciate the scope and significance of Zheng He's voyages
- understand the theory behind the tribute system
- compare and contrast European and Chinese maritime technology
- learn about some of the people, places, and products that figured in the voyages of the Ming treasure fleets
- ask why these spectacular voyages are not well known in the West

Key Questions

- What had the Chinese accomplished in terms of maritime technology and travel before the voyages of Zheng He?
- Where did Zheng He and the treasures ships go?
- What are some of the skills, inventions, and technological advancements that made these voyages possible?
- How did Zheng He's expeditions help establish the legitimacy of Chengzu's rule?
- What was the Chinese attitude toward the people and countries they encountered?
- Why were the Chinese officials opposed to the treasure ships and future voyages?
- What did the Chinese state gain from the maritime expeditions?
- What if the Chinese had made it all the way to Europe? How might history have been different?

Vocabulary

barbarians
blue-and-white ware
commerce
commodities
compass
edict
envoy
eunuch
junks
latitude
li (unit of measure)
monsoon
treasure ships
tribute
usurper

Supplementary Materials

Item 20.A: Additional vocabulary for primary sources
Item 20.B: Zheng He's treasure ship and Columbus's *Santa Maria*
Item 20.C: Outline map of the world
Item 20.D: Suggested activities for Ma Huan's account

Student Activities

>> Activity 1: Orienting Ourselves in Time

Ask students what they know about the great age of European maritime exploration. In addition to the voyages of Columbus, what other European explorers and discoveries of that era can they name? As a class or in small groups, generate a list of important dates from the European voyages of exploration. Students may want to consult an encyclopedia, a European history text or a Web site. The following sites will prove helpful:

http://international.loc.gov/intldl/awkbhtml/kb-1/kb-1-1-3.html
http://www.twingroves.district96.k12.il.us/Renaissance/GeneralFiles/C_DisTrade.html

Using materials in Teacher Resources on the CD-ROM, plot the important dates and events of the European maritime discoveries on a time line that can be displayed in the classroom. Using this time line and a good map of the world, lead the class in an analysis and discussion of the European voyages of discovery. Questions that might begin a good discussion:

- Which European nation first rounded the tip of Africa? When?
- Which European first sailed to India? To China? When?
- Europeans had been sailing the waters of the Mediterranean for thousands of years. Why did it take until the end of the 15th century for them to sail down the coast of Africa and around the Cape of Good Hope?
- What kinds of skills, navigational tools, and nautical expertise would they have had to develop in order to make such voyages?
- Why did it take so long for the Europeans to develop these tools and techniques?

Finally, outline for the students the story of Zheng He and his expeditions (or have students read the introductory material). Plot the dates of Zheng He's seven voyages on the time line. Given what the students already know about Chinese technology and inventions (see Lessons 16 and 17), ask them why they think the Chinese were able to sail such great distances so many years before the voyages of Dias, da Gama, Cabral, and Columbus. (Students will be able to better answer the last question later in the lesson.)

PRIMARY SOURCE related to Activity 2

Document 20.1: "Ships, Chinese and Western, on the World Map of Fra Mauro," 1459

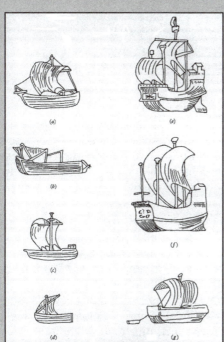

According to Joseph Needham, Fra Mauro's world map was based upon Marco Polo's information about China that had been spreading in Europe. The map included small drawings of ships. Vessels a–d are shown in European seas. Vessels e–g are in the eastern seas, including the Indian Ocean and the Yellow Sea.

» Activity 2: Making Comparisons and Drawing Conclusions

Ask students to break up into pairs or groups of three. Give each a copy of Document 20.1. Explain to the students that the size of each drawing corresponds to its relative size on the original map.

- What do the students notice about the relative size of the ships in European waters as opposed to the ships in Asian waters?
- What other differences do they see between the two categories of ships (for example, number of masts, size of sails, a rudder)?
- Do these differences help to answer some of the questions raised in Activity 1?

Item 20.B: Zheng He's treasure ship and Columbus's *Santa Maria*

» Activity 3: Further Investigation of Zheng He's Treasure Ships

An even more dramatic comparison of the difference in size between Zheng He's largest treasure ships and European vessels of the era can be seen in Item 20.B. Project this contemporary artist's drawing on the wall or distribute copies to students. (The image, in color, can also be found at: http://www.janadkins.com/treasure.html.) Students should respond to the same set of questions as in Activity 2.

Students may want to do further research on the treasure ships. There is a great deal of information available on the Web and in some of the books listed in the section on Further Resources for Teachers and Students. Wei Wenxi, a Chinese amateur expert on ancient ships, has built a model of one of the vessels in the Treasure Fleet. Excellent photos of it are available at http://english.people.com.cn/200506/21/eng20050621_191504.html.

After doing their research, have students make a drawing, poster or, if time allows, a model of one of the treasure ships. Alternately, if someone has a model of one of Columbus's ships, they might bring it in for display, and the class could determine how much larger Zheng He's vessel would have been.

PRIMARY SOURCE *related to Activity 4*

Document 20.2: A sailing chart from *Wu Bei Zhi* (《武备志》, *Treatise on Military Preparation*), 1621

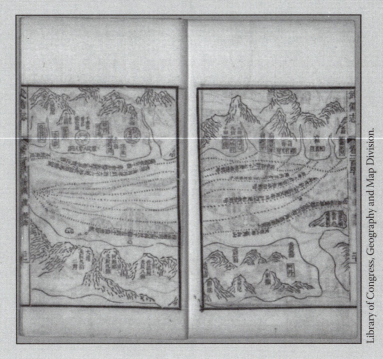

Library of Congress, Geography and Map Division.

» Activity 4: Examining One of Zheng He's Sailing Charts

Project on a screen or give students copies of Document 20.2. Explain to the students that this is a later edition of one of the sailing charts that Zheng He used on his voyages. It is not a map but a "schematic corridor" that indicates the routes for sailing, compass bearings, and other information. The land at the top of the map is the west coast of India; the land at the bottom is Arabia.

Ask the students to break up into pairs or small groups. Working with a copy of the chart, have them answer the following:

- What do they see on the chart?
- What seems to be the most prominent feature(s) on the chart?
- Comparing the chart to a modern map of the Arabian Sea (the area between Western India and Arabia), what differences do they notice?

- The chart is not an accurate map. Would it still have been helpful to Zheng He and his sailors? How?
- Who would have supplied the original information about sailing in this region to the Chinese chart makers? Where could students find more information about maritime voyages in the Arabian Sea during the 15th century?

Activity 5: Making a Big Map of Zheng He's Expeditions

Review the story of Zheng He and his expeditions (or have students read the introductory material). Using the Teacher Resources for Big Maps (available on the CD-ROM), and an outline map of the world (Item 20.C), have the students (1) trace the outline of Ming dynasty China; (2) locate Nanjing, the capital of China at the time and the port from which all seven expeditions began; (3) map the routes of the seven voyages of Zheng He. Sources of information for the routes can be found in several of the publications listed in Further Resources for Teachers and Students. An additional activity is to add the routes of some of the European explorers (e.g., Dias, 1488; Columbus, 1492; Da Gama, 1498) from the time line in Activity 1. As the class continues its study of Zheng He and his voyages, other things can be added to the map. For example, you could label the various ports where Zheng He stopped and mark them with illustrations of characteristic products and trade items from that region.

PRIMARY SOURCE related to Activity 6

Document 20.3: Stone inscription on stele erected by Zheng He (郑和), 1431–1432

The Emperor, approving of their loyalty and sincerity, has ordered us (Zheng He) and others at the head of several tens of thousands of officers and flagtroops to ascend more than a hundred large ships to go and confer presents on them in order to make manifest the transforming power of the (imperial) virtue and to treat distant people with kindness. From...[1405] till now we have several times received the commission of ambassadors to the countries of the Western Ocean...all together more than thirty countries large and small. We have traversed more than one hundred thousand *li* of immense waterspaces and have beheld in the ocean the huge waves like mountains rising sky-high, and we have set eyes on barbarian regions far away hidden in a blue transparency of light vapors, while our sails, loftily unfurled like clouds, day and night continued their course (rapid like that) of a star, traversing those savage waves as if we were treading a public thoroughfare...

• Full text available on CD-ROM •

>> Activity 6: Analyzing an Inscription

Ask students to read Document 20.3. (Reading this aloud may prove to be particularly impressive and helpful to the aims of this activity.) Follow this up with a discussion:

- What might be some reasons why Zheng He would have erected this stele?
- How does the inscription portray Emperor Chengzu?
- How does the inscription portray the countries and peoples that Zheng He visited?
- Do you detect examples of exaggeration? Where? How might you go about determining whether the claims really are exaggerated?
- How does the inscription explain the fleet surviving a hurricane?

PRIMARY SOURCES related to Activity 7

Document 20.4: Fei Xin's description of the country of Champa (part of present-day Vietnam), 1436

They do not understand New Year's Day but when the moon emerges, they take it to be the beginning, and when it disappears, they take it to be the end. When [the moon] has thus waxed and waned ten times they take it to be one year. They have a system of [dividing] day and night into ten watches by skillful beating of a drum. The principal chief and the populace do not rise before noon and they do not sleep before midnight. When they see the moon, they drink wine and sing and dance to celebrate it...

• Full text available on CD-ROM •

Document 20.5: Fei Xin's description of Calicut, India in 1436

This is an important [place] of the oceans. It is very near to Ceylon, and it is also a [principal] port for all the foreigners of the Western Ocean. The mountains are wide and the fields barren, [but] wheat and cereals are [available] in quite sufficient quantity...

The principal chief is rich and lives in the depth of the hills. By the side of the sea are the markets; [here] are collected [all] the commodities for trade.

• Full text available on CD-ROM •

≫ Activity 7: Reading and Interpreting Accounts of Zheng He's Voyages

Have students read Document 20.4. Lead the students in a discussion and analysis of Fei Xin's account of the visit to Champa (one of the first stops on Zheng He's third voyage).

- How is the chief of Champa portrayed? How is his residence described? How does the chief behave toward Zheng He and the Chinese?
- What products does Fei Xin mention? Ask the students to speculate about what these commodities were used for.
- How does Fei Xin characterize the people of Champa and their customs? What prejudices do you detect in his description? Why might these prejudices have crept into Fei Xin's account? (The teacher may want to remind the students of the discussions and discoveries they made in Lesson 1: Stereotypes.)

Now have students read Document 20.5. Tell them that Calicut, known as the "Metropolis of the Spice Trade," was the most important port in South Asia. Using the same set of discussion questions that you used for Document 20.4, compare and contrast Fei Xin's account of and attitudes toward Calicut and Champa. Which one does he seem to have admired more? Why might this be?

PRIMARY SOURCE related to Activity 8
Document 20.6: Introduction to Fei Xin's "Overall Survey of the Star Raft," 1436

Third. In…[1415], in the suite of the principal envoy, the Grand Eunuch Zheng He, and others, I went to Bengal and all the foreigners, and I arrived at Hormuz and other countries, to publish the imperial edicts and to confer rewards. In…[1416], I returned to the capital…

• *Full text available on CD-ROM* •

≫ Activity 8: Extended Research

In the introduction to his account of his travels (see Document 20.6), Fei Xin gives us a list of the places he visited with the admiral. Using the places listed in Fei Xin's account and the places mentioned on the stele (Document 20.3), have students break up into pairs and select one place that they would like to research. Emphasize that their research should concentrate on what that place was like in the 15th century, when the Chinese arrived. Students could publish the results of their research in a short report, a poster, a PowerPoint show, or some other means. As a follow-up to these reports, ask students to consider why each of these countries would have wanted to exchange goods with China.

PRIMARY SOURCE related to Activity 9

Document 20.7: Description of Calicut, India, in *Yingyai shenglan* (*The Overall Survey of the Ocean's Shores*) by Ma Huan (马欢), published mid-15th century

The king of the country is a Nan-k'un man; he is a firm believer in the Buddhist religion; and he venerates the elephant and the ox.

The population of the country includes five classes, the Muslim people, the Nan-k'un people, the Che-ti people, the Ko-ling people, and the Mu-kua people.

The king of the country and the people of the country all refrain from eating the flesh of the ox. The great chiefs are Muslim people; and they all refrain from eating the flesh of the pig. Formerly there was a king who made a sworn compact with the Muslim people, saying, "You do not eat the ox; I do not eat the pig; we will reciprocally respect the taboo"; and this compact has been honoured right down to the present day.

• Full text available on CD-ROM •

≫ Activity 9: Examining Another Eyewitness Account

Ma Huan was another traveler who accompanied Zheng He on his voyages and left an eyewitness account. Document 20.7 gives his description of Calicut. As it is much more extensive than Fei Xin's, it is probably best to assign portions to various groups. Item 20.D (on the CD-ROM) includes suggested activities keyed to various portions of the text. Not all portions need be assigned.

≫ Activity 10: Creative Extension—Describing a Foreign Place

Ask the students what is the most foreign place that they have visited. The place need not be a foreign country. It can be a place in this country or even in their town, city, or state that simply felt unfamiliar and foreign. Ask them to write a description of that place—what it looks like, the people who live there, the food, the customs, etc.—as if they were writing for a friend who had never seen it and might never see it. What should they emphasize? What will the overall tone of their description be like?

Alternately, students might be asked to imagine themselves as sailors on Zheng He's ship. Have them write a letter, first-person essay, or journal entry expressing their observations and impressions of Calicut, Champa, or some other place that Zheng He visited. They can base their letter on the descriptions from Fei Xin and Ma Huan, or on the research they did for Activity 8.

PRIMARY SOURCES *related to Activity 11*

Document 20.8: "Tribute Giraffe with Attendant," 1414

Philadelphia Museum of Art: Gift of John T. Dorrance, 1977.

Document 20.9: Hymn of Praise to Emperor Chengzu (明成祖), 1414

Oh how glorious is the Sacred Emperor who excels both in literary
and military virtues,
Who has succeeded to the Precious Throne and has accomplished
Perfect Order and imitated the Ancients!
The myriad countries are thoroughly at rest and the Three Luminaries
follow their due course,
Rain and heat are seasonable and rice and millet are yearly harvested.
The people in their customs are joyful and there is no hindrance or
rift between them,
Consequently auspicious signs have abundantly descended to the world…

• Full text available on CD-ROM •

›› Activity 11: Interpreting a Tribute Gift

Pass around copies of Documents 20.8 and 20.9. Explain to the students that the giraffe was a tribute gift to the emperor. Discuss:

- How has the painter made the giraffe seem special?
- Why might the Chinese have been so delighted with this gift?
- What do students notice about the man leading the giraffe? Is he Chinese?
- Next read the hymn in praise of the emperor:
- How is the emperor praised?
- What are some of the other marvelous signs that indicate that Heaven is pleased with the emperor?
- How is the giraffe (*jilin*) described? How are its qualities a mirror of the emperor's qualities?

In 1972, after President Nixon's visit to China, the Chinese government gave two pandas to the Washington National Zoo as a gift from the Chinese people. In what ways was this gift similar to the gift of the giraffe from Bengal? In what ways was it different?

If students were in charge of giving the gift of an animal from their country to the Beijing Zoo, what would it be, and why?

›› Activity 12: Closing Discussion

"How does a country forget its greatest adventurer-hero?" asks Adi Ignatius in his *Time* magazine article "The Asian Voyage: In the Wake of the Admiral." Ask students to read the entire article at http://www.time.com/time/asia/features/journey2001/intro.html. Afterwards, have a class discussion or a debate about why, as Ignatius writes, "Zheng He is largely unknown outside of China." This is also an excellent opportunity to review all that the class has learned about China. What do they know now that they did not when they started their study of China? Why do they think that so few Western students know about China? Why is it important to know about China and its long and rich history?

Further Teacher and Student Resources

Brook, Timothy. *The Confucians of Pleasure: Commerce and Culture in Ming China.* Berkeley: University of California Press, 1998.

Chang Kuei-sheng, "Cheng Ho" entry in L. Carrington Goodrich and Fang Chaoying eds., *Dictionary of Ming Biography 1368-1644*, New York: Columbia University Press, 1976, pp. 194-200.

Kristof, Nicholas D. "1492: The Prequel." *The New York Times,* June 6, 1999.

Levathes, Louise. *When China Ruled the Seas: The Treasure Fleeet of the Dragon Throne, 1405-1433.* New York: Oxford University Press, 1996.

Menzies, Gavin. *1421: The Year China Discovered America.* New York: HarperCollins, 2002.

Snow, Philip. *The Star Raft: China's Encounter with Africa.* Ithaca, N.Y.: Cornell University Press, 1989.

Viviano, Frank. "China's Great Armada." *National Geographic*, July 2005.

Note: Levathes', Menzies', and Viviano's works include excellent maps of the voyages.

Web Sites

http://www.vancouvermaritimemuseum.com/watery/treasure_fleet.htm (on China's maritime history, shipbuilding, etc.)

http://www.cronab.demon.co.uk/china.htm (part of a much more extensive Web site on maritime history)

http://www.chinapage.com/history/zhenghe2.html ("Zheng He" by Siu-Leung Lee)

http://afe.easia.columbia.edu (Asia for Educators site. Enter Zheng He in the search box for excellent background of the voyages during the Ming dynasty.)

A black and white version of the map in Document 20.2 can be viewed at:

http://www.atmos.washington.edu/~earth/earth1/Earthmap1.jpg

http://www.time.com/time/asia/features/journey2001/greatship.html (a more realistic mast height is illustrated by Philip Nicholson for TIME Inc 2001)

http://www.time.com/time/asia/features/journey2001/intro.html ("The Asian Voyage: In the Wake of the Admiral" *Time Magazine* article, includes model of ship with various parts labeled; also links to other sites)

http://www.pbs.org/wgbh/nova/sultan/media/expl_01q.html (for a terrific animation of Zheng He's treasure ships)

www.hist.umn.edu/hist1012/primarysource/feihsin.htm (Compares Fei Xin's accounts of the east coast of Africa with those of the Muslim traveler Ibn Battuta (1304-1369), the 16th-century Portuguese commercial agent Duarte Barbosa, and the Swahili oral tradition.)

http://cf.hum.uva.nl/galle/galle/trilingual.html ("The Trilingual Inscription of Zheng He")

www.nytimes.com/library/magazine/millennium/m3/kristof.html ("1492: The Prequel": Nicholas D. Kristof travels to Africa to look for traces of Zheng He's voyages)

http://english.peopledaily.com.cn/200506/21/eng20050621_191504.html (excellent photos of Wei Wenxi's model ship)

http://www.chinaheritagenewsletter.org/articles.php?searchterm=002_zhenghe.inc&issue =002 (a superb article on the Zheng He sexcentenary, including an extensive bibliography)

http://www.international.ucla.edu/article.asp?parentid=10387 (more on Professor Jin Wu)

Video

Sultan's Lost Treasure, NOVA (ISBN 1-57807-580-7), 2001. 60 mins. (documentary on the discovery of a Ming dynasty trading ship off the coast of Borneo that contained a large cache of porcelain. Includes a segment on Zheng He's treasure ships.)

Elsewhere in the World

- In the 14th century, Ibn Battuta (ca. 1304–ca. 1378) traveled extensively in Africa and Asia.

- 1403: A 23,000-volume encyclopedia was published in China.

- 1428: Joanne of Arc gathered an army to attack the English.

- 1438: Incas began imperial rule in Peru.

- In the mid-15th century, Aztec culture peaked.

- 1441: European slave trade in Africa began.

- 1453: Turks conquered Constantinople, and the Byzantine Empire ended.

- 1454: Gutenberg printed the Bible with movable type.

- 1492: Jews and Muslims were expelled from Spain.

- At the end of the 15th century, the Portuguese, followed by the Spanish and the English, began their voyages of exploration.

In the World Today

A Controversial Claim

In 2002, *1421: The Year China Discovered America* was published. Written by Ian Menzies, a former submarine commander in the British Royal Navy, the book claims to prove that Zheng He's fleet not only visited the lands mentioned on the steles and in the accounts of Fei Xin and Ma Huan, but in fact "explored virtually the whole world between 1421 and 1423." Despite criticisms by many scholars (some have called him "dead wrong"), Menzies' assertion that the Chinese discovered the Americas is popularly accepted in China. Whatever the actual case, one thing is absolutely certain: China today is no longer the isolated "sleeping dragon" that she became in the centuries following the end of Zheng He's voyages. The People's Republic is very much a major player in the cultural and economic globalization that defines our world today.

Menzies' Web site, which outlines his case in plenty of detail, can be found at:
http://www.1421.tv.

For a refutation of Menzies' conclusions, see:
www.kenspy.com/Menzies

Two book reviews that also debunk Menzies are at:
http://www.asianreviewofbooks.com/arb/article.php?article=201 and
http://enjoyment.independent.co.uk/books/reviews/article127872.ece

Ask students why they think this book got so much attention. Encourage them to read both sides of the argument to understand how historians evaluate books that propose new historical theories.

In the World Today

Zheng He Six Centuries Later

In recent years, interest in Zheng He has grown tremendously. The year 2005 marked the 600th anniversary of Zheng's first voyage, an opportunity for China and other countries to mount exhibitions, conferences, seminars, and symposia that focused on the latest research into the person many call "the greatest sailor in history."

Among recent scholars who have promoted further study of Zheng He's voyages is Jin Wu, a professor of marine studies and civil engineering. Recognizing that written and archaeological evidence of Zheng He's voyages is scanty, Professor Wu supports a multidisciplinary approach—engineers, scientists and historians working together—to uncover answers to some of the remaining questions concerning the voyages of the Treasure Fleet.

"Ocean-going sailing ships sailed mainly by wind and ocean currents," Professor Wu points out. "With the combined effort of historians, navigators, and oceanographers, Zheng He's expedition routes can be more convincingly verified." The technology to build, sail, and support the fleet, he says, "required advanced management skills and systems and certainly deserves our intensive study…What was achieved was comparable to what we did in our day to go to the moon."

None of Zheng He's ships has survived. But descriptions, written and pictorial, exist, and these have helped shipbuilders to reconstruct replicas. Wei Wenxi, an amateur student of ancient ships, has built a one-fortieth scale model of one of the treasure ships. There are also plans to build full replicas of one of Zheng He's treasure ships. In Singapore, the Friends of Admiral Zheng He has embarked on such a project. China, too, is building a replica and, according to an article in the BBC News, "hopes to use it to retrace the original journeys." The man in charge of the project is, appropriately enough, another Admiral Zheng—this one, Zheng Ming, a retired naval officer.

More on Professor Jin Wu can be found at: http://www.international.ucla.edu/article.asp?parentid=10387. Take a look at the chart that Professor Jin Wu has provided comparing Zheng He's voyages with three early European voyages of discovery. Students might want to create a similar chart, adding additional information (size of the ships, places explored, etc.) based on further research.

たち妻もり家かの風り春ふる日ぐ

Glossary

admonition: a warning

alloy: a substance that is a mixture of two or more metals, or of a metal and something else

ancestor: any person from whom one is descended

ancestral tablet: a piece of wood or stone on which were written the names of ancestors, sometimes with a brief description of special achievements; placed in an important location in a home

arable: suitable for farming

archaeology: the scientific study of the life and culture of past, especially ancient, peoples, by excavation of ancient cities, artifacts, etc. (see Lesson 4)

archetype: the original pattern, or model, from which all things of the same kind are made

aristocracy: a wealthy social class; in agricultural societies the aristocracy owned large tracts of land, held political power, and passed their control to future generations through inheritance

balance of power: a distribution of military and economic power among branches of government, states and/or nations that is sufficiently even to keep any one of them from being too strong or dangerous

bamboo: a giant woody grass with a hollow stem, very hardy; in China symbolic of a long life, endurance and strength; a very popular subject for painting

barbarian: a term used by Han Chinese to describe anyone non-Chinese; a foreigner

benevolent: wishing to do good; kind

bronze: an alloy (or mixture) of copper or tin

brush stroke: work done with a brush in calligraphy and painting

Buddhism: a world religion founded in India in the 5th century B.C.E. (see Lesson 8)

bureaucracy: a government with a central administration; non-elected officials of such a government, often seen as inflexible

calligraphy: fine writing; practiced in China for more than two thousand years; long considered an art form (see Lesson 12)

cauldron: a large kettle or boiler

cavalry: combat troops riding horses

ceremonial: including a system of rites or formal actions connected with an occasion, often religious

character: in Chinese a single written symbol that represents a word or part of a word (see Lesson 5)

civilization: an advanced stage of social development; state-level society (see Lesson 3)

climate: the prevailing or average weather conditions of a place, as determined by the temperature and meteorological conditions over a period of years

commerce: the buying and selling of goods, especially when done on a large scale, between cities, states, and nations

commodities: anything bought or sold, any articles of commerce

compass: an instrument used to determine the direction of magnetic north

concubine: a woman who lives with a man who is already married; in China and other Asian countries concubines often lived in the same household with the man's wife and children

Confucianism: a Chinese philosophy of life based on the teachings of Confucius in the 5th century B.C.E.; emphasizes ethical, respectful relationships between individuals (Lesson 7)

copper: a reddish-brown, easily bent, metallic element that is corrosion-resistant and an excellent conductor of electricity and heat

courtyard dwelling (*siheyuan*): the traditional layout of a house, especially in north China, where buildings surround a courtyard (see Lesson 11)

creation myths: stories that explain the origins of human beings (see Lesson 6)

cun: brush strokes used in traditional Chinese painting, similar to ones used in calligraphy

Daoism: a Chinese philosophy of living that emphasizes a life of simplicity, naturalness, and harmony with the universe, developed in the 5th century B.C.E. (see Lesson 8)

deity: a god

dialect: a regional form of speech; in China the dialects, though they share the same written language, are completely different spoken languages

dike: an obstacle/defense built to protect against flooding

diplomacy: a way of managing relations between nations, often quite formal

diplomat: a representative of government who conducts relations with the governments of other nations

divine: of or like a god

diviner: an individual believed to have special powers, who could understand messages from ancestors or gods; for example, by reading the cracks in an oracle bone

dragon boat: boats shaped to look like a dragon, especially in the bow and stern, used in traditional races held on the fifth day of the fifth month (see Lesson 9)

drought: a long period of dry weather

duty: the obedience that someone shows towards his or her parents, older people, etc.

dynasty: a succession of rulers from the same family who inherit leadership

edict: an official public order issued by an authority, such as an emperor

elite: a group seen as the finest, best educated, most distinguished, most powerful, etc.

empire: a group of nations, territories, or peoples ruled by a single authority, who is usually called an emperor or empress

enlighten: to help someone understand

ensemble: [in music] a group of performers

envoy: a diplomat; less important than an ambassador

ethnic: having a common national or cultural heritage

ethnocentrism: the belief that one's own ethnic group, nation, or culture is superior

eunuch: a man who has been castrated (testicles removed); in imperial China, eunuchs served the emperor in his palace

excavation: (in archaeology) a dig (see Lesson 4)

fengshui: the art of siting a building in the "best" location, seeking harmony between the structure and the physical environment (see Lesson 11)

festival: a time or day of feasting and celebration

filial piety: respect from a son or daughter

fu: good fortune

geomancy: sometimes used to define *fengshui*

grotto: a small cave

hand scroll: long horizontal paper with wooden dowels on each end used for calligraphy or painting; meant to be held in both hands, unrolled, and looked at one section at a time

hanging scroll: a painting on paper or silk hung vertically

hangtu: a method used for almost three thousand years to build walls and homes. The name comes from two Chinese words: *hang* (meaning pounded or beaten), and *tu* (which means earth)

harmony: a situation where there is agreement

hero: a person admired for courage or nobility

hierarchy: a group of persons arranged in order of rank, grade, class, etc.

Huang He: Yellow River, known as "China's Sorrow" for its role in so many floods (see Lesson 2)

Huangdi: emperor; also the mythological Yellow Emperor (see Lesson 6)

infantry: foot soldiers

inscription: symbols or words carved into stone or metal, for example bronze

irrigation: a system by which water is controlled or diverted into channels and used for watering

junk: a Chinese flat-bottomed sailing vessel

junzi: a term used by Confucius to describe a gentleman, someone of excellent character

karma: the effect of a person's actions during his or her lifetime

kowtow: the act of kneeling and touching the ground with the forehead to show great deference, submissive respect, etc.

latitude: the distance north or south of the equator

Legalism: an approach to government promoted by advisors to Qin Shi Huangdi, using harsh punishments to control people (see Lesson 8)

li: Chinese unit of measurement; equals about one-third of a mile

literati-artists: painters who believed art should be expressive, and like calligraphy and poetry an outlet for the painter's emotions (see Lesson 14)

loess: a fine-grained, yellowish-brown, extremely fertile loam deposited by the wind and sometimes by floods (see Lesson 2)

lunar: having to do with the moon

Mandarin: the official spoken language in China

manor: the main residence of a large estate

merchant: a businessman who buys and sells goods for profit

moat: a deep, broad ditch dug around a fortress or castle, and often filled with water, for protection against invasion

monk: a male member of a religious order living in a monastery or hermitage

monsoon: a seasonal wind of the Indian Ocean and South Asia, blowing from the southwest from April to October, and from the northeast during the rest of the year

mooncake: a flaky pastry with many different fillings, a traditional food of the mid-Autumn Festival (15th day of the 8th lunar month)

moral: concerned with deciding between right and wrong behavior

mural: art on a wall

myth: a traditional story, the author of which is not known; serves usually to explain the origin of human beings, customs, beliefs, religious rites, etc. of a people (see Lesson 6)

name chop: seal used to stamp documents, art, calligraphy etc.; usually made out of soapstone, jade, or ivory (see Lesson 5)

nirvana: a state of bliss, great peace

nomads: people who have no permanent home, but move about in search of food, pasture, etc. (see Lesson 19)

oracle bone: animal bone, often inscribed, used to ask ancestors and/or gods for guidance regarding the future (see Lesson 5)

pagoda: a sacred building in the Buddhist religion, originally built to house a relic of Buddha; later built to commemorate a sacred place, to house objects used in worship, or to help balance life forces

patriarchal: a society or organization in which the father or the eldest male is recognized as the head

perspective: the place (physical or mental) from which someone looks at or sees a scene or situation

pictograph: a picture or picture-like symbol representing an idea, as in primitive writing

pilgrim: a person who journeys to a sacred place

plateau: an elevated tract of more or less level land

prejudice: a judgment or opinion formed before the facts are known; can be positive but usually is not

propriety: the quality of being proper, fitting, or suitable

provenance: origin; source; where, for example, an artifact comes from

qi: energy, "breath of life," spirit

reincarnation: rebirth of the soul in another body

rite: a solemn and formal ceremony, often done according to strict rules or customs

ritual: the way in which a rite is performed

river basin: an area drained/formed by a river

sage: a wise person

scholar-official: a civil servant (government employee) who had passed the required difficult exams; his education included knowledge of classic Chinese literature, history, and philosophy and skill in calligraphy, painting, and poetry; he had the responsibility to use his knowledge to serve the emperor, and to improve society

shaman: a priest or medicine man, who is believed to be able to heal and to foretell the future by communicating with spirits

Shi Huangdi: also referred to as Qin Shi Huangdi; the name King Zheng of Qin gave himself after he conquered and unified other states. It means "august lord"; traditionally Shi Huangdi is thought of as China's first emperor

site: (noun) the setting; (verb) to place

smelt: to refine or extract metals

solar: having to do with the sun

specialization: separating jobs by specialty

steppe: the great plains of Southeast Asia; this area has few trees

stereotype: a fixed idea or set of ideas about a person or a group of people; it allows for no individuality or critical judgment

stratification: the process of arranging in layers or strata

submit: to yield, to give in (noun: submission)

subsistence: a level of living where a person has the barest minimum in terms of food, clothing, and shelter that is needed to survive

surplus: more than what is needed; excess

sutra: sacred Buddhist writings believed to be records of the oral teachings of the Buddha

symbol: something that represents another thing (e.g. a heart is a symbol of love)

temperate: moderate; temperate zones lie between the tropics and the polar circles

terrace: a series of flat platforms of earth created on a hillside; allows for farming of previously steep terrain

terracotta: hard, brown-red earthenware used for pottery and sculptures

Three Perfections (*sanjue*): calligraphy, painting, and poetry; mastery of all three showed an individual was an educated, cultured person in imperial China

tin: a soft, silver-white, crystalline, metallic chemical element, malleable at ordinary temperatures

tomb: grave, vault, or chamber for the dead

topography: the detailed description of a place, often on a map, that shows the surface features, such as mountains, valleys, rivers, lakes, etc.

tradition: the handing down of stories, beliefs, customs, etc. from generation to generation

treasure ships: the largest vessels in Zheng He's fleet which combined the best features of several kinds of reliable Chinese ships of his day

tribute: a regular payment of money or goods made by one ruler or nation to another

tribute system: an arrangement where one nation or ruler pays tributes to show they accept another nation as superior or more powerful, and/or to protect themselves from invasion

usurper: a person who takes power by force or without right

vessel: a container, such as a bowl or jug; or, a boat or ship

virtue: goodness or morality; right action and thinking

The Way (*Dao*): the natural, unseen forces of the universe with which man should live in harmony (see Lesson 8)

Xiongnu: nomadic ethnic groups or tribes that lived to the north of China

yang: represents male, day, brightness, positivity, hardness, and hills; complements yin

yin: represents female, night, negativity, softness, and valleys; complements yang

zodiac: a figure or diagram with signs and symbols used in astrology

Credits

Documents 1.3, 9.4, 9.6, and 11.8: Copyright © 1975 by Laurence Yep. Used by permission of HarperCollins Publishers.

Documents 1.4, 2.2, 9.2, and 9.5: From *River Town: Two Years on the Yangtze* by Peter Hessler. Copyright © 2001 by Peter Hessler. Reprinted by permission of HarperCollins Publishers.

Documents 2.1a, 2.1c, 2.1d, 2.1e, 12.4, 12.5, and 16.1e: Photos by Renee Covalucci

Document 2.1b: Photo by Kongli Liu

Documents 2.1f–j, 16.1c, and 19.1a–f : Photos by Michael Abraham

Documents 2.1k, 11.4a, 11.5, 11.11, 11.14, and 16.4 (top): Photos by Ronald G. Knapp

Documents 2.4, 8.9, 8.10, 8.11, 8.12, and 10.7: From *Chinese Fairy Tales and Fantasies* by Moss Roberts, copyright © 1979 by Moss Roberts. Used by permission of Pantheon Books, a division of Random House, Inc.

Document 2.6: Smithsonian Freer Gallery of Art.

Document 2.7: Wang Hui (1632–1717), Yang Jin (ca. 1644–1726), and Gu Fang (active ca. 1700). Emperor Kangxi inspecting the dams of the Yellow River. Photo: Thierry Ollivier. Location: Musée des Arts Asiatiques-Guimet, Paris, France. Réunion des Musées Nationaux/Art Resource, NY.

Item 2.D, Documents 7.9 and 9.1: Reprinted with permission of Pocket Books, an imprint of Simon & Schuster Adult Publishing Group, and by permission of Harold Ober Associates from *The Good Earth* by Pearl S. Buck. Copyright 1931, and renewed © 1958, by Pearl S. Buck.

Item 2.E and Document 7.9: Excerpts from *The Examination* by Malcolm Bosse. Copyright © 1994 by Marie-Clause Bosse. Reprinted by permission of Farrar, Straus and Giroux, LLC.

Documents 3.3, 6.1, 6.2, 6.4, 6.6, and 6.7: Birrell, Anne. *Chinese Mythology: An Introduction.* pp. 32, 35, 46–47, 71–72, 132, 133–134, 147–148, 155. © 1993 The Johns Hopkins University Press; All Rights Reserved. Reprinted with permission of The Johns Hopkins University Press.

Document 3.4: Three-legged wine vessel (*jue*), 15th–14th century B.C. (Zhengzhou-Anyang transition), Height 15⅛ in., weight 3 lb. 12 oz. Found 1965, Feixi Xian, Anhui Province, Anhui Provincial Museum. Courtesy of the Cultural Relics Bureau, Beijing and The Metropolitan Museum of Art.

Document 3.5: Wine vessel (*lei*), 15th–14th century B.C. (Zhengzhou-Anyang transition), Height 20½ in., weight 112 lb. 10 oz. Palace Museum Beijing. Courtesy of the Cultural Relics Bureau, Beijing and The Metropolitan Museum of Art.

Document 3.6: Square wine vessel (*fang zun*), Anyang period (ca. 1300–ca. 1030 B.C.), Height 23 in., weight 75 lb. 14 oz. Found 1938, Ningxiang Xian, Hunan Province, Historical Museum, Beijing. Courtesy of the Cultural Relics Bureau, Beijing and The Metropolitan Museum of Art.

Document 13.2: Used by permission of Acorn Alliance/Moyer Bell.

Document 13.3: Used by permission of Duke University Press.

Document 13.4: From *The Art of Chinese Poetry* translated by James J. Y. Liu. University of Chicago Press, 1962. Copyright 1962 James J. Y. Liu. Used by permission of The University of Chicago Press.

Document 13.6: Li Po, "Zazen on Ching-t'ing Mountain" from *Crossing the Yellow River: Three Hundred Poems from the Chinese*, translated by Sam Hamill. Copyright © 2000 by Sam Hamill. Reprinted with the permission of BOA Editions, Ltd., www.BOAEditions.org.

Document 13.7: "Tune 'Pure Serene Music'" from *Sunflower Splendor: Three Hundred Years of Chinese Poetry* used by permission of Eugene Eoyang.

Documents 14.1 and 17.1: © Copyright the Trustees of the British Museum.

Documents 14.2, 14.3, 14.4, and 14.5: National Palace Museum, Taiwan, Republic of China.

Document 14.6: The Metropolitan Museum of Art, Bequest of John M. Crawford, Jr., 1988. (1989.363.33) Photograph by Malcolm Varon. Photograph © 1991 The Metropolitan Museum of Art.

Documents 15.2 and 15.3: Hubei Provincial Museum.

Document 15.4: "Gentle Girl," translated by Stephen Owen, from *An Anthology of Chinese Literature: Beginnings to 1911* by Stephen Owen, Editor & Translator. Copyright © 1996 by Stephen Owen and The Council for Cultural Planning and Development of the Executive Yuan of the Republic of China. Used by permission of W.W. Norton & Company, Inc.

Documents 15.5 and 18.3: Courtesy of Dunhuang Academy.

Documents 15.6 and 15.7: Shaanxi Provincial Museum.

Documents 15.8 and 15.9: Hebei Provincial Cultural Relics.

Lesson 15, Selections of Music:

Jiangnan sizhu performed by the Chinese Performing Arts of North America.

Guangdong music: *Gaohu* solo performed by Jiang Ke Mei, China Broadcast Folk Orchestra.

Music for wind and percussion: *Guanzi* solo performed by Hu Zhi Hou, China Central Music Academy Folk Orchestra.

Sheng solo performed by Hu Jian Bing, Chinese Performing Arts of North America.

Qin solo performed by Shin-Yi Yang, Boston Guzheng Ensemble.

Document 16.1a: Photo by Pamela Tuffley

Document 16.1b: Photo by Eugene Dorgan

Document 16.1d: Photo by Jie Miao

Document 16.1f: Photo by Mark Lyons

Documents 16.5a and 16.5b: Copyright © Kathleen Cohen. All rights reserved. Used by permission of San Jose State University.

Document 17.3: Used by permission of the Ontario Science Centre.

Content Indices

- Dynasty Index

- Place-Name Index

- "Listen & Learn" Pronunciation Index

- CD-ROM Lesson Contents Index

Lesson Pages

- Quick, easy access to each lesson's Primary Sources, Supplementary Materials, and Further Resources.

Your explorer's guide to the rich resources found on

THE ENDURING LEGACY OF
ANCIENT CHINA
Primary Source Lessons for Teachers and Students

CD–ROM

Image Index

- Browse through 100+ images, arranged by lesson, to view on screen or print for class handouts and projects!

Teacher Resources

- Guides and instructions

- Bibliographies

- Suggestions for dealing with challenging material in class

- Time Lines and Maps